The Complete Book of
AMERICAN
Facts & Games
Grades 3–5

AMERICAN
EDUCATION
PUBLISHING™

Columbus, Ohio

Credits:

School Specialty Children's Publishing Editorial/Art & Design Team
Vincent F. Douglas, President
Tracey E. Dils, Publisher
Jennifer Blashkiw Pawley, Joanna M. Schmalz, Lindsay A. Mizer,
  Teresa A. Domnauer; Project Editors
Robert Sanford, Art Director
Nancy Allton, Interior Design and Production

Author:

Cathryn J. Long

Also Thanks to:

Larry Nolte, Joan Clapsadle; Interior Illustration

School Specialty
Children's Publishing

Send all inquiries to:
School Specialty Children's Publishing
8720 Orion Place
Columbus, OH 43240-2111

ISBN 1-56189-208-4

9 10 11 12 13 14 15 WAL 09 08 07 06 05 04

The Complete Book of
AMERICAN
Facts & Games
Table of Contents

Section 1

AMERICAN HISTORY TO 1900

Did you know that a hazard of living on the frontier was having snakes fall from the ceiling? Have you heard of the Wizard of Menlo Park? Did you know teddy bears were named for a president? This section will help you review these and many other amazing facts about the U.S. from the days of its first inhabitants through the twentieth century.

The activities in this section are a practical and fun review of the U.S.'s early history. You can use these activities to review a history topic or to learn about a subject you never knew about. This book presents a fun way to learn and reinforces what you are learning in school. You will also practice important skills like reading comprehension, vocabulary, and spelling.

To complete each activity, you will need to read and understand the reading selection, as well as locate information in illustrations or maps that may accompany each reading passage or activity. You can also find an appropriate word in the alphabetical list of words provided with most of the activities as another helpful tool in completing each activity.

If you have already learned about the topic that is featured, you may want to challenge yourself to complete as much of the activity as you can without reading the introduction, looking at the illustrations, or using the word lists.

Each activity focuses on a specific topic, and the topics are arranged in chronological order and by theme. Of course, not every history topic could be covered, but we have included those that are most often taught, and some that are simply most interesting and enjoyable. If a topic you want to explore is not included, you may wish to do some research on your own and create your own activities—complete with clues and/or word lists. We have included extra pages at the end of this section with suggestions for topics to explore.

Section 1
AMERICAN HISTORY TO 1900
Table of Contents

Natives of North America

The first people to live in America came from Asia. Many thousands of years ago, during the Ice Age, a land bridge connected Asia to North America (where Alaska is today). Hunters most likely followed herds of large animals, such as the elephant-like woolly mammoth, across the land bridge. In time, groups of people were living across North and South America. These people are called natives because they were the first to live there.

Land bridge, connecting Asia to North America

At first, all Native Americans survived by hunting and gathering plant foods. Later, some discovered they could save seeds from these foods and plant them to grow more. In Mexico, native people first grew corn. After that, farming became very important to many tribes.

The Native American way of life depended on the area where each tribe lived. In North America east of the Mississippi River, Eastern Woodlands people hunted deer and used logs and bark to build homes and fences. On the Great Plains between the Mississippi River and the Rocky Mountains, buffalo were a source of food, clothing, and shelter. Buffalo hunting became easier for these tribes when Native Americans first got horses from the Spanish in the 1600s. Great Plains people made everything from tepees to bone tools from parts of the buffalo.

Northwest Coast people were rich—they had plentiful foods like salmon and resources like timber. These people thought it was a sign of strength and dignity to give away food and presents in big celebrations called potlatches. In the Southwest, natives grew corn and often lived in pueblos—apartment houses made of adobe (clay and straw bricks).

Most tribes had a chief—a wise man who helped the people make decisions. The shaman (SHAH-mun) was the tribe's spiritual leader and healer. Many members of the tribe helped educate the children through stories and rituals. These traditions remain among many Native American tribes today.

The first Europeans to reach America called the natives Indians. That was because they thought they had come to some Asian islands called the Indies! Even though the name was given by mistake, it continued to be used.

Read the clues about the natives of North America.
Then complete the puzzle using the word list on the next page.

★ Across ★

1. Northwest Native American celebration in which gifts and food are given away

5. In the Eastern _____, deer hunting was important.
6. This animal helped feed, clothe, and shelter Plains Indians.
7. An apartment building created by Southwest Native Americans
9. Continent from which people first came to America
10. Native American children listened to these as part of their education.

★ *Down* ★

1. We make French fries from this vegetable, grown by Native Americans.
2. Term for a Native American leader
3. Material from which pueblos are built
4. Fish that helped make Northwest people wealthy
6. The first Americans came from Asia on a land _____.
7. Horses changed the lives of people living in this area.
8. An elephant-like animal hunted in the Ice Age
10. A Native American spiritual leader

*Foods Native
Americans first grew*

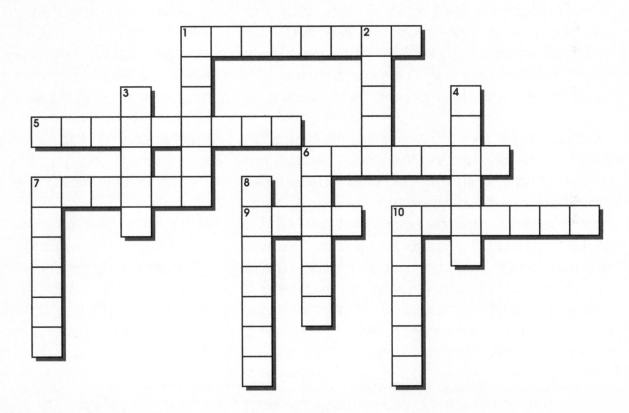

Word List

ADOBE	BUFFALO	POTATO	SHAMAN
ASIA	CHIEF	POTLATCH	STORIES
BRIDGE	MAMMOTH	PUEBLO	WOODLANDS
	PLAINS	SALMON	

European Explorers

About a thousand years ago, Viking tales told of Vinland, a mysterious country across the sea. Leif Eriksson led Viking ships from Greenland to find Vinland. Eriksson and his Vikings arrived at the North American coast and settled briefly on the island now called Newfoundland.

Most of Europe, however, had not heard about the Viking adventure. Leaders of the strongest nations were trying to find a good way to reach Asia, where valuable silks and spices were traded. The Portuguese found a

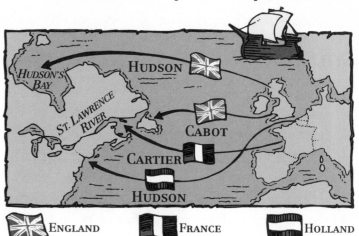

Northern European Explorers

route by sea around southern Africa in the 1400s. But Christopher Columbus thought he could reach Asia by sailing west. Columbus looked for royal backing; he got it from Ferdinand and Isabella, monarchs of Spain. Even though he actually had found America, and made four voyages there, Columbus continued to believe it was Asia to his dying day.

Spanish and Portuguese explorers helped draw a true map of the world. Vasco Nunez de Balboa crossed Central America and found the Pacific Ocean on the other side. He claimed all the land bordering the ocean for Spain. Ferdinand Magellan's ships sailed all the way around the world. Soon, Spanish expeditions found gold and silver in Central and South America and claimed the land. But it was an Italian explorer, Amerigo Vespucci, whose name was used for the new continents.

Spanish treasure seekers also explored North America. Hernando de Soto failed to find riches in the Southeast. Francisco Vásquez de Coronado searched the Southwest for gold but found none. Juan Rodríguez Cabrillo claimed the land of California for Spain. Along the East Coast, French and British explorers such as Henry Hudson, John Cabot, and Jacques Cartier looked for a water route, which some called the Northwest Passage. This waterway supposedly led from the north Atlantic to the riches of Asia. Though they never found it, they made land claims that became the foundation of Canada and the United States.

Read the clues about the European explorers.
Then complete the puzzle using the word list on the next page.

★ Across ★

2. Initials of the state now on the land Cabrillo claimed for Spain
4. Last name of the Viking explorer who first reached America
7. Name of an explorer who worked for England and Holland

9. His ships were the first to go around the world.
11. Number of trips to the New World made by Columbus
12. Cabrillo and Balboa claimed land bordering this ocean for Spain.
13. Viking name for Newfoundland
15. The explorer America is named for (his first name)

★ *Down* ★

1. The Spanish failed to find gold in ____ America.
2. This Spaniard explored the Southwest.
3. The explorer who tried to reach Asia by sailing west
5. The Spanish queen who backed Columbus's voyage
6. This man found that the Pacific lay on the other side of America.
8. A French explorer who entered the St. Lawrence River
10. The Portuguese reached Asia by sailing around this continent.
14. Initials of a passage between the Atlantic and Pacific sought by French and British explorers

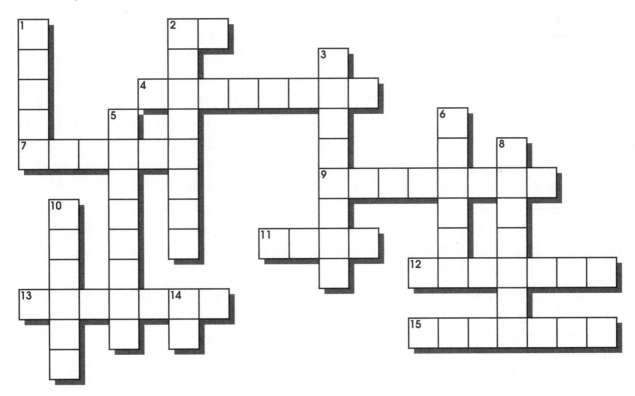

Word List

AFRICA	CARTIER	FOUR	NORTH
AMERIGO	COLUMBUS	HUDSON	NW
BALBOA	CORONADO	ISABELLA	PACIFIC
CA	ERIKSSON	MAGELLAN	VINLAND

Colonial Life

English settlers began to arrive in North America in the early 1600s. They came for many reasons, though most hoped to become richer than they were in Europe. The gentlemen who founded the first permanent English colony at Jamestown, Virginia, thought they would find gold lying on the ground. They had no such luck, and many of the settlers died before the colony finally made a profit from growing tobacco. Later arrivals on the East Coast found farming and trading were the best ways to gain prosperity.

The Triangular Trade

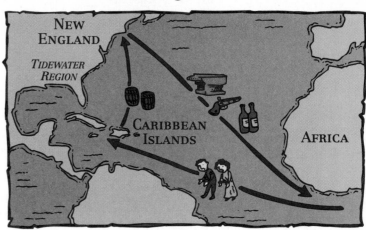

Other settlers came to escape certain laws and rulers. For instance, the Pilgrims, who founded Plymouth, disagreed with the Church of England. They wanted a simpler church in which worshippers had a say. To them, the right to worship in their own way was worth the hardships they might find in the new land.

Along the Atlantic coast, colonies began as small settlements and, in time, were organized into large areas like the states we know today. The northeastern colonies, called New England, were home to a way of life brought by the Pilgrims and by the Puritans who founded Boston. Work, church, and education were important, and male church members could vote in town meetings. Shipbuilding and trade helped New Englanders make money. New England traders first organized the triangular trade in which rum was exchanged for slaves, who were exchanged in the Caribbean islands for molasses (made from the sugar cane grown there). The molasses was in turn brought to New England to be made into rum.

The middle colonies included New York, New Jersey, Delaware, and Pennsylvania. William Penn, an English Quaker, advertised religious freedom and good farmland in the colony he founded, Pennsylvania (meaning "Penn's Woods"). Huge crops of wheat were milled into flour and shipped out of Philadelphia, the capital. New settlers and lively business helped make Philadelphia the largest city in the colonies. New York also grew quickly as a trade city.

To the south, in the coastal Tidewater region, large crops of rice, indigo (a blue dye), and tobacco grew well because of the climate. Africans were forced to work as slaves on the region's large farms, called plantations.

Use the word list to help you find the words
about colonial life that are hidden in the block below.
Some of the words are hidden backward or diagonally.

```
S H I P B U I L D I N G P Y M I
A L X D O C C A B O T O L A U E
Q U A K E R F Q O H W L A T D T
C Q E V L S P H G C M D N E N O
P M F J E H L N D R P A T W A W
H O Z R I S I R O U I N A O L N
B L U U C M W J R H L M T R G M
K A B J R B X I P C G D I O N E
H S V A K T T L C T R X O G E E
T S F D B A E N S S I C N P W T
U E T M N D Y V G N M O S K E I
O S Q S A Z J A M E S T O W N N
M K J L I N B H V P L G Y G Q G
Y F I M S E T T L E M E N T S F
L H L Z S G N I D A R T F E A I
P E N N S W O O D S R A R I C E
```

Word List

CHURCH   NEW ENGLAND   PLYMOUTH   SHIPBUILDING

FARMING   PENNS WOODS   PURITANS   SLAVES

GOLD   PHILADELPHIA   QUAKER   TOBACCO

JAMESTOWN   PILGRIMS   RICE   TOWN MEETING

MOLASSES   PLANTATIONS   SETTLEMENTS   TRADING

The Spanish Southwest

In some parts of the United States, the colonial past is Spanish instead of English. That is because Spain had an early claim on parts of North America. The oldest European-founded city in the United States is Spanish—St. Augustine, Florida, which dates from 1565. Most Spanish lands were in the Southwest. Spain ruled areas that are now part of Texas, Arizona, New Mexico, Nevada, Utah, Colorado, and California. The United States won or bought these lands piece by piece during the 1800s.

Missionaries were the pioneers of Spanish America. A mission was a church and settlement surrounded by its own farms and orchards where Native Americans were taught Christianity by Catholic priests. Native people worked at mission farms for little or no pay. To keep order, soldiers were often stationed near the mission at a fort called a presidio. In California, Father Junípero Serra founded a string of missions along the coast. Later, many of them helped form the beginning of California cities, including Los Angeles and San Francisco.

Santa Fe ("Holy Faith"), today the capital of the state of New Mexico, was once the capital of Spain's northern territories. Spanish ranch owners brought the first cattle, sheep, and horses to the area. Stray horses, called mustangs, formed wild herds that roamed far distances. Spanish farmers also introduced orchard crops, such as oranges, olives, and peaches. Some Native Americans grew tired of Spanish rule. A Tewa Indian leader named Pope (poh-PAY) led a rebellion in 1680 that drove the Spanish out of the area we now call New Mexico for several years.

TORNADO

RANCH

PATIO

MUSTANG

CORRAL

A few words from the Spanish

Words about the Spanish Southwest have been scrambled.
Rearrange the letters and write the correct word on each line.
Use the word list if you need help.

NHPSASI

_____

TS UTENGUASI

_____

TSAAN EF

_____

IRSPEIOD

_____

LNRBLOEEI

_____

THNTYICRAISI

_____

NATSGUM

_____

IRLADOF

_____

NADINI

_____

ERPNIOE

_____

SMINOIS

_____

RAFILOCIAN

_____

Word List

CALIFORNIA	INDIAN	PIONEER	SANTA FE
CHRISTIANITY	MISSION	PRESIDIO	SPANISH
FLORIDA	MUSTANG	REBELLION	ST AUGUSTINE

Indians and Settlers

When Europeans and Native Americans first met, they were often friendly. Columbus exchanged gifts with the Arawak (AHR-uh-wok) people when he landed on the Caribbean island of Hispaniola (hiss-pah-NYO-luh). A Native American named Squanto helped the Pilgrims survive by teaching them to plant corn and showing them ways to catch fish. At Jamestown, a group of tribes led by Chief Powhatan (pow-HAH-tuhn) gave corn to the starving colonists.

Quickly, however, conflict became the rule between settlers and Indians. The settlers tried to buy land, or they simply took it. Most Indians thought land could not be bought or sold but belonged to those who were using it at the moment. As settlers built and farmed farther west, Indians fought them, raiding villages and farms. Settlers also raided Indian settlements. At times, the conflict became real war. One example is King Philip's War, in which the son of a chief who had welcomed the Pilgrims fought New Englanders.

A greater conflict between Indians and English settlers began in the mid 1700s. The French were fighting the British in a war in Europe. At the time, French traders were buying furs from American Indians in territory north and west of the English colonies.

France claimed that territory, as did Britain. The European war spread to North America, where it was called the French and Indian War. Many Indians joined the French in fighting the British. The British won the war in 1763, but they agreed to keep settlers east of the Appalachian Mountains.

The American Revolution put an end to the British agreement, and settlers began moving west. The Shawnee leader Tecumseh

Fur Trade

(teh-CUM-seh) desperately tried to keep back the tide of settlement. He tried to unite all the tribes west of the Appalachians to stop the settlement. He did not succeed, and the tribes were pushed farther westward.

The greatest European weapon against the Indians turned out to be disease. Some historians think as many as two-thirds of all Native Americans in North America were killed by European diseases such as smallpox and the flu.

Use the word list to help you find the words
about the Indians and settlers that are hidden in the block below.
Some of the words are hidden backward or diagonally.

```
B  F  G  T  O  T  N  A  U  Q  S  F  N  Q  T  L
I  H  I  S  P  A  N  I  O  L  A  P  C  U  R  D
M  R  E  Z  C  J  C  O  A  N  T  S  L  I  E  W
O  S  P  I  O  O  R  D  A  K  Y  O  X  C  M  N
H  N  O  K  N  W  R  I  J  W  V  B  P  I  A  A
S  A  R  E  F  S  D  N  D  E  S  E  B  I  R  T
M  I  U  V  L  N  N  Q  R  V  O  P  C  K  I  A
A  H  E  A  I  R  E  V  O  L  U  T  I  O  N  H
L  C  N  K  C  P  L  A  P  H  K  T  L  N  S  W
L  A  U  A  T  D  A  J  R  H  O  E  E  O  R  O
P  L  R  W  D  T  S  D  N  A  L  C  S  M  E  P
O  A  S  A  T  L  M  B  D  E  N  U  A  H  L  F
X  P  V  R  T  Z  B  O  E  A  L  M  E  Q  T  E
I  P  E  A  G  M  W  A  R  T  F  S  S  U  T  I
B  A  G  L  O  E  R  F  U  I  X  E  I  C  E  H
C  O  L  U  M  B  U  S  F  Y  N  H  D  A  S  C
```

Word List

APPALACHIANS	CONFLICT	FRANCE	LAND	SQUANTO
ARAWAK	CORN	FUR	REVOLUTION	TECUMSEH
CHIEF	DISEASE	HISPANIOLA	SETTLERS	TRIBES
POWHATAN	EUROPE	INDIAN	SMALLPOX	WAR
COLUMBUS				

The Colonists Protest

In 1765, the British government decided to tax the thirteen English colonies to help pay for the French and Indian War. The government ordered a stamp tax. This tax required colonists to pay to get a stamp on newspapers, calendars, and every sort of public paper. People were upset at having to pay the tax, but they were even more disturbed by the way the government had created the tax. Every colony had an elected assembly led by a governor. Normally, colonial money matters were decided by the assembly in each colony. But this time, no assembly had been allowed to help decide. Angry assembly members, such as Patrick Henry, protested in every colony.

The British, surprised by this outcry, decided to take back, or repeal, the law that created the stamp tax. However, they soon passed the Townsend Acts, which taxed many goods such as cloth, glass, and tea sent from England to the colonies.

Colonists, especially in Boston, objected. Anger grew when British soldiers shot several protesting colonists in what was named the Boston Massacre. Samuel Adams led a secret society of colonial men called the Sons of Liberty in anti-British acts. Disguised as Indians, the Sons of Liberty threw tea off a British ship into the harbor water. This event became known as the Boston Tea Party. Neighbors divided depending on their view of England. Loyalist Tories were supporters of the British government, and Patriots protested against it. As war threatened, many Tories left the colonies and moved north to Canada. Some who remained in the colonies were covered with hot tar and feathers by unruly Patriots.

The colonies drew together under the British threat. In 1774, they organized the first Continental Congress, with delegates from all the colonies (except, at first, Georgia). As the Revolutionary War began, this congress served as the first form of American government.

Boston Tea Party

Words about the colonists' protest have been scrambled.
Rearrange the letters and write the correct word on each line.
Use the word list if you need help.

LERPEA

_____

SNICOLEO

_____

TXA

_____

NTOBSO

_____

MULESA MADAS

_____

PMATS

_____

STIROTPA

_____

NDANELG

_____

SROIET

_____

BLIRTEY

_____

SANDIIN

_____

MOGRNTEVEN

_____

Word List

BOSTON	GOVERNMENT	PATRIOTS	STAMP
COLONIES	INDIANS	REPEAL	TAX
ENGLAND	LIBERTY	SAMUEL ADAMS	TORIES

The Revolutionary War

On April 18, 1775, Paul Revere rode hard along the road from Boston to the nearby towns of Lexington and Concord. His job was to warn people that British soldiers were coming to take the colonists' ammunition and to arrest Patriot leaders. Local "minutemen," farmers who had trained as Patriot soldiers, were prepared for the announcement. As the British approached the towns, the minutemen turned out to exchange fire. These were the first shots of the Revolutionary War.

The Continental Congress met in Philadelphia and decided to ask Britain's King George for peace. But they also decided to prepare for possible all-out war. They hired George Washington, formerly an army officer under the British, to lead a Continental army. At their first full battle, called the Battle of Bunker Hill, Patriot soldiers fought well—but their ammunition ran out and they were defeated.

Even as the army went into action, many colonists remained doubtful about rebelling. In 1776, a pamphlet by Thomas Paine called Common Sense helped colonists decide that independence from England was the best idea. The Continental Congress approved a Declaration of Independence on July 4, 1776. That day, the United States of America was born.

The Revolutionary War was hard-fought. Washington was responsible for pulling the army together and training them. Yet the men had to fight not only the well-trained and -supplied British but also German soldiers called Hessians. King George of England hired the Hessians to help him win the war.

Washington led his army across the Delaware River to surprise the Hessians with a victory at Trenton, New Jersey. Another major win at Saratoga helped convince the French to enter the war on the side of the new United States. In spite of the help, the Continental army suffered a long, cold winter at Valley Forge when the British took over Philadelphia.

After many more battles, the Americans and French trapped the British at Yorktown, Virginia, in 1781 and won the war.

> Mary McCauley, nicknamed "Molly Pitcher," brought soldiers water and helped load their cannons.

Read the clues about the Revolutionary War.
Then complete the puzzle using the word list on the next page.

★ Across ★

4. The allies who joined the United States to fight the British
6. When the Continental army won this battle, the French decided to enter the war as American allies.
8. Last name of the messenger who warned people between Boston and Lexington

10. She was called "Molly _____" because she brought water to thirsty soldiers.
12. Name given to men trained to fight the British at a moment's notice
13. Term for a hired German soldier in the Revolutionary War
14. Location of the final battle of the Revolution

Down

1. River crossed by Washington and his men to get to Trenton
2. Paul Revere warned people that the _____ were coming.
3. In 1776, the Continental Congress issued the _____ of Independence.
5. Washington's army surprised the Hessians at this city.
7. Name of the king of England at the time of the Revolution
9. Where Washington's army spent a long, cold winter—_____ Forge
11. Last name of the author of *Common Sense*

Word List

BRITISH	**FRENCH**	**PAINE**	**TRENTON**
DECLARATION	**GEORGE**	**PITCHER**	**VALLEY**
DELAWARE	**HESSIAN**	**REVERE**	**YORKTOWN**
	MINUTEMEN	**SARATOGA**	

Thomas Jefferson

Born on a Virginia plantation, Thomas Jefferson was well educated at the College of William and Mary in Williamsburg. He was good at many things, including languages, music, writing, and architecture, but he decided to enter the law profession. As a young lawyer, he was elected to the Virginia colonial assembly, called the House of Burgesses. He was soon sent to the Continental Congress and placed on the committee to write the Declaration of Independence. His friend John Adams, also on the committee, asked him to write the first draft. The most important statement of the Declaration was that the colonies were separate from Britain, declared independent states. Jefferson also included the belief that "all men are created equal" with certain rights that cannot be taken away. That belief has helped guide Americans in self-government ever since.

After the Revolutionary War, Jefferson served in other government offices. He wrote a statute, or law, of religious freedom for Virginia, which set a standard for all the other states. Then he served as President Washington's Secretary of State, in charge of foreign affairs. As an adviser to the president, Jefferson favored little government and a nation made up mostly of farmers. His point of view became the basis of one of the first American political parties, the Democratic Republican Party, an earlier form of today's Democratic Party.

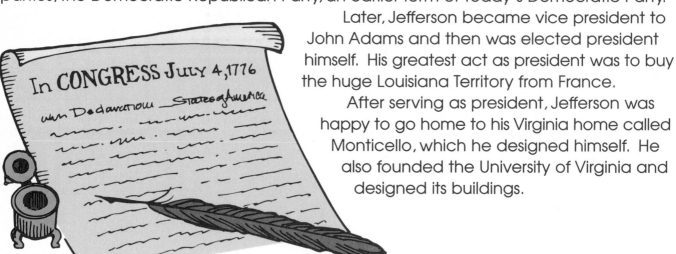

Later, Jefferson became vice president to John Adams and then was elected president himself. His greatest act as president was to buy the huge Louisiana Territory from France.

After serving as president, Jefferson was happy to go home to his Virginia home called Monticello, which he designed himself. He also founded the University of Virginia and designed its buildings.

Words about Thomas Jefferson have been scrambled.
Rearrange the letters and write the correct word on each line.
Use the word list if you need help.

TSSATE

_____

SIVERAD

_____

CEHTRIRCAUTE

_____

INCRALTADOE

_____

TUSETAT

_____

DIRTESPEN

_____

NOUSAILIA

_____

TANOTNALPI

_____

LEMLIOTONC

_____

LIPTALICO

_____

PNDICEENNDEE

_____

AWREYL

_____

Word List

ADVISER	**INDEPENDENCE**	**MONTICELLO**	**PRESIDENT**
ARCHITECTURE	**LAWYER**	**PLANTATION**	**STATES**
DECLARATION	**LOUISIANA**	**POLITICAL**	**STATUTE**

George Washington

George Washington was born on a Virginia farm. He was given a primary education, then, as a young man, worked as a surveyor measuring land. When his half-brother died, Washington inherited his land and a home, Mount Vernon. Tall and strong, he liked outdoor work and the army. He became an officer in the Virginia militia and fought to push the French out of the upper Ohio River valley. In fighting at Fort Duquesne (now Pittsburgh, Pennsylvania), Washington learned Indian techniques and battle strategies.

Towns, schools, and buildings have been named after the first president, including the state of Washington.

By the end of the French and Indian War, Washington was a well-known officer. The Continental Congress asked him to become Commander in Chief of the Continental army in the Revolutionary War. Outnumbered by the enemy, the army never had enough supplies and was not as well trained as the British. Washington trained the army, gave them discipline, and kept up their hopes. Even in the winter of 1777-1778, when he and his men were nearly starving and freezing at Valley Forge, Washington refused to give up. His wife, Martha, joined him there and helped nurse sick soldiers. Training continued through the winter. In June 1778, the army followed Washington to a victory over the British in Monmouth, New Jersey. It was such determination, along with luck and good allies, that allowed Washington and his army to win the war.

After the Revolution, Washington tried to retire to Mount Vernon. But he was called back to become chairman of the Constitutional Convention—the gathering of delegates responsible for creating a fresh plan of government for the United States. When this plan, the Constitution, was approved, he was elected the first president of the United States and served two terms. As president, Washington helped unite the new country. He listened to arguments from all sides, then steered a middle course. He was so well known for his strength and fairness that foreign countries were willing to accept and trade with the new nation. There is little wonder that Congress decided to name the new capital city in the District of Columbia after him.

Read the clues about George Washington.
Then complete the puzzle using the word list on the next page.

★ Across ★

1. Washington was asked to take this position at the Constitutional Convention.
3. Name of George Washington's wife
5. Colonial army; Washington joined it as a young man
7. Settlers of a new _____ on the Pacific named it after Washington.

9. Name of the fort where Washington fought during the French and Indian War
10. Mount _____ was Washington's home.
11. At Valley Forge, Washington and his men nearly starved and were almost _____.
14. Washington was the first to hold this elected position.
15. Before the Revolution, Washington was a well-known _____.

★ *Down* ★

1. Washington's position in the Continental army
2. As president, Washington helped _____ the new country.
4. The city of Washington is in the _____ of Columbia.
6. George Washington's first job
8. Number of terms Washington served as president
12. What Washington hoped to do after the Revolution
13. Martha Washington worked at this job at Valley Forge.

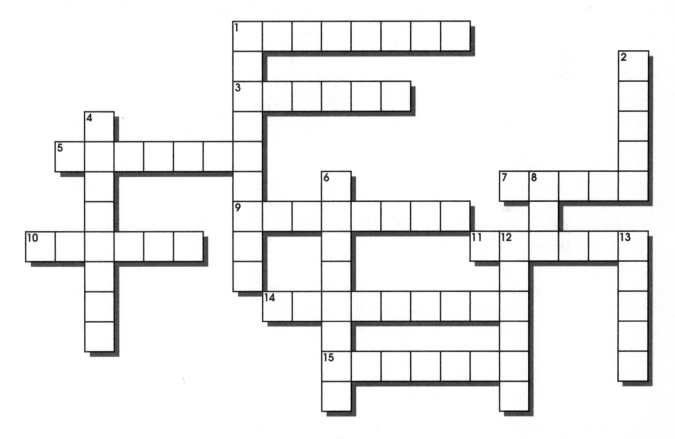

Word List

CHAIRMAN	FROZEN	OFFICER	SURVEYOR
COMMANDER	MARTHA	PRESIDENT	TWO
DISTRICT	MILITIA	RETIRE	UNITE
DUQUESNE	NURSE	STATE	VERNON

The Constitution

Soon after the Revolutionary War, the states began to argue with each other over trade, taxes, boundaries, and more. The Continental Congress had created a plan of government for the United States called the Articles of Confederation. But this plan made the national government so weak that it could not resolve the states' disputes. Congress decided to have a special meeting called the Constitutional Convention. The convention was held in Philadelphia in the summer of 1787 and lasted four months. There, delegates from the states created a new plan of national government—the Constitution. Delegate James Madison of Virginia kept careful notes at the Convention and offered many good ideas. For that reason, he is sometimes called the Father of the Constitution.

The Constitution created a federal system, in which states share power with a strong national government. The national government is divided into three branches. The powers of each branch are set up with checks and balances so no single part of the government becomes too powerful.

The delegates did not easily agree on this system or on other parts of the Constitution. Benjamin Franklin of Pennsylvania told the delegates they would have to compromise, just as a carpenter joins two boards by taking a little off each one. One of the most

Government Under the Constitution

Legislative branch makes the laws (Senate, House of Representatives) *Executive branch carries out the laws (president, departments, and agencies)* *Judicial branch decides what is lawful (Supreme Court, other courts)*

important compromises of the meeting was an agreement that small states made with the large states. All states were to have equal representation in the Senate. But the number of representatives in the House of Representatives would depend on the population of each state. This arrangement was called the Great Compromise.

Before the Constitution was approved by the states, ten amendments were added, called the Bill of Rights. The Bill of Rights gives us rights that include free speech, freedom of the press, a fair trial, and freedom of religion.

Read the clues about the Constitution.
Then complete the puzzle using the word list on the next page.

★ Across ★

1. Meeting that created the Constitution—the Constitutional _____
4. Kind of system in which states and a national government share power

5. Agreement in which each side gives up a little
8. Parts of the Constitution added after it was written
9. Number of branches of government
11. Name of the branch of government that makes laws
12. In this part of Congress, states are represented equally.
13. The Father of the Constitution

★ *Down* ★

1. The government did not work well under the Articles of _____.
2. Branch of government headed by the president.
3. Branch of government that decides what is lawful.
6. The _____ Court heads the judicial branch.
7. Number of amendments in the Bill of Rights
10. The Constitution uses _____ and balances to keep any one part of the government from becoming too powerful.

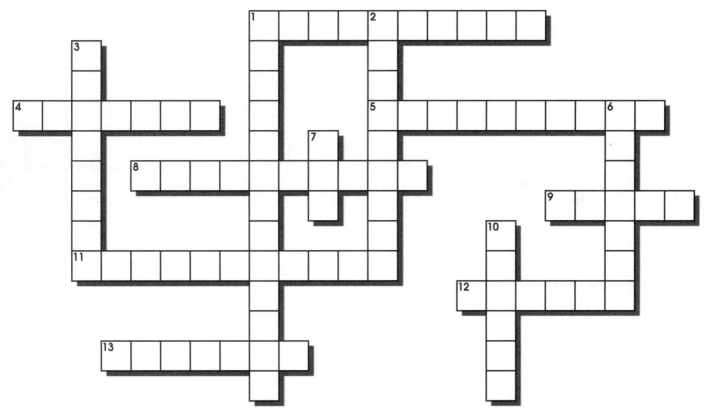

Word List

AMENDMENTS	CONFEDERATION	JUDICIAL	SUPREME
CHECKS	CONVENTION	LEGISLATIVE	TEN
COMPROMISE	EXECUTIVE	MADISON	THREE
	FEDERAL	SENATE	

Lewis and Clark

In 1803, Thomas Jefferson made a deal to buy the Louisiana Territory from the French for $15 million. The land of the United States would be more than doubled. Some senators feared that this New West would overpower their eastern states, but the Senate finally approved the purchase.

Jefferson hired Meriwether Lewis and William Clark, seasoned army officers, to explore part of the purchase. Their mission was to try to find a way across the territory to the Pacific Ocean. The leaders, along with nearly fifty soldiers and assistants, headed up the Missouri River from St. Louis. They spent their first winter on the Great Plains, with the Mandan Indians. They made notes on all they saw, collected sample plants and animals, and created maps. They also hired a French Canadian guide, Toussaint Charbonneau (too-SAN shar-bohn-OH). His wife, Sacajawea (sah-kuh-juh-WEE-uh), a Shoshone (shuh-SHOH-nee), also worked as guide and interpreter.

The Lewis and Clark Expedition

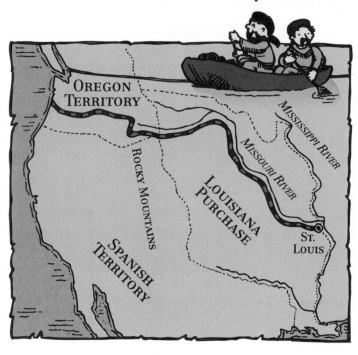

That spring, Lewis and Clark and their group got stuck at the foot of the Rocky Mountains. They needed horses and a good route to follow. By chance, a small group of Shoshone appeared. Sacajawea recognized her brother, now a chief. Sacajawea and her brother helped the expedition cross the mountains. When at last they reached the Pacific, Clark wrote in his journal, "Great joy!"

Lewis and Clark returned to St. Louis two years after they started, loaded with valuable information about the land they had crossed.

Read the clues about Lewis and Clark.
Then complete the puzzle using the word list on the next page.

★ Across ★

1. Lewis's first name
4. The Shoshone woman who helped Lewis and Clark
6. Lewis and Clark brought back samples of plants and _____.
9. Relation of Sacajawea who served as guide across the Rockies

10. River that formed the eastern boundary of the Louisiana Territory
12. Tribe with whom Lewis and Clark spent their first winter
13. Lewis and Clark wintered on the Great _____.

★ *Down* ★

1. Lewis and Clark traveled on this river upon leaving St. Louis.
2. Mountains Lewis and Clark had to cross
3. Jefferson asked Lewis and Clark to seek a route to this ocean.
5. Senators from some _____ states feared the new land would overpower them.
7. Beyond the Rockies, the expedition had to cross part of the _____ Territory.
8. Country that sold the Louisiana Territory to the United States
11. This government body had to approve the Louisiana Purchase.

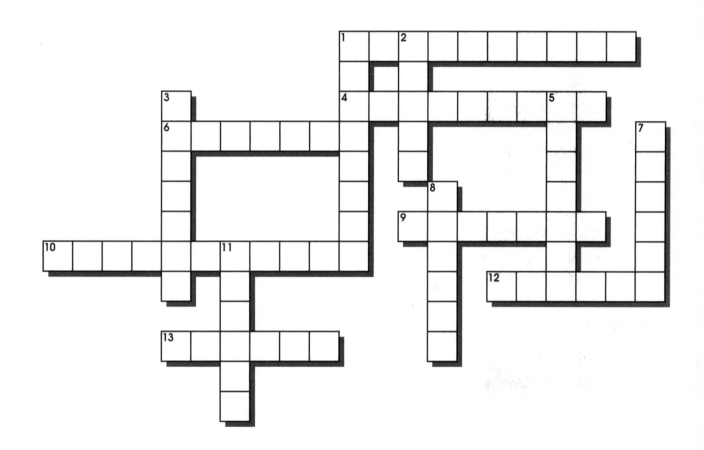

Word List

ANIMALS	FRANCE	MISSOURI	ROCKY
BROTHER	MANDAN	OREGON	SACAJAWEA
EASTERN	MERIWETHER	PACIFIC	SENATE
	MISSISSIPPI	PLAINS	

The Oregon Trail

Nature at its most beautiful! Rich land for farming! Plenty of wood, water, and game! Claims like these drew many people to the Oregon Territory in the 1840s. This area included today's Washington, Oregon, Idaho, and the Canadian province of British Columbia. The very first Americans in the Oregon Territory came to trap beaver. Some of them helped to blaze the trail route from Independence, Missouri, across the plains, over the Rocky Mountains, to the Pacific. Called the Oregon Trail, this path made it possible for settlers to reach the Oregon Territory by wagon.

In the spring, families traveled to Independence to buy trail supplies and join a "train" of perhaps a hundred wagons. Most wagon trains included a whole herd of cattle and extra horses. Strong oxen pulled covered wagons, called prairie "schooners," because they looked like sailing schooners on an ocean of grass.

On the open plains, wagon trains were often met by Native American bands of Kansa, Sioux, Crow, and others who traveled the land on horseback, hunting buffalo. Sometimes these people traded with the pioneers and gave them directions.

The pioneers faced many dangers on the trail—steep mountain slopes, rushing rivers that had to be forded or crossed by raft, bad weather, and illnesses such as cholera.

Life on the Oregon Trail could also be enjoyable—people walked and talked alongside the wagons, played music around the fire, and swam in cool streams. When pioneers saw the streams flowing west instead of east, it meant they had crossed the Continental Divide and were on the last leg of their journey.

The Oregon Trail

Use the word list to help you find the words
about the Oregon Trail that are hidden in the block below.
Some of the words are hidden backward or diagonally.

```
G A P Q S C H O O N E R S W E Y
R T I L P B L C P W T M N T R E
P D N E A S F J I R U J O O O N
I I D A H I P B D L Q P T K C R
O V E O T O N J A S P I G L K U
N I P F S U T S H A R P N D Y O
E D E V Y X Q U O R J T I X M J
E E N C D S W N E E N S H F O S
R B D E H U N T I N G E S A U D
S K E O C O N A H R U H A R N I
E O N S I O L I N O G A W M T H
J N C R G L P E A B L Q X I A M
M E E E C G B T R R N U A N I Z
V X R B E A V E R A T Y O G N A
Z O R E G O N T R A I L R N S A
D N F X B M D B V O L A F F U B
```

Word List

BEAVER	HUNTING	OREGON TRAIL	SCHOONERS
BUFFALO	IDAHO	OXEN	SIOUX
CHOLERA	INDEPENDENCE	PIONEERS	TRAIN
DIVIDE	JOURNEY	PLAINS	WAGON
FARMING	OREGON TERRITORY	ROCKY MOUNTAINS	WASHINGTON

Texas

"G. T. T." was written on many house and barn doors in the South during the 1820s. It meant, "Gone to Texas." Even though Texas belonged to Mexico, Americans moved there for cheap land and the freedom of the frontier.

Some of the first Americans to arrive were led by Stephen Austin, an American with a dream of founding a new western community. Unlike others, Austin had permission from Mexico to create a settlement. To get approval from Mexico, settlers were supposed to learn Spanish, become Catholic, and bring no slaves.

Soon, there were more Americans than Mexicans in Texas. Many of the Americans did not want to follow Mexican laws about religion and slavery. A new Mexican president named Antonio Lopez de Santa Anna decided to stop the flow of Americans into Texas. He sent soldiers to take a cannon away from American Texans in the town of Gonzales, but a group of Americans fired on the soldiers. War began. In San Antonio, a small group of Americans held out for almost two weeks against the Mexican army at an old mission called the Alamo. In the end, however, Mexican soldiers killed every one of them, including two famous frontiersmen, Davy Crockett and Jim Bowie.

During the Alamo battle, other settlers were meeting in the town of San Felipe to declare Texas independent and to ask Sam Houston to lead their new army. Houston was a Texas newcomer who had been a congressman and governor of Tennessee. Houston and the army of settlers crying "Remember the Alamo!" quickly defeated Santa Anna. Texas remained an independent nation for nine years. Then, in 1845, it was made part of the United States. This action and others angered Mexico and led to war between the U.S. and Mexico the following year. When the United States won, it gained California and a huge territory between California and Texas.

Texas's First Flag

Words about Texas have been scrambled.
Rearrange the letters and write the correct word on each line.
Use the word list if you need help.

AAMLO

_____

RENROIFT

_____

PETINDNNEED

_____

SHOUTON

_____

SLEGZONA

_____

LIGONEIR

_____

LETBAT

_____

LEMESTNTTE

_____

NUTISA

_____

TROKECCT

_____

XCOMEI

_____

MISONIS

_____

Word List

ALAMO	CROCKETT	HOUSTON	MISSION
AUSTIN	FRONTIER	INDEPENDENT	RELIGION
BATTLE	GONZALES	MEXICO	SETTLEMENT

The California Gold Rush

"GOLD!" The headline was enough to draw more than 70,000 gold seekers to California in 1849. These "forty-niners" came from all over the world. Some followed the California Trail from the east across the Nevada desert. Others came by boat around Cape Horn at the foot of South America. The demand for fast sailing ships, called clipper ships, was so great that it helped America's shipbuilding industry grow.

Gold sinks to the bottom of pan as forty-niner drains out stream water

The first gold was found by James Marshall, a mill worker, in the stream water used to run a sawmill near Sacramento. The mill owner, John Sutter, had little time to celebrate before a stampede of prospectors ruined his land and business. The forty-niners hunted gold all through the foothills of the Sierra Nevada, creating mining camps and towns overnight. One result of the gold rush was the near destruction of the local Pomo Indian tribe. The Pomo were driven off the land, and many died of diseases brought by the miners.

Few forty-niners made a fortune, but the merchants who sold goods to miners at high prices did well. San Francisco, the port where many people entered California mushroomed into a sizable city. Gambling, stealing (or "jumping") someone's land claim, cheating, and other crimes and violence became common in the territory. There were not enough laws, courts, or police to handle these problems, which is one reason Californians voted to become a state in 1850. Sacramento, gateway to the gold region, became the state capital.

Read the clues about the California Gold Rush.
Then complete the puzzle using the word list on the next page.

★ *Across* ★

3. Capital of California
6. Gold seekers would pan for gold in a river or _____.
7. Gold was found in the foothills of the Sierra _____.
9. Prospectors coming over land from the east generally used the California _____.
10. A fast sailing ship popular with forty-niners

11. Last name of the person who first found gold in California
13. Native American tribe badly harmed by the gold rush

★ *Down* ★

1. Building at which gold was first discovered
2. Many gold seekers came by ship around the cape of this name.
3. Last name of the owner of the land where gold was first found
4. Gold seekers were called forty-_____.
5. This port city mushroomed during the gold rush—San _____.
8. These were kept very high by merchants during the gold rush
12. California became a _____ in 1850.

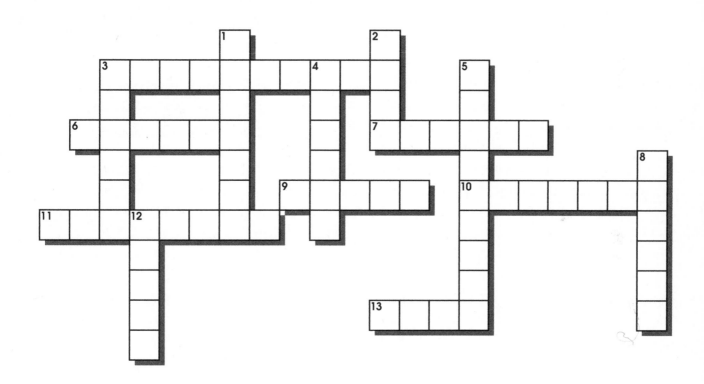

Word List

CLIPPER	MARSHALL	PRICES	STREAM
FRANCISCO	NEVADA	SACRAMENTO	SUTTER
HORN	NINERS	SAWMILL	TRAIL
	POMO	STATE	

Slavery

Slavery might have died out sooner in the United States were it not for Eli Whitney's invention of the cotton gin in 1793. This machine cleaned the seeds out of cotton so well that it made growing cotton a more profitable business. While northern states largely gave up slavery and built mills and factories, southern states became a land of cotton and other crops grown on large farms called plantations. So much cotton grew in the South that people there called it King Cotton.

One in four southern families kept slaves, most holding only a few as farmhands or servants. But the big plantation owners kept many. Most slaves there worked as field hands in groups of thirty to forty men, women, and children. They were directed by a white overseer or by another slave called the driver. Other slaves worked in their owner's household or at crafts like woodworking. Slaves had little free time and were not allowed education except for some churchgoing. However, slaves developed their own arts and traditions, based partly on the African ways of their ancestors. Music sung and played by slaves became the basis of jazz, the blues, and much of modern American popular music.

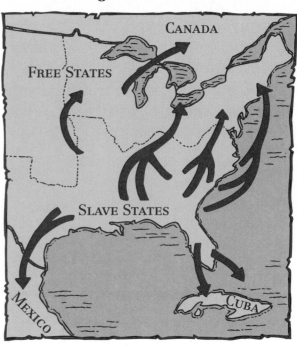

Some Routes of the Underground Railroad

Some slaves tried to revolt. Nat Turner led a slave revolt in which some white families were killed. It resulted in harsher laws to control slaves. Others escaped to northern states or non-slavery countries. A network of black and white people who helped slaves escape was called the Underground Railroad. Former slave Harriet Tubman helped lead more than 300 people to freedom through that system. Even though no actual railroad existed, such helpers were called conductors, and houses where escaping slaves could rest in hiding were called stations.

Read the sentences about slavery.
Then complete the sentences by filling in each blank.
Use the word list if you need help.

★ The cotton gin made growing cotton more _____.

★ Eli _____ invented the cotton gin.

★ Nat _____ led a slave rebellion.

★ The _____ Railroad helped slaves escape.

★ Those who helped slaves escape on the Underground Railroad were known as

_____.

★ One of every _____ families in the South
owned slaves.

★ _____, a country north of the United States, was
one of the areas to which some slaves escaped.

★ Plantation slaves worked in the fields, as craftsmen, or in the owner's

_____.

★ Harriet _____ is known as a famous African
American conductor on the Underground Railroad.

★ Slave drivers were usually _____ themselves.

★ The _____ created by slaves became the basis
of jazz and the blues.

Word List

Canada	household	slaves	Underground
conductors	music	Tubman	Whitney
four	profitable	Turner	

Frederick Douglass

Frederick Douglass was a great African American speaker. He was a leader in the abolition movement to end slavery in the United States. Douglass was born a slave with the name Frederick Bailey on a plantation in Maryland. As a boy he was sent to serve in a city house in Baltimore. There, his master's wife began to teach him to read and write—until her husband stopped her. Douglass kept learning on his own. He blacked, or polished, boots to earn money, then paid a white boy to get his first book. Soon he was writing out passes, allowing runaway slaves to claim they were free.

As a young man, Douglass was sent to learn ship caulking. He managed to escape his place of work, taking a train to New York. For safety, he changed his name from Bailey to Douglass and moved farther north into Massachusetts. There he worked as a day laborer. One day, he spoke up at an abolition meeting. He spoke so well that he was hired by the Massachusetts Anti-Slavery Society to lecture in other towns. Douglass told about the evils of slavery, especially the breaking up of slave families. He had in mind the master who had split him from his own mother at birth, then separated him from a loving grandmother when he was a child.

Douglass wrote a book telling the story of his life and started his own paper, the *North Star*. He believed African Americans should lead in the struggle for their freedom. He used his house in Rochester, New York, as a station in the Underground Railroad to hide escaping slaves.

When the Civil War began, Douglass was one of the first to urge that African Americans be allowed to serve in the Union army. He was too old to fight himself, but his two sons joined the army. In old age, he lived an honored life in Washington, D.C., where he held various offices, including U.S. minister to Haiti.

Read the clues about Frederick Douglass.
Then complete the puzzle using the word list on the next page.

★ Across ★

5. Douglass was most famous as a _____ for the abolition of slavery.
6. City where Douglass lived in old age
9. City where Douglass grew up and learned to read

10. Relatives of Douglass who fought in the Civil War
11. State where Douglass was born on a plantation
12. Douglass especially hated the _____ of slave families.
14. Two-letter abbreviation of the state to which Douglass went to escape slavery

★ Down ★

1. Douglass's job when he first escaped slavery
2. Country to which Douglass served as U.S. minister
3. Douglass's last name when he was a slave
4. In Rochester, Douglass used his home as an Underground Railroad _____.
7. Term used for the idea of ending slavery
8. Young Douglass wrote free _____ for runaway slaves.
13. Douglass urged that African Americans be allowed to join this.

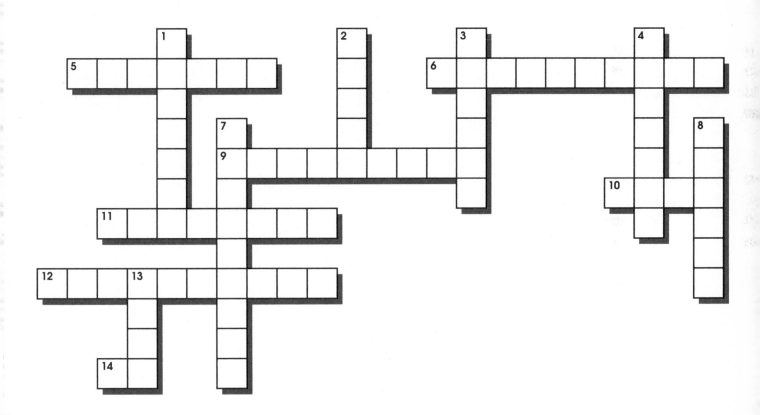

Word List

ABOLITION	BALTIMORE	NY	SPEAKER
ARMY	HAITI	PASSES	STATION
BAILEY	LABORER	SEPARATION	WASHINGTON
	MARYLAND	SONS	

Abraham Lincoln

Abraham Lincoln was born in 1809 in a Kentucky log cabin, and then moved with his family to farms on the frontier in Indiana and in Illinois. He educated himself by reading, and in 1834, he became a legislator, helping make laws for the state of Illinois. In 1836, he became a lawyer. Lincoln married a Kentucky woman, Mary Todd, and in time they had four sons. Lincoln became nationally famous when he ran for U.S. Senate against Stephen Douglas. In a series of public arguments called the Lincoln-Douglas Debates, Lincoln declared the nation could not last "half slave and half free."

The Republican Party made Lincoln their candidate for president in 1860. He won, and only a month after his election, the rebel Confederate states were at war with the United States. On January 1, 1863, he freed the slaves in the rebelling states with the Emancipation Proclamation. His aim was to discourage the South with the proclamation. Lincoln always said he was personally against slavery, but he thought the union of the states was the most important issue. Midway through the war, Lincoln spoke at a battlefield near Gettysburg, Pennsylvania. He asked Americans to stick to the ideals of freedom and equality for which many men had died.

The Lincoln Memorial in Washington, D.C.

When he was reelected as president toward the end of the war, Lincoln promised that the government would act "with malice (meanness) toward none, with charity (kindness, generosity) for all." However, Lincoln was shot while he sat in a theater shortly after the end of the war by John Wilkes Booth, a man still angry about the South's loss. The assassin's bullet did not stop the ideals Lincoln worked for—freedom, equality, and national unity.

Use the word list to help you find the words
about Abraham Lincoln that are hidden in the block below.
Some of the words are hidden backward or diagonally.

```
R L E M A N C I P A T I O N O R
B E C Q M F A N I R R H S I E C
C G P U T N I B A C G O L P U W
I I H U C D O U G L A S A L L G
G S J I B X H I S E N B X F T E
L L R P N L S D M A H O H L N T
A A M J W R I L L I N O I S E T
W T A C G A K C S W X T A L M Y
Y O R R N M Q D A E S H T A N S
E R Y L S C E K E N T I L V R B
R M T N E D I S E R P D J E E U
T O O U T H E A T E R A L R V R
L T D C A C T H V Y A P R Y O G
G E D T B Y K C U T N E K T G O
S S B Z E Q U A L I T Y W S Y U
F R E E D O M E U N I T Y H D A
```

Word List

BOOTH	FREEDOM	LAWYER	REPUBLICAN PARTY
DEBATES	GETTYSBURG	LEGISLATOR	SLAVERY
DOUGLAS	GOVERNMENT	LOG CABIN	THEATER
EMANCIPATION	ILLINOIS	MARY TODD	UNITY
EQUALITY	KENTUCKY	PRESIDENT	WAR

Fighting the Civil War

When Abraham Lincoln was elected president in 1860, South Carolina decided to leave, or secede from, the Union. However, Fort Sumter, on the Carolina coast, remained in the hands of the U.S. Army. Angry state officials had the fort bombarded, and the Civil War began.

Eleven states in the South united to form the Confederacy, headed by Jefferson Davis. Robert E. Lee, once a U.S. Army officer, agreed to lead the Confederate army. Lincoln named several generals to lead the Union army, but finally he came to depend most on Ulysses S. Grant.

Lincoln decided to weaken the South by cutting off its oceangoing trade with a naval blockade. Meanwhile, the North, with its many factories and people, was well supplied.

Many soldiers were killed in the war, partly because improved rifles and cannons killed more efficiently than the older models. Even more men died, however, because of infected wounds and diseases that swept the camps and military prisons.

Midway through the war, Lincoln freed slaves in the rebelling states with the Emancipation Proclamation. Since slaves in the rebelling states were under the power of the Confederacy, the Proclamation did not set slaves free immediately. However, it paved the way for a complete end to slavery after the war.

Although the South won major battles early in the war, the tide turned at Gettysburg, Pennsylvania. There, the Union held back General Lee's attempt to invade the northern states. In battles at Vicksburg and Chattanooga, the Union gained control of western Confederate states. Then, while Grant pushed southward, Union General William Sherman's men made a long march through Georgia to the sea. His troops burned crops and houses, destroying anything that could help the Confederate army stay alive. Finally, Lee surrendered to Grant at the Appomattox Courthouse in Virginia, on April 9, 1865.

Read the clues about the Civil War. Then complete the puzzle using the word list on the next page.

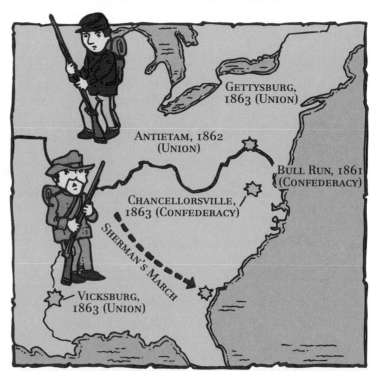

Important Civil War Battles and Who Won Them

GETTYSBURG, 1863 (UNION)

ANTIETAM, 1862 (UNION)

BULL RUN, 1861 (CONFEDERACY)

CHANCELLORSVILLE, 1863 (CONFEDERACY)

SHERMAN'S MARCH

VICKSBURG, 1863 (UNION)

★ Across ★

1. The first full battle of the Civil War was at _____ Run, near Washington, D.C.

4. The North had more of these to make arms and supplies.
6. Location of an important battle in Mississippi
8. Initials of the most important Union general
10. Number of states in the Confederacy
11. Lee did this at Appomattox Courthouse.
12. Last name of the Union general who destroyed property across the South
13. Last name of the leader of the Confederacy

★ *Down* ★

1. Line of ships used to stop trade with the South
2. Last name of the general who led the Confederate army
3. State where the Confederates surrendered
5. The Emancipation Proclamation ended this in the Confederacy.
7. Lincoln had several of these but depended most on Grant.
8. The side that won the battle at Gettysburg
9. Name of the fort where the Civil War started
12. Initials of the state that was first to secede

Word List

BLOCKADE	FACTORIES	SHERMAN	UNION
BULL	GENERALS	SLAVERY	USG
DAVIS	LEE	SUMTER	VICKSBURG
ELEVEN	SC	SURRENDER	VIRGINIA

Reconstruction

Reconstruction means, "rebuilding." After the Civil War, the president and Congress struggled over the best way to rebuild the South. President Andrew Johnson put in place a plan of reconstruction that allowed states of the old Confederacy to rejoin the Union easily. Soon most Southern states had passed laws called the black codes, which kept freedmen (former slaves) from voting, assembling, or working at many jobs. Congress did establish a Freedmen's Bureau to help the former slaves. The bureau founded over 4,000 schools in five years. Adults often attended these schools along with the children to learn how to read and write.

Congress grew angry over the way the new state governments were treating the freedmen. It passed amendments to the Constitution to guarantee citizens' rights. When some states refused to accept the amendments, Congress sent the army back to the South to enforce them. Congress also passed Reconstruction Acts in 1867 that required real changes. Under the acts, new representatives were elected in the South, including the first African Americans in government. The new state governments raised taxes to pay for rebuilding, though some of the money went into the pockets of selfish politicians. Northerners came south to help with the reconstruction—or to make a profit. White Southerners named them all after the cheap suitcase of the day—carpetbaggers.

By 1877, Reconstruction had died out in the South. Why? White Southerners in general resented Reconstruction bitterly. Some people were making unfair profits from it. And Congress lost interest. Then, violence by secret groups like the Ku Klux Klan kept African Americans from voting or getting good jobs. Many black people lived in poverty as sharecroppers, working the land for a share of the crop. Most of them were always paying off debts—money borrowed so they could live until harvest time.

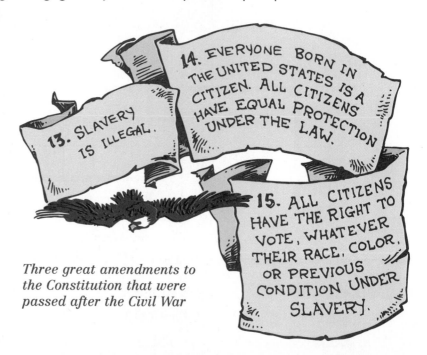

13. SLAVERY IS ILLEGAL.

14. EVERYONE BORN IN THE UNITED STATES IS A CITIZEN. ALL CITIZENS HAVE EQUAL PROTECTION UNDER THE LAW.

15. ALL CITIZENS HAVE THE RIGHT TO VOTE, WHATEVER THEIR RACE, COLOR, OR PREVIOUS CONDITION UNDER SLAVERY.

Three great amendments to the Constitution that were passed after the Civil War

Words about Reconstruction have been scrambled.
Rearrange the letters and write the correct word on each line.
Use the word list if you need help.

MARY

_____

PROSREHRESCAP

_____

ERENDMEF

_____

DECREFNOYCA

_____

THIGRS

_____

SREGNOSC

_____

TBSED

_____

PGRETSBAREGAC

_____

NMESTANDME

_____

REPOVYT

_____

NNIOU

_____

OSJHONN

_____

Word List

AMENDMENTS	CONFEDERACY	FREEDMEN	RIGHTS
ARMY	CONGRESS	JOHNSON	SHARECROPPERS
CARPETBAGGERS	DEBTS	POVERTY	UNION

Women's Rights

"All men and women are created equal." This statement was at the heart of a declaration made at the first women's rights convention, held at Seneca Falls, New York, in 1848. The organizers of the conference, Lucretia Mott and Elizabeth Cady Stanton, were active in the abolition movement. As they argued that slaves should have freedom and rights, they realized that women should, too.

American women were not allowed to vote. In many states, women were not even allowed to own property or keep their own wages. Most jobs and colleges were closed to them.

Important Places for Women's Rights

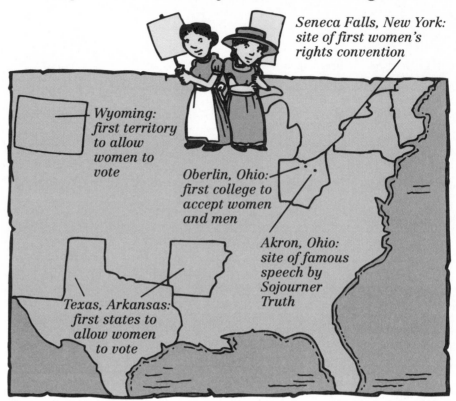

Seneca Falls, New York: site of first women's rights convention

Wyoming: first territory to allow women to vote

Oberlin, Ohio: first college to accept women and men

Akron, Ohio: site of famous speech by Sojourner Truth

Texas, Arkansas: first states to allow women to vote

Many women took part in the struggle to change all this. The Grimké sisters, Sarah and Angelina, asked lawmakers to consider freedom for women as well as freedom for slaves. Sojourner Truth, herself a former slave, pointed out that women could work as hard as men could.

One of the greatest workers for women's rights was Susan B. Anthony. She lectured and organized tirelessly all her life. Anthony met Elizabeth Cady Stanton soon after the Seneca Falls conference. Stanton became Anthony's speechwriter and good friend. They led the struggle for a New York law allowing women to keep their own wages. It became a model for laws in other states.

The fight for woman suffrage, or the right of women to vote, lasted many decades. Anthony and other early leaders did not live to see their ideal gained. At last in 1920, the Nineteenth Amendment was passed, allowing all women in the United States the right to vote.

Words about women's rights have been scrambled.
Rearrange the letters and write the correct word on each line.
Use the word list if you need help.

TEOV

_____

VINCENTOON

_____

TOMT

_____

NSTONTA

_____

DERMOFE

_____

UJRSNREOO

_____

FGUSRAFE

_____

THRIGS

_____

NITENETENH

_____

YNOTAHN

_____

ECANES SLALF

_____

ITILNOOAB

_____

Word List

ABOLITION	FREEDOM	RIGHTS	STANTON
ANTHONY	MOTT	SENECA FALLS	SUFFRAGE
CONVENTION	NINETEENTH	SOJOURNER	VOTE

The Fate of the Indians

From the first arrival of Europeans on the East Coast, Indians were pushed westward. In 1830, Congress tried to end problems between settlers and Indians. The Indian Removal Act forced all Indians living east of the Mississippi River to move far west to the land that is now Oklahoma. Earlier agreements and treaties were broken as many tribes were forced to leave their homelands. The Cherokee Indians lost about a quarter of their people on the trail, to disease, cold, and hunger. For that reason, the journey to Oklahoma was called the Trail of Tears.

After the Civil War, the buffalo-hunting tribes of the Great Plains lost more and more game and land to settlers. The government tried to keep the Indians on plots of land set aside for them, called reservations. There, they were supposed to farm instead of hunt. But the Sioux and other tribes wanted freedom to move and hunt as they had done before. The U.S. Army came to the plains to protect settlers and enforce the reservation law. Full battles between the army and various tribes sometimes resulted. In 1876, in what is now Montana, Sioux warriors wiped out General George Custer and all of his men at the Battle of the Little Bighorn (also called Custer's Last Stand). Within a year, though, the Sioux leader, Crazy Horse, had to surrender to the army. Nez Percé people, from Oregon, fled across Idaho and Montana to try to escape into Canada. The army caught them and their leader, Chief Joseph, just before they reached the border. Chief Joseph spoke for many Indians when he said, "My heart is sick and sad."

As America expanded, Native American tribes were forced to move farther west.

The Nez Percé were sent to a reservation.

In 1887, Congress passed the Dawes Act. The act said only individual Indians, not tribes, had the right to hold land. Millions of acres of reservation land were sold off to non-Indians. It was not until the 1930's that this policy ended. Then, a new law stopped the breakup of tribal lands, allowed native peoples to govern themselves on reservations, and encouraged tribes to keep their traditions and customs.

Read the clues about the fate of the Indians. Then complete the puzzle using the word list on the next page.

★ Across ★

2. Plains tribe, most living north of the Canadian border

7. Tribe living in the farthest southwest part of the plains
8. State on land where eastern tribes were forced to move
9. Chief of the Nez Percé
10. Areas set aside for tribes by the government
12. Tribe that (with some Cheyenne) defeated Custer
13. Tribe that lost a quarter of its people on the way to Oklahoma

★ Down ★

1. The Nez _____ originally lived on the northeast edge of the plains.
2. Custer was defeated at the Battle of the Little _____.
3. The Trail of Tears resulted from the Indian _____ Act.
4. Custer's position in the U.S. Army
5. Second word in the name of the Sioux chief who defeated Custer
6. Name of the act that allowed only individual Indians to own land
11. These groups could no longer own land under the Dawes Act.

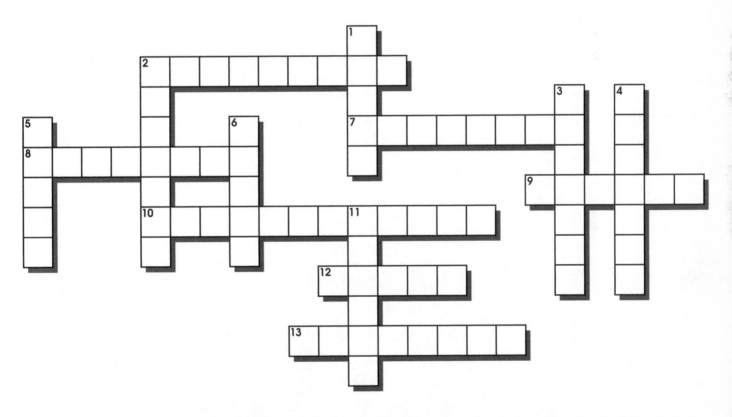

Word List

BIGHORN   COMANCHE   JOSEPH   RESERVATIONS

BLACKFEET   DAWES   OKLAHOMA   SIOUX

CHEROKEE   GENERAL   PERCE   TRIBES

HORSE   REMOVAL

Homesteading

During the Civil War, Congress passed the Homestead Act. It gave citizens or immigrants 160 acres of land on the Great Plains if they settled there for five years. The aim was to create many small farms from Wisconsin westward. At the same time, new railroads tried to encourage settlement in order to get more business. They sold land they had bought or that had been granted to them by the government when their lines were built.

People came from the eastern United States and from many other countries to homestead. They found treeless prairie covered with tough-rooted grass. A steel plow could cut through the roots, but often there was not enough water. Homesteaders learned "dry farming," in which grains are planted deep to catch moisture low in the soil. Homesteaders learned other ways to get along on the plains. Without enough wood, they built houses called "soddies" from blocks of root-filled earth. Their fires burned with dry buffalo droppings called chips. To pump up drinking water, they built windmills to catch the prairie wind. They learned the importance of planting trees to hold the soil once the prairie grass was plowed.

The new farmers faced many problems—blizzards, fires, drought, and sometimes grasshoppers that ate everything from crops to boots! Even at home in their sod houses, people were irritated by snakes and insects falling from the ceiling. Yet homesteading still drew people. In 1893, a last bit of land was opened for homesteading—the Cherokee Outlet in Oklahoma. Over 100,000 people lined the Kansas border to rush in when the signal was given.

Use the word list to help you find the words
about homesteading that are hidden in the block below.
Some of the words are hidden backward or diagonally.

```
P  S  R  E  P  P  O  H  S  S  A  R  G  E  D  W
D  R  Y  F  A  R  M  I  N  G  I  S  U  S  K  A
B  A  E  I  H  D  S  E  T  T  L  E  M  E  N  T
D  S  V  R  S  O  L  B  M  D  W  R  L  G  C  E
J  M  K  E  D  B  L  I  Z  Z  A  R  D  R  O  R
A  Y  S  D  R  T  I  M  D  T  P  O  W  E  S  R
H  P  I  N  O  D  M  S  R  H  T  C  O  A  I  A
I  E  U  P  U  M  D  H  J  B  D  I  B  T  T  I
S  A  M  F  G  A  N  B  R  A  C  D  A  P  B  L
C  K  I  A  H  J  I  A  E  F  Q  M  R  L  D  R
U  V  S  R  T  C  W  T  K  T  O  L  O  A  T  O
E  S  Q  M  B  L  S  M  R  H  A  F  B  I  S  A
M  P  F  S  I  E  S  C  A  J  E  G  J  N  E  D
K  O  K  V  M  D  O  L  C  M  P  B  D  S  E  S
B  R  I  O  D  P  K  T  B  E  I  R  I  A  R  P
S  C  H  E  R  O  K  E  E  O  U  T  L  E  T  C
```

Word List

BLIZZARD	DRY FARMING	GREAT PLAINS	SETTLEMENT
CHEROKEE OUTLET	FARMS	HOMESTEAD	SODDIES
CIVIL WAR	FIRE	OKLAHOMA	TREES
CROPS	FIVE	PRAIRIE	WATER
DROUGHT	GRASSHOPPERS	RAILROADS	WINDMILLS

Cowboys

The first American cowboys were really Mexicans. They raised longhorn cattle in Texas while it was still part of Mexico. Most features of cowboy life developed there. The main job of a cowboy was to move herds of steer from place to place and to protect the animals on the open land. Texas cowboys used a well-trained small horse that could turn easily to stop and steer the cattle. They threw a rope loop called a lasso to catch individual animals. They marked cows with a branding iron to show who owned them.

Branding was necessary because herds often mixed on the plains, and land ownership was not clear. Texas cowboys wore leather leggings called chaps to protect their legs from brush and cactus. Cowboy hats developed from the broad Mexican sombrero.

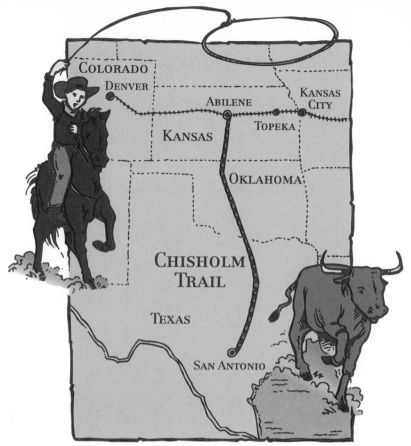

Cattle drives were made each spring on trails such as the Chisholm Trail.

Cowboys moved north when the first railroads came to Kansas and Missouri. Texan cattle owners realized that if they could get animals to the railroad, they could ship them to Chicago for slaughter and sale to eastern cities. People there paid well for good beef. Every spring, cowboys were hired by the cattle owners to drive huge herds north to the railroad.

A cattle drive took many weeks, since a herd could only travel about fifteen miles a day. Cowboys kept the thousands of cows together and guarded against rustlers, thieves, and stampedes. To calm the herd, cowboys sang to them. Cowboy songs became an important part of American popular music.

As the nation expanded westward, longhorns were kept not only in Texas, but also on huge open grasslands called ranges all over the plains. In some sparsely settled areas, cattle owners took the place of government. Their decisions were called "cow custom," which meant the law of the herd owners. After barbed wire was invented in 1873, farmers fenced their land to keep out cattle. Soon the herd owners and cowboys themselves were building fences to create enclosed ranches, and the wandering cowboy life came to an end.

Read the sentences about cowboys.
Then complete each sentence by filling in each blank.
Use the word list if you need help.

★ An uncontrolled rush of cattle is called a _____.

★ Cattle thieves were called _____.

★ Cowboys used a well-trained _____ to help herd cows.

★ Cowboys threw a rope called a _____ to catch cows.

★ Texas cowboys used a branding _____ to mark the cows to show ownership.

★ Cowboys wore leather leggings called _____ to protect against brush.

★ A herd could travel about _____ miles in a day.

★ Community decisions made by cattle owners were called cow _____.

★ Cowboys raised _____ cattle in Texas.

★ Taking a herd to a distant location is known as a cattle _____.

Word List

chaps	drive	iron	rustlers
custom	fifteen	lasso	stampede
	horse	longhorn	

Inventions

Thomas Edison was called the Wizard of Menlo Park because he and the people working in his Menlo Park, New Jersey, laboratory produced over 1,000 inventions after the Civil War. The greatest was the electric light bulb. Edison also invented the phonograph and one of the first motion picture cameras.

Edison was not the only inventor hard at work between the middle 1800s and into the early twentieth century. Alexander Graham Bell invented the telephone in 1876. Guglielmo Marconi (gool-YEL-moh mar-COH-nee), an Italian, invented the wireless telegraph, which led to radio. The American press gave huge coverage to Marconi's experiment in which a signal from England was received in North America. And Dr. John Kellogg invented cornflakes! His first cold cereal went along with other inventions that made food easier to keep and prepare, such as home canning and refrigeration.

These and many other inventions helped a great change to come about called the Industrial Revolution. This revolution was a change from work done by hand to work done by machines. The Industrial Revolution was first set in motion in England, where the steam engine was invented. The first American factories, built in the early 1800s in New England, spun yarn and wove cloth using power from a wheel turned by water. Beginning in the middle 1800s, steam engines powered factories, boats, and trains. In Pennsylvania, Edwin Drake first drilled for oil that was used to grease the engines and served as a valuable fuel. Trains began to roll on steel rails instead of iron because the new Bessemer process created long-lasting steel more quickly and inexpensively than old style steel. Strong steel lay at the heart of many inventions, from the typewriter to the skyscraper to the barbed wire used especially by farmers and ranchers in the west.

Some Inventions of the 19th Century

PHONOGRAPH, 1863

SEWING MACHINE, 1846

TELEPHONE, 1876

Read the clues about inventions.
Then complete the puzzle using the word list on the next page.

★ Across ★

1. Last name of the inventor of cornflakes
5. The Industrial _____ expanded in the United States after the Civil War.
8. Kind of wire used to keep animals in or out

11. Edison invented the _____bulb.
12. This invention helped people talk over long distances.
13. Process that made steel quicker and cheaper to produce
14. Edison was called this as a nickname.

★ Down ★

2. Last name of the inventor who, with his laboratory partners, invented over 1,000 things
3. With a _____ machine, clothes could be made more quickly.
4. Substance that powered engines in the second half of the 1800s
6. Last name of the inventor of the wireless telegraph
7. Made of steel, these were laid all over the United States after the Civil War.
9. Substance that powered the first American factories
10. Strong, long-lasting material used in many inventions

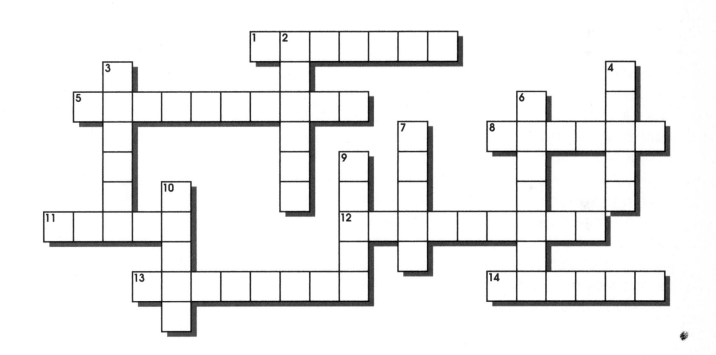

Word List

BARBED	KELLOGG	REVOLUTION	TELEPHONE
BESSEMER	LIGHT	SEWING	WATER
EDISON	MARCONI	STEAM	WIZARD
	RAILS	STEEL	

Big Business

The late 1800's brought a huge growth spurt to American business. American stores, for instance, became larger to sell the many new products being invented and produced. Before, people had to go to several small shops to find what they wanted. Now, large department stores opened in cities, offering such items as clothes, shoes, furniture, and food, all under one roof. Woolworth's and J.C. Penney also appeared as early chain stores, which were nearly identical stores under the same ownership, sprinkled all across the country. Sears, Roebuck and Co. and other stores sold their products for the first time through catalogs sent nationwide. This was the beginning of the mail-order catalog business, today a multibillion-dollar industry.

This cartoon from the late 19th century shows how rich business owners had the reputation for caring about nothing except money and golf.

Larger and larger companies were creating the products people bought. John D. Rockefeller founded one of the largest—the Standard Oil Company. Standard Oil first grew by buying up other oil producers and oil refiners. Rockefeller joined these companies into a new type of business organization called a trust. In a trust, a central board of directors reduces competition among its companies and sets prices. When one organization sells nearly all of the available supply of one product, as Rockefeller did with American oil, it is called a monopoly. A monopoly can be dangerous because it can keep prices for its goods high without worrying about another business selling the same thing for less.

Many people were upset when big businesses destroyed smaller ones and forced buyers to pay high prices. The government responded to the public feeling with the Sherman Antitrust Act of 1890. The law was supposed to keep trusts from ending competition. The law turned out to be difficult to enforce, but it showed that government could have a role in setting business rules.

Business owners defended themselves against public criticism by saying they increased economic activity and so helped the nation. Andrew Carnegie, owner of a huge steel company, argued that rich businesspeople should use their money to help other people. At the end of his life, Carnegie gave his money to found public libraries all over the nation and to help build hospitals and schools.

Read the clues about big business.
Then complete the puzzle using the word list on the next page.

★ *Across* ★

1. Name of the oil company Rockefeller founded
2. One set of officers controls competition and prices among several companies in

this form of business.

4. From this book, customers could order goods by mail.
6. Building full of books; Carnegie paid for many
7. A monopoly can control the _____ of goods.
9. A business controlling all of one product
11. Kind of store selling many sorts of things under one roof
12. Rockefeller bought out both oil producers and oil _____.
13. A place where early department stores were located

★ *Down* ★

1. Product that made Carnegie rich
3. John D. _____ created one of the first trusts.
4. This man made a fortune in steel, then gave much of it away.
5. The Sherman Antitrust Act showed that _____ had a role in making rules for business.
10. Kind of store that sells the same items in many locations

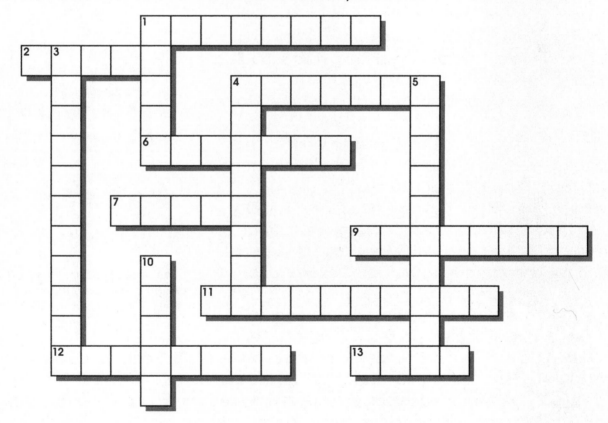

Word List

CARNEGIE	CITY	MONOPOLY	STANDARD
CATALOG	DEPARTMENT	PRICE	STEEL
CHAIN	GOVERNMENT	REFINERS	TRUST
	LIBRARY	ROCKEFELLER	

Immigration

After the Civil War and through the early years of the twentieth century, a great wave of people came to live in the United States from other countries. Before 1880, most of these immigrants were from northwestern European countries including Ireland, Britain, Germany, and the Scandinavian nations. After 1880, more and more came from southeastern Europe, from such countries as Italy, Greece, Poland, and Russia.

Late in the 1800s, little open land remained for farming, but the rapidly growing cities offered jobs in factories. Poor immigrants lived in crowded conditions, many in poorly built apartment buildings called tenements. They worked for low wages, often in sweatshops. These were small factories where hours were long and the pay low. Most immigrants felt that education was the key to a better life. Immigrant children filled the public schools, and many adults went to school at night.

Many of the immigrants who settled on the West Coast were Asian. Chinese people first arrived in large numbers to prospect for gold in 1849, and, later, to work on the railroads. Chinese workers laid most of the track for the Central Pacific Railroad, which ran from California eastward to Utah, where it joined the Union Pacific to become the first transcontinental railroad—a railroad spanning across the continent. Many Japanese people came to the United States to work on orchards and farms. Both Japanese and Chinese immigrants faced prejudice—negative opinions about them because of their race. In 1882, Congress passed the first of a set of

The Statue of Liberty, a gift from France, greets immigrants in New York harbor.

laws to keep Chinese people out of the country. In the 1920s, Congress decided to control all immigration through quotas—limits on the number of immigrants from a region or country. The quotas ended three centuries of unlimited immigration. The quota system based on country of origin was done away with in 1965.

Read the sentences about immigration.
Then complete the sentences by filling in each blank.
Use the word list if you need help.

★ _____ gave the Statue of Liberty to the United States as a gift in 1886.

★ Chinese workers helped build the first _____ railroad.

★ In sweatshops, hours were _____.

★ The _____ of Liberty stands in New York harbor.

★ Congress passed the first _____ to keep Chinese people out of the U.S. in 1882.

★ Someone who comes from another country to live permanently in a new country

is called an _____.

★ Most immigrants came from _____ Europe before 1880.

★ A negative opinion of a group of people based on race is known as

_____.

★ The quota system was designed to _____ all immigration.

★ Many Asian immigrants settled on the _____ Coast.

Word List

control	**immigrant**	**northwestern**	**transcontinental**
France	**law**	**prejudice**	**West**
	long	**Statue**	

Jane Addams

Jane Addams helped make life better in American cities. She was born into a wealthy family in Cedarville, Illinois. As a young woman, she visited London. In a poor neighborhood there, she visited Toynbee Hall, a "settlement house" where students from Oxford University were helping people. Addams decided to try to do something similar in her home state. She used her own inherited money to start the project.

Jane Addams, a woman who was devoted to helping others, especially poor children.

With a friend, Ellen Gates Starr, she leased a house in a run-down, rat-infested neighborhood in Chicago and called it Hull House. The two friends opened a reading room and a kindergarten. Soon, Hull House was offering cooking, health, and English classes for poor immigrants. Neighborhood people were welcome to come for help in everything from finding a place to live to learning to sew. Addams worked to get the city to improve garbage collection and sewers. Hull House also acted as a center for the arts, with an art gallery and a music school. People paid a small amount for Hull House services. The point was not to give away charity but to help people become independent. By 1895, Addams's idea had been imitated in fifty more settlement houses in American cities. Many such houses exist today.

Addams did more than run Hull House. She worked especially hard for poor children. She helped end child labor in Illinois and worked to create juvenile courts, where children accused of crimes could be treated differently from adults. Addams thought fun was important, too. She sent city children to country summer camps and helped create the first public playground in Chicago.

Read the clues about Jane Addams.
Then complete the puzzle using the word list on the next page.

★ *Across* ★

2. Addams helped set up _____ courts for children.
5. Immigrants could learn this language at Hull House.
6. City where Hull House was founded
8. Hull House had an art _____.
9. Term used for a city social services institution—_____house
11. Students from this university helped run Toynbee Hall.

12. A room for this was one of the first things Addams established at Hull House.

Down

1. What Addams used to pay for Hull House
3. Addams helped improve life in these.
4. Addams established the first of these in Chicago, just for children.
7. First word in name of Addams's settlement house
8. Addams convinced the city to collect this better.
9. Last name of the friend who helped Addams set up Hull House
10. First word in the name of the London house that inspired Addams

Word List

CHICAGO	GALLERY	JUVENILE	SETTLEMENT
CITIES	GARBAGE	OXFORD	STARR
ENGLISH	HULL	PLAYGROUND	TOYNBEE
	INHERITANCE	READING	

Theodore Roosevelt

Theodore Roosevelt's life spanned both the nineteenth and twentieth centuries. He helped the nation move into modern times. Born in New York City in 1858, Roosevelt was, as he said himself, a "sickly" boy. He learned to box, wrestle, and hunt to become stronger. He threw himself into all he did with great energy. He attended Harvard College, then divided his time between New York politics and writing. For two years he ran a ranch in the Dakota Territory.

Roosevelt became nationally known during the Spanish-American War of 1898. The war began when Spain refused to give Cuba independence, and the United States sided with Cuba. Roosevelt collected friends, some of them western cowboys, to go and fight in Cuba. These "Rough Riders" helped win the war against Spain.

Famous as a Rough Rider, Roosevelt was elected governor of New York, then vice president of the United States. He became the youngest president in history when President McKinley was shot in 1901. Roosevelt was popular and liked to have fun. On a hunting trip, he refused to shoot a bear cub. Quickly, a toy maker created the "Teddy Bear" to remember the event. The stuffed bear became a popular American toy.

Roosevelt liked to say people should have a fair, or "square," deal. He became the first president to step between owners and workers when a coal strike created hardships. He threatened to seize the mines if owners would not agree to talk. The owners did agree, and finally the two sides settled fairly. Roosevelt had the Justice Department sue a northwestern railroad monopoly for stopping business competition. It was the first of his many moves to "bust trusts," which means to break up combinations of businesses that are controlling prices. He also worked to set up the Pure Food and Drug Act, which still protects American food safety. Finally, he loved nature; he added to the national parks and created national forests and wildlife refuges—places where animals could not be hunted.

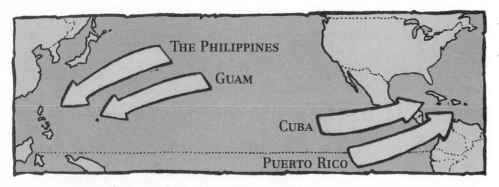

Land acquired by the United States in the Spanish-American War

Industry Builds

Use the word list to help you find the words
about Theodore Roosevelt that are hidden in the block below.
Some of the words are hidden backward or diagonally.

```
D P U R E F O O D A N D D R U G
F A I N A T I O N A L P A R K S
O S K H S R O U G H R I D E R S
R T G O V E R N O R E D Y B A F
E A J X T E D D Y B E A R U N H
S T H L T A Y L E F R N S D C J
T S P A I N T T D R A V R A H U
S A F E A O W E T E Q D E L I Q
W R L D M I S E R E T U H E Z S
R Y P E E T W H U R U K S N O L
I O C R R E C V S V I E H A E M
T M B A U G U H T C G T R U T F
I C O U T O B M S B P E O Z N L
N I H Q A T A P O P U L A R X T
G Z H S N E W Y O R K C I T Y U
M S P A N I S H A M E R I C A N
```

Word List

CUBA	**GOVERNOR**	**NATURE**	**RANCH**	**SQUARE DEAL**
DAKOTA TERRITORY	**HARVARD**	**NEW YORK CITY**	**ROUGH RIDERS**	**TEDDY BEAR**
FORESTS	**HUNT**	**POPULAR**	**SPAIN**	**TRUSTS**
	NATIONAL PARKS	**PURE FOOD AND DRUG**	**SPANISH AMERICAN**	**WRITING**

American History to 1900—Topics to Explore

You have read only a sampling of the events and people that shaped America's early history. Below, you will find a list of more topics related to American History to 1900. Choose some topics from the list, or think of other subjects on your own, that you would like to learn more about. Use the following pages to take notes and create your own activities.

Other Topics in American History to 1900:

- The American flag

- Sojourner Truth, evangelist, abolitionist, and feminist

- Native American societies and cultures

- The Statue of Liberty

- Railroads and the Great Railroad Strike

- Benjamin Franklin

- The Dred Scott case

- Clara Barton, founder of the American Red Cross

- Freedom of Speech

- The Alaska Purchase

Notes Page

Choose one of the topics from page 65, or think of a topic on your own, and write about what you know in the space below. Research your chosen topic further, using the library or the Internet to help you find information. Take lots of notes, as you will use these notes to create your own activity on the next page.

★ NOTES ★

Create Your Own Activity

Use this page to create your own activity based on the notes you took on the previous page. Share your activity with a friend.

Notes Page

Choose one of the topics from page 65, or think of a topic on your own, and write about what you know in the space below. Research your chosen topic further, using the library or the Internet to help you find information. Take lots of notes, as you will use these notes to create your own activity on the next page.

★ **NOTES** ★

Create Your Own Activity

Use this page to create your own activity based on the notes you took on the previous page. Share your activity with a friend.

Notes Page

Choose one of the topics from page 65, or think of a topic on your own, and write about what you know in the space below. Research your chosen topic further, using the library or the Internet to help you find information. Take lots of notes, as you will use these notes to create your own activity on the next page.

★ NOTES ★

Create Your Own Activity

Use this page to create your own activity based on the notes you took on the previous page. Share your activity with a friend.

AMERICAN HISTORY FROM 1900 TO THE PRESENT

Do you know why America's superhighways were built? Or how a Russian satellite transformed American education? Or why a sheep named Dolly may foretell the future of the human race? This section will help you review these and many other amazing facts about the U.S. from the early days of the twentieth century to the present.

The activities in this section are a practical and fun review of the U.S.'s history in the last 100 years to the present. You can use these activities to review a history topic or to learn about a subject you never knew about. Here is a fun way to learn that also reinforces what you are learning in school. You will also practice important skills like reading comprehension, vocabulary, and spelling.

To complete each activity, you will need to read and understand the reading selection, as well as locate information in illustrations or maps that may accompany each reading passage or activity. You can also find an appropriate word in the alphabetical list of words provided with most of the activities as another helpful tool in completing each activity.

If you have already learned about the topic that is featured, you may want to challenge yourself to complete as much of the activity as you can without reading the introduction, looking at the illustrations, or using the word lists.

Each activity focuses on a specific topic, and the topics are arranged in chronological order and by theme. Of course, not every history topic could be covered, but we have included those that are most often taught, and some that are simply most interesting and enjoyable. If a topic you want to explore is not included, you may wish to do some research on your own and create your own activities — complete with clues and/or word lists. We have included extra pages at the end of this section with suggestions for topics to explore.

Section 2

AMERICAN HISTORY FROM 1900 TO THE PRESENT

Table of Contents

Henry Ford and the Automobile

Henry Ford did not invent the automobile. In about 1900, when he started making his own cars, several kinds were already available for sale. However, automobiles cost so much that only rich people could afford them. Ford thought that he could make plenty of money selling cars if he could make them cheaply enough so that many people could afford to buy them.

Ford knew that the key to making less expensive cars was to make manufacturing more efficient. That meant making each worker's effort go further. When Ford first started, his workers spent a lot of time collecting the various auto parts from around the factory before they could assemble them. Ford had a better idea.

In Chicago, Ford had seen meat packers working in a line. Big pieces of meat hung from hooks attached to an overhead rope. Each worker did one thing to the meat, and then the meat was moved along the rope to the next worker. Ford decided to try this assembly line method in his factory.

He put his workers in a line along a conveyor belt. The auto traveled on the belt from person to person, and each worker added a part. The first time they tried this assembly line, car-building time was cut from about 12 hours to only 6. By the 1920s Ford factories turned out a car every ten seconds!

The assembly line soon became a standard feature in nearly every kind of factory. Because Ford's Model T was inexpensive, many people could afford it, and it became the most popular car in history. Owning a car allowed people to commute to the city more easily, which speeded the growth of suburbs. Driving also made it possible for families to travel more easily and to take more pleasure trips.

The automobile made businesses like motels and drive-thrus possible.

Words about Henry Ford and the automobile have been scrambled.
Rearrange the letters and write the correct word on each line.
Use the word list if you need help.

SRUBBUS

_____

TROYCAF

_____

MITE

_____

KORREW

_____

DOTHEM

_____

OMABILETOU

_____

MESBLASY ELNI

_____

VROCENOY TELB

_____

SEENEINPXIV

_____

STARP

_____

GAURNIFMUTCAN

_____

FENICTIFE

_____

Word List

ASSEMBLY LINE	EFFICIENT	MANUFACTURING	SUBURBS
AUTOMOBILE	FACTORY	METHOD	TIME
CONVEYOR BELT	INEXPENSIVE	PARTS	WORKER

The Wright Brothers Fly

As the twentieth century began, people around the world were trying to figure out how to fly. Already, some adventurers had attempted flight in "gliders"—machines that resembled airplanes but had no engines. Glider flights were short because these early flying machines had to be launched from a hilltop or set in motion by a towing vehicle. Gliders were so unreliable that most flights ended in crashes. Still, the idea of flying piqued the interest of Wilbur and Orville Wright of Dayton, Ohio. The brothers ran a print business and a bicycle shop, but their real love was looking for a way to fly.

Many glider flights ended in crashes.

The brothers tackled the question of flying methodically. First they worked to build a glider with wings bent so they would lift and hold the machine in flight. Then they practiced controlling and maneuvering the glider in flight. The brothers took their machines all the way to the shores of the Atlantic at Kitty Hawk, North Carolina, to practice. There the land was flat and free of people, with strong winds that could help a glider to fly. After years of work, the brothers added an engine to their glider, transforming it into a real airplane. On December 17, 1903, they successfully flew the first self-powered airplane at Kitty Hawk. Orville flew the first of four trial flights and Wilbur piloted the last and longest flight.

The invention of the airplane thrilled most Americans. In 1927, U.S. pilot Charles Lindbergh made the first solo flight across the Atlantic, becoming a hero around the world. Airplanes played a small but dramatic part in World War I and a large part in World War II. Since the 1950s, air travel has helped the nation's businesses, reduced travel time between parts of the country, and opened doors to the world.

Read the clues about the Wright Brothers and their attempts at flight. Then complete the puzzle using the word list on the next page.

★ Across ★

3. Early glider flights often ended in these accidents.
5. An American made the first _____ flight across the Atlantic.
9. Kitty Hawk is located near this ocean.
10. The first person to cross the Atlantic alone in an airplane
12. The Wright brothers owned this kind of shop.

13. Name of the first woman pilot to fly solo across the Atlantic

★ *Down* ★

1. First name of the Wright brother who piloted the first of a set of successful airplane flights
2. The buying and selling of goods and services; airplanes helped this grow
4. A glider could be launched from this landscape feature.
6. The month in which the first successful airplane flew
7. Hometown of the Wright brothers
8. First word in the North Carolina town where the Wrights tested their planes
11. Flying machines without engines

Amelia Earhart was the first woman to fly solo across the Atlantic—one year after Charles Lindbergh.

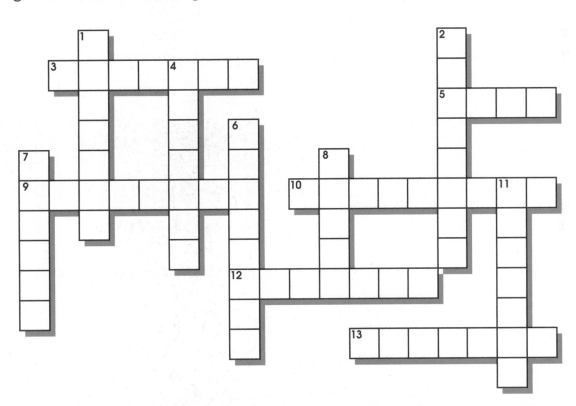

Word List

ATLANTIC	DAYTON	GLIDERS	LINDBERGH
BICYCLE	DECEMBER	HILLTOP	ORVILLE
BUSINESS	EARHART	KITTY	SOLO
CRASHES			

World War I

U.S. President Woodrow Wilson wanted to stay out of the fighting when World War I began in 1914. The conflict started as a small squabble, but mushroomed because so many countries were tied together in alliances. By 1917, the "Central Powers," led by Germany, were fighting against Britain, France, and other allies around the world. Then German submarines called U-boats began to sink American ships, and a telegram was uncovered in which Germany invited Mexico to join an attack on the United States. Wilson asked Congress to declare war in order to "end all wars."

World War I began with an assassination in Bosnia.

About two million American troops helped make a difference on fields where exhausted soldiers had been shooting at one another from trenches for years. The U.S. and its allies defeated the Central Powers in 1918.

World War I helped bring on important changes in the United States. Women, who were important to the war effort at home and in the field (especially as nurses), were granted the right to vote in 1920 after decades of effort. A second important change was the migration of African Americans northward in search of jobs and better conditions. This "Great Migration" began when many men in the North left their jobs to go to war, and newcomers from the South took their places.

After World War I, the nation remained unwilling to get involved in world affairs. The U.S refused to join the "League of Nations," an alliance of countries that would unite to help resolve conflicts peacefully. When Germany returned to war two decades after World War I, there was no organization in place to help stop World War II.

Many died at the end of World War I from a disease called the Spanish Flu.

Use the word list to help you find the words about
World War I that are hidden in the block on the next page.
Some of the words are hidden backward or diagonally.

```
V W J T C U P S O L D I E R G M
A O L E N F O R K S E G D E R R
R M T L A L D I W L A P R C E L
Q E P E B T S A T O I M H A A N
U N M G R G R F V R A J O L T P
L P C R I A E F O N O C M L M S
N H L A T L W A Y E V O R I I T
I H R M A L O D N G W N P E G A
R T B T I I P L B N F F J S R O
A A H T N A L R I A W L M O A B
W I L S O N A O S H O I U C T U
D N B E H C R W Y C U C M X I F
L L S J S E T H I T Z T D A O N
R G D M T S N X E C N A R F N I
O L E A G U E O F N A T I O N S
W F S B R M C R T B R C A B T K
```

Word List

ALLIANCES	CONFLICT	MEXICO	VOTE
ALLIES	FRANCE	SOLDIER	WILSON
BRITAIN	GERMANY	TELEGRAM	WOMEN
CENTRAL POWERS	GREAT MIGRATION	TROOPS	WORLD AFFAIRS
CHANGE	LEAGUE OF NATIONS	UBOATS	WORLD WAR I

The Jazz Age

After World War I ended, a new mood swept the United States—and much of the rest of the world. The misery and death of the war were over, and it felt like time to celebrate and take life less seriously. In New Orleans, African-American and European musical influences had already mixed to create "jazz," a new kind of music played at first in funeral processions. Soon great performers like trumpeter Louis Armstrong and singer Bessie Smith showed the whole country how good jazz could sound. The radio, developed for communication during the war, brought jazz and other entertainment to people at home for the first time.

During the 1920s, a Constitutional amendment made the sale of alcoholic beverages illegal. But this "Prohibition" was ignored in many bars called "speakeasies" where people met to talk, drink, and dance to jazz. At large, private homes, party-goers swung to the music, too, as the wealthy grew richer during the prosperous decade. Writers like F. Scott Fitzgerald recorded their

Organized crime increased in the 1920s when the sale of alcohol became illegal.

carefree and careless lives in fiction. At any party there were likely to be "flappers," daring young women who wore their hair in the fashionable "bob," raised the hems of their skirts to the knee, and did dances like the "Charleston" to the new music. American women in general gained confidence as they entered the work force in greater numbers than ever and exercised their right to vote.

Electricity reached about two thirds of homes by 1929, allowing people to use many new labor saving devices, including vacuum cleaners, washing machines, toasters, and refrigerators. With the arrival of phonograph records, people could work or play while listening to music.

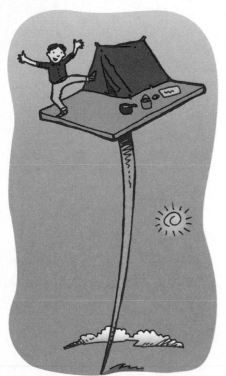

Fads like flagpole sitting swept the country in the 1920s.

Words about the Jazz Age have been scrambled.
Rearrange the letters and write the correct word on each line.
Use the word list if you need help.

GROMSNART

_____

SKIEPEASAES

_____

WNE SRLONAE

_____

IMCSU

_____

EDROCSR

_____

DORAI

_____

DIGAFZETRL

_____

OTHBIROPINI

_____

PLARESFP

_____

LANRUFE

_____

WHATELY

_____

IEITRYELCCT

_____

Word List

ARMSTRONG	FLAPPERS	NEW ORLEANS	RECORDS
ELECTRICITY	FUNERAL	PROHIBITION	SPEAKEASIES
FITZGERALD	MUSIC	RADIO	WEALTHY

The Movies

The first motion pictures flickered across the screen for less than a minute. These black and white "living photographs" were made possible by the work of many inventors, including the American Thomas Edison and the Lumiere brothers of France, in the last years of the 1800s. Short movies were shown together at theaters with 5-cent admission, called "nickelodeons." As the new century began, longer movies were made, and they were shown as part of "vaudeville" performances along with singers, comics, and skit actors.

Charlie Chaplin

Douglas Fairbanks

Mary Pickford

These were the first "stars" to work for the first major movie studio, United Artists.

Filmmaking took a big step in 1903 when Edwin Porter created the first film that told a story, The Great Train Robbery. Soon actors and comics like Charlie Chaplin were turning out movie after movie. Thomas Edison built the first film studio in the United States in West Orange, New Jersey, and in 1918, producer D.W. Griffith created United Artists, the first studio that kept actors on contract.

People flocked to the movies in the 1920s, but even more viewers came after 1927 to see the first feature picture that had sound, The Jazz Singer, starring Al Jolson. The "talkies" captured an American audience of about 100 million every week by 1930. By the mid-1930s color movies appeared on the scene.

Most American films were produced in Hollywood, California, where the major studios were located. Movies were especially popular in the 1930s during the Great Depression, because they provided a way for people to forget their troubles. The coming of television in the 1950s reduced ticket sales, but movies revived when large theater complexes were built in the 1970s and when films on videocassette became available in the same decade.

**Read the clues about the movies.
Then complete the puzzle using the word list on the next page.**

★ Across ★

4. A place where films are produced and filmed
6. Charlie _____ was a great early film comic.
7. Name for an early movie theater where admission was 5 cents
9. The town where most films were—and continue to be—produced
11. Term for famous movie actors
12. Name of an American inventor who contributed to movie technology

★ *Down* ★

1. The first talking motion picture was about this kind of singer
2. Last name of the first female studio star
3. Country of the Lumiere Brothers, who helped develop motion pictures
5. Nickname for an early motion picture with sound
6. In the mid 1930s, this made movies more appealing.
8. Name of the star of The Jazz Singer
10. Name of the producer who founded United Artists

Word List

CHAPLIN	GRIFFITH	JOLSON	STARS
COLOR	HOLLYWOOD	NICKELODEON	STUDIO
EDISON	JAZZ	PICKFORD	TALKIE
FRANCE			

The Crash of '29

New York City's Wall Street was a very busy place during the 1920s. Flourishing business encouraged people to buy stocks (shares in a company), because stock values kept increasing. Unlike any time in history, people who had never bought stocks before began to do so. As stock values quickly rose, more people felt safe borrowing money to buy stocks, which was called "buying on margin." These people felt sure they could sell the stocks shortly to pay their debt and earn a quick profit.

On October 24, 1929, now called "Black Thursday," the stock market crash began as stock values dropped rapidly, and 13 million shares of stock were sold. Stock prices fell again on Monday, and on the next day, called "Black Tuesday," over 16 million shares of stock changed hands. People panicked, and more people wanted to sell than to buy. The giant Morgan Bank tried to restore confidence in the economic situation by buying millions of shares. After Black Tuesday, the market lost another $10 to $15 million in value and did not recover for a long time.

The stock market crash helped open the way to the worst economic downturn the U.S. has ever known. Many investors suffered financial ruin, especially those who had bought stocks on margin. When companies lost money as their stock prices fell, they let workers go or went out of business. Panic spread, and banks failed so that even people with savings often lost what they had. The stock market crash was not the sole cause of the poverty and misery that spread across the land, but it was a major marker of the start of the Great Depression.

President Herbert Hoover did not know what to do to keep the nation from depression.

Read the clues about the Crash of '29.
Then complete the puzzle using the word list on the next page.

★ *Across* ★

1. Effort given in exchange for pay; this was hard to find during the Great Depression
3. Word used for a unit of stock
4. Term for a prolonged, severe time of economic inactivity and want

8. State of having little money; this spread after the stock market crash.
10. Color associated with the Tuesday and following Thursday of the stock market crash
11. Term used for the practice of borrowing to buy stocks: "on _____"
12. U.S. president during the stock market crash and the beginning of the Depression

★ *Down* ★

1. The Great Depression struck not just one nation but most of the _____.
2. Day of the week in October when the stock market fell the most
5. Month of the stock market crash of 1929
6. An investment in a company, which can be bought or sold
7. Name of the bank that tried to keep stock prices up when the Crash of '29 began
9. Name of the street where the chief stock market is located

Word List

BLACK	MORGAN	SHARE	WALL
DEPRESSION	OCTOBER	STOCK	WORK
HOOVER	POVERTY	THURSDAY	WORLD
MARGIN			

The Dust Bowl

Beginning in 1934, dust storms struck across the Midwest. Huge clouds darkened the sky, and dirt and dust blew in and coated everything. Dust clouds even blew as far east as New York City and Washington, D.C. People closed up their houses and covered the windows with wet blankets, but still the dust seeped in, stopping up machinery, coating hair and skin, dirtying everything. In the western plains states of Texas, Oklahoma, Colorado, New Mexico, and Kansas the storms were so common that the area was nicknamed the "Dust Bowl."

Dorothea Lange's photographs and John Steinbeck's novel helped show the nation the plight of the Okies.

The Dust Bowl was partly the result of an extended drought (years of very little rain) and high temperatures. Another reason for the Dust Bowl, though, was that farmers were plowing up the soil without knowing how to preserve the land. Many of these farmers were homesteaders who received small farms from the government after the turn of the century. They planted wheat because it needed little rain and few workers for harvesting, but the roots of the wheat did not hold the soil well. Most farmers did not bother to plant trees, and they burned stubble (stalks that remain after harvest) to the ground. All these factors led to dry, dusty soil that would easily blow whenever a dry spell came.

The Dust Bowl gave birth to a huge migration of farm families. Many people simply gave up their land, piled their possessions on a car or truck, and headed west. Because many of these people were from Oklahoma, they were nicknamed "Okies." Poor and largely uneducated, most Okies could find work only in the California migrant labor camps, harvesting vegetables, fruit, and cotton.

The government responded to the Dust Bowl by creating the Soil Conservation Service. This organization educated farmers about farming methods that would protect the soil and harmonize with the climate.

Read the sentences about Dust Bowl.
Then complete the sentences by filling in each blank.
Use the word list if you need help.

★ Most migrants traveled _____ after dust storms struck their farms.

★ A prolonged dry spell is called a _____.

★ A settler would dampen a _____ to cover his windows during a dust storm.

★ The Soil _____ Service taught farmers to save soil.

★ The nickname given to migrants from Oklahoma was

_____.

★ The Grapes of Wrath was an important _____ that helped show the plight of migrant workers.

★ Small farmers who got land from the government were known as

_____.

★ The famous photographer, Dorothea _____, took pictures of migrant workers.

★ Dust storms destroyed this essential farm resource:

_____.

★ The western plains states of Texas, Oklahoma, Colorado, New Mexico, and

_____ were nicknamed the Dust Bowl.

Word List

blanket	Conservation	Kansas	soil
book	drought	Lange	west
	homesteaders	Okies	

Franklin and Eleanor Roosevelt

Franklin and Eleanor Roosevelt were distant cousins from the same Roosevelt clan, and both were used to wealth and privilege when they married in 1905. Eleanor worked at raising their six children, while Franklin became an attorney and entered New York state government. He was governor of New York when the Great Depression struck, and his record in helping the people of the city helped him win the U.S. presidency in 1933. His achievements were all the more remarkable because he had been crippled by polio years before, and could not walk without crutches.

The Civilian Conservation Corps put young men to work in national forests.

Franklin Roosevelt had promised Americans a "New Deal" that he hoped would end the Great Depression. With tremendous energy, he pushed through many new laws in the famous "first hundred days" of his presidency. Some of these laws, such as the one that created deposit insurance for bank accounts, were great successes. Other programs included the Works Progress Administration (WPA) and the National Recovery Administration (NRA). The WPA provided jobs building roads, parks, and bridges. It also gave work to writers and artists. The NRA aimed to enforce fair practice codes among businesses. The Supreme Court ultimately found the NRA program unconstitutional, but Roosevelt and his advisors kept on working to bring Americans hope. "The only thing we have to fear," he said, "is fear itself."

Eleanor Roosevelt became the most active First Lady in history. She made it her singular job to see how changes were affecting the people. She worked especially hard for equal treatment of women and minorities. Her influence helped convince the president to name Frances Perkins as Secretary of Labor. Perkins was the first woman to be appointed to a cabinet post. Both Eleanor and Franklin helped keep American spirits up during World War II, and a grateful nation re-elected Franklin a record four times. He died as the war ended, but Eleanor went on to do the work for which she may be best remembered. She headed a committee that drafted the Universal Declaration of Human Rights for the newly born United Nations.

The Works Progress Administration sponsored public works and art.

Words about Franklin and Eleanor Roosevelt have been scrambled.
Rearrange the letters and write the correct word on each line.
Use the word list if you need help.

OSSUNIC

_____

YETNORTA

_____

REGVNROO

_____

TREAG SIREONPEDS

_____

LOPOI

_____

WNE LEDA

_____

ISANGVS

_____

TOLRNCO

_____

RAFE

_____

NEWMO

_____

NOTIRISEIM

_____

SPINKER

_____

Word List

ATTORNEY	FEAR	MINORITIES	POLIO
CONTROL	GOVERNOR	NEW DEAL	SAVINGS
COUSINS	GREAT DEPRESSION	PERKINS	WOMEN

World War II

The United States was not involved in World War II when the war began. In the late 1930s, Germany and Italy started to take other nations by force. Japan invaded China. President Franklin D. Roosevelt arranged aid and supplies for Britain and stopped trade that benefited Japan. Congress did not declare war until December 7, 1941, the day the Japanese attacked the U.S. naval base at Pearl Harbor, Hawaii.

During World War II, children collected scrap iron and rubber to help the war effort.

In the U.S., World War II had a variety of effects. The production of war materials stimulated the American economy and put an end to the Depression. Meanwhile, Americans of Japanese ancestry, called the "Nisei," were sent to isolated camps. (In the 1960s, the government admitted that this was wrong, and paid compensation to the victims.)

In Europe, American troops fought in Africa and Italy. Under General Dwight D. Eisenhower, they invaded Europe and landed on the beaches of Normandy, France, on "D-Day" in 1944. In hard fought battles, the U.S., Britain, Russia, and other allies retook Europe. When the allied soldiers marched into Germany at last, they found the death camps where dictator Adolf Hitler had organized the murder of six million Jews and others.

On the Pacific front, Americans fought in China and from island to island trying to beat back the Japanese. By 1944, the Japanese were desperate but refused to give up; many

Japanese "kamikaze" pilots flew suicide bombing missions. In August 1945, American bombers dropped newly invented atomic bombs on the Japanese cities of Hiroshima and Nagasaki, killing thousands of civilians. The Japanese surrendered soon after.

World War II made most Americans realize that isolation from other nations was not possible. After the war, the U.S. played a major role in global affairs.

Words about World War II have been scrambled.
Rearrange the letters and write the correct word on each line.
Use the word list if you need help.

BOLLAG

_____

NAPJA

_____

BECREEMD

_____

REPLA RAHRBO

_____

SMAPC

_____

TENSONCIMAOP

_____

ANDORMNY

_____

ENSWEHIREO

_____

GARYMNE

_____

LISTOP

_____

CMOATI

_____

AISRHMHOI

_____

Word List

ATOMIC	DECEMBER	GLOBAL	NORMANDY
CAMPS	EISENHOWER	HIROSHIMA	PEARL HARBOR
COMPENSATION	GERMANY	JAPAN	PILOTS

Suburbia

After World War II, the marriage rate doubled. So many children were born from 1946 through the early 1960s that this trend was called a "baby boom." At first, new families were doubled up in their parents' houses or spilled out of small city apartments. William Levitt was one of the first to think of mass-producing houses in areas just outside the cities. The houses he built on Long Island, New York, all looked the same, but people were glad to have their own homes surrounded by green grass. Between 1950 and 1960, a quarter of the U.S. population moved to the suburbs—and today, this migration continues.

Many families could afford suburban houses because of the "G.I. Bill of Rights." This bill, passed by Congress just after the war, guaranteed veterans good terms for buying a house (along with hospital care and funding for college). These benefits helped individuals, but they also helped stimulate the economy, which blossomed in the postwar years. Large corporations hired many people, but not everyone benefited from the boom. The suburbs were largely white and middle class because prejudice and poverty kept most minorities in the inner cities or rural areas.

The rise of the suburbs led to increased land and roadway development. Roads and road-dependent businesses including fast food restaurants and shopping strips covered land that was formerly farmed or ranched. Living in the suburbs caused people to rely heavily on their cars for transportation. In the mid-1950s, the federal highway system linked every part of the nation. Now trucks could deliver products more easily to the suburbs nationwide.

The growth of the suburbs brought many Americans a higher standard of living, but it has also brought problems, including: air pollution; sprawl over rural space; loss of community feel; deterioration of cities; and sameness to life across the nation.

Malls became part of the suburban landscape beginning in the 1970s.

Use the word list to help you find the words about suburbia
that are hidden in the block on the next page.
Some of the words are hidden backward or diagonally.

```
I G J U S E I T I R O N I M G C
E A H N S N F E D E R A L A S O
B H O R P R Z N H L E C D K V L
S A U T O S S N A E T H I R N L
M R S A U R S S U B U R B S E E
F C E H A P O L L U T I O N T G
A R S C O R P O R A T I O N S E
M N I N L C E C A Y M O N O C E
I A H L W A R P S Y A Z E B O T
L E V I T T A M I N O R S T G V
I J O R S H S A J R A K H P U N
E L V M E M E L H E C R U R A L
S M I A J X I C A U L A E B L K
W O N C O A T L R N P R M T S O
C O M M U N I T Y D S E B O E T
A B G Y N L C A Y A W H G I H V
```

Word List

BOOM	CORPORATIONS	HIGHWAY	RURAL
CARS	ECONOMY	HOUSES	SPRAWL
CITIES	FAMILIES	LEVITT	SUBURBS
COLLEGE	FEDERAL	MINORITIES	TRUCKS
COMMUNITY	GI	POLLUTION	VETERANS

The Cold War

After World War II ended, the Soviet Union and its Communist allies faced off against the United States and its allies in a long period of hostility called the Cold War. Each side tried to keep the other from world domination. Berlin, Germany, was divided into Communist East Berlin and non-Communist West Berlin. In 1961, East Berlin authorities built a wall across the city to keep their own citizens from escaping to the non-Communist world via West Berlin.

Winston Churchill, Prime Minister of Britain, declared that an "iron curtain" had fallen between Soviet-dominated Eastern Europe and nations of the West. Elsewhere in the world, the U.S. sent more and more aid and troops to help keep small countries from falling under Communist influence. Full war broke out when Communist North Korea invaded South Korea in 1950. The U.S. convinced the United Nations to sponsor American and other troops there for three years. The battle ended with the border between North and South Korea unchanged.

Anticommunists like Senator Joe McCarthy encouraged "blacklists" to deny work to suspected Communists.

The Cold War was made worse by a nuclear arms race. Treaties seemed to do little to slow it down, partly because neither side trusted the other. Additionally, there was what President Dwight D. Eisenhower called the "military-industrial complex" in the United States— many jobs and companies had come to depend on weapons production for their survival.

When the Soviet Union itself fell apart in the late 1980s, the Cold War ended abruptly. A wave of democracy and private economic development swept over the former Soviet-dominated countries. Russia, the strongest remaining republic of the former Soviet Union, faced new problems including how to re-invent its economy. Aging bombs and missile systems reminded the world, however, that Russia could still threaten people beyond its borders.

The fall of the Berlin Wall in 1989 symbolized the end of the Cold War.

Words about the Cold War have been scrambled.
Rearrange the letters and write the correct word on each line.
Use the word list if you need help.

LODWR

_____

TEOVIS

_____

ARKOE

_____

LICRUHHLC

_____

TIMCOUSMN

_____

SPONAEW

_____

ENWHORISEE

_____

ETHER

_____

NRIO

_____

ERUNCLA

_____

ONECYMO

_____

LINERB

_____

Word List

BERLIN	ECONOMY	KOREA	THREE
CHURCHILL	EISENHOWER	NUCLEAR	WEAPONS
COMMUNIST	IRON	SOVIET	WORLD

Television

Television was invented in the 1920s, with experiments both in the U.S and Britain. However, T.V. was not well established in the United States until after World War II. By 1960, when color television arrived, over 90 percent of homes had a T.V. set.

The first broadcast networks were originally radio companies, and T.V. programs imitated radio, with comedies, mysteries, Westerns, and variety shows. Commercial sponsors in general refused to pay for cultural programs that few people seemed to want to watch. The federal government stepped into this role by creating National Educational Television, which later became the Public Broadcasting System.

Howdy Doody was the star of a popular early children's show.

Americans soon learned to depend on television for evening news. T.V. began to influence politics as candidates' debates were televised and paid political ads became common. Coverage of events like the Vietnam War and President Richard Nixon's Watergate scandal helped to form public opinion.

By the 1970s, Americans were watching over six hours of television a day. This was partly because cable service was now available (at extra cost), and families were able to get clear reception on many channels. Previously, people depended on house antennae that allowed them get only a few channels. More recently, new high definition television broadcasting promised an even more sparkling picture.

Videocassettes and the videocassette recorder (VCR), introduced in about 1980, allowed people still more choices of programs and movies on T.V. Programming became more varied, and some was improved. By the 1990s, the Internet was drawing viewers to still more entertainment and information on computer screens. However, added violence and sex on T.V. and the Internet continues to worry many people. Educators warn that Americans, and children in particular, are losing the ability to read or think independently amid the flood of mindless television programs and videogames.

Read the clues about television.
Then complete the puzzle using the word list on the next page.

★ *Across* ★

5. The government created National _____ Television.
8. Initials of the machine that allows videos to play on a television
9. Early TV shows used the formulas of this familiar entertainment form
11. This captures a few local TV channels from air waves

13. Decade in which the Internet began to steal some time from TV watching

★ *Down* ★

1. Discussions between presidential candidates, often televised
2. Category of shows with athletic competition, very popular on TV
3. High _____ television promises a clearer picture.
4. Televised investigation of this Nixon scandal helped put him out of office
6. Next TV development after black and white
7. European country where early TV experiments were made
10. Initials of the public TV programming network
12. Average hours Americans spent watching TV in 1970

Sports on TV helped bring it attention.

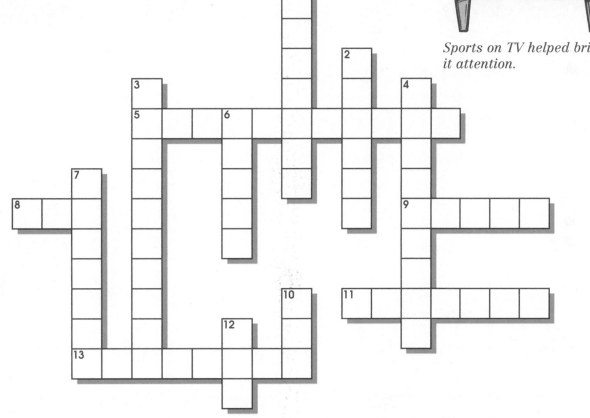

Word List

ANTENNA	**DEFINITION**	**PBS**	**SPORTS**
BRITAIN	**EDUCATIONAL**	**RADIO**	**VCR**
COLOR	**NINETIES**	**SIX**	**WATERGATE**
DEBATE			

Rock Music

"Rock Around the Clock" was the name of the first widely popular song in the style of music called "rock-and-roll." Rock-and-roll, or "rock" for short, began in the 1950s, when African-American musicians were recording a kind music called "rhythm and blues." Rhythm and blues has its origins in blues, jazz, and gospel music. As white performers began to record "covers" (their own versions) of these rhythm and blues songs, they added elements of country and western music to the mix. Radio disc jockey Alan Freed helped make this new music popular among white teenagers and renamed it in 1951 as rock-and-roll. The loud, driving beat and the often rebellious lyrics marked rock as music for adolescents—but not for adults.

Aretha Franklin was the top performer of soul music.

Elvis Presley recorded covers and other rock songs such as "All Shook Up" and became such a popular sensation that he was called "the king of rock-and-roll." During the 1950s, rock radio stations multiplied. Much rock music was sinking into novelty songs and dull repetition. It was revived by a British group called The Beatles in the early 1960s. During that decade many kinds of rock flowered, including rhythmic African-American Motown and soul, blues, acid rock, and folk rock. In 1969, the Woodstock festival, held in New York fields owned by farmer Max Yasgur, drew an enormous crowd. It signified rock as the voice of the youth "counter culture," which opposed the Vietnam War and the other ills of society.

In the 1970s, the dance music movement called "disco" became popular, then faded. Many more kinds of rock developed in the 1970s, 1980s, and 1990s, each with its own following. "Oldies" stations remain on the radio and play rock-n-roll and a variety of music styles from the past.

The Beach Boys played surf music, a form of rock.

Words about rock music have been scrambled.
Rearrange the letters and write the correct word on each line.
Use the word list if you need help.

SCROEV

_____

NOTWOM

_____

MYRHTH

_____

RHISITB

_____

SUBLE

_____

LIVES

_____

DOCKSTOOW

_____

UTNYROC

_____

TOLSSENADEC

_____

LOPESG

_____

ORIDA

_____

EDREF

_____

Word List

ADOLESCENTS	COUNTRY	FREED	RADIO
BLUES	COVERS	GOSPEL	RHYTHM
BRITISH	ELVIS	MOTOWN	WOODSTOCK

Modern Art

Beautiful works of art were produced in the United States before 1900, but in general they followed styles first developed in Europe. During the twentieth century, American artists took a leading role in creating world-class modern art.

In the first decades of the century, Alfred Stieglitz helped gain acceptance for photography as an art form. He also introduced new art from Europe and America at his New York gallery called 291. Among those displayed was a highly original artist, Stieglitz's wife, Georgia O'Keeffe. O'Keeffe painted flowers and other familiar objects in enlarged close-up, or in settings that made them look quite different.

Sculpture by artists like Frank Stella were based on abstract forms.

During World War II, a number of European painters arrived as refugees in New York City. They joined with the artists already there to make the city a source of exciting new art. Much of it was abstract art, which uses lines, shapes, and colors as subjects instead of recognizable objects and scenes.

One unique group of artists, called "abstract expressionists," worked to bring emotional expression to their work. Jackson Pollock, for example, poured or dripped paint onto canvases, so that his paintings reflected the energy of his moving arm. Another group of artists were called "field" or "color field" painters. They presented colors in large blocks or stripes.

Quilts and other folk arts were taken seriously as art at the end of the century.

During the 1960s, artists like Andy Warhol began to create "pop art"—cartoon-like pictures that questioned the gap between fine art and popular art. At the same time, minimalists were showing work that depended on very simple essentials of line and shape.

After the late 1970s, more realistic art returned to the scene amid an explosion of styles. "Postmodern" ideas, popular around the world, said that art of any era, place, or social group deserved serious attention.

Use the word list to help you find the words about
modern art that are hidden in the block on the next page.
Some of the words are hidden backward or diagonally.

```
P A B S T R A C T P G O W U G C
N O A E N E T B A H Q U A L R O
E X P R E S S I O N I S T S E L
T K T T O F L O Z R R E O F B O
H N O K E E F F E Y U Q I O D R
O S W S T O K N W L T W J L E S
Y H P A R G O T O H P A E K I T
E M A N P A I N T E R S D M S H
S T I E G L I T Z R E I M C E B
D I T O A R D E W A R H O L E K
W R O P L M N O D C F L D H G C
A H L C L N X J I L T V E M U O
D O T K E Q U F L O W E R S F L
T E E U R O P E O M X C N E E L
H S E L Y T S M R S R D S H R O
O I R E M B N R E D O M T S O P
```

Word List

ABSTRACT	FLOWERS	PAINTERS	REFUGEES
ART	FOLK	PHOTOGRAPHY	STIEGLITZ
COLORS	GALLERY	POLLOCK	STYLES
EUROPE	MODERN	POP	WARHOL
EXPRESSIONISTS	OKEEFFE	POSTMODERN	WIFE

John F. Kennedy

Jackie, Caroline, and John Jr. added to President John F. Kennedy's charm.

John Fitzgerald Kennedy was president of the United States for less than three years. Yet he made such an impression that some people called his time in office "Camelot," after the homeland of the legendary King Arthur.

Young, energetic, and witty, Kennedy promised a fresh start for America. His Democratic party was taking over after eight years of the Republican administration under President Eisenhower. Kennedy founded the Peace Corps, the government program in which Americans work to improve living standards in needy nations. He favored new laws that would enforce rights and help the poor in the United States. Unfortunately, Congress did not pass many of these laws before he was killed.

Kennedy faced his first crisis soon after taking office. He agreed to send a small American force to try to invade Communist Cuba in hopes of starting a revolution there against the leader, Fidel Castro. However, the invasion at Cuba's Bay of Pigs failed, giving Castro a public relations victory. Later, in 1962, Cuba began to stock nuclear missiles from the Soviet Union. When Kennedy found out about it, he ordered U.S. ships to stop Soviet ships that were approaching Cuba. He told Cuba to dismantle the missile sites or face nuclear war, and he placed the United States on nuclear alert. After days of worldwide fear and worry, Castro backed down.

John F. Kennedy was in a parade in Dallas, Texas, in an open car, when assassin Lee Harvey Oswald, shot him dead. Decades of investigation and talk about the killing followed, with few solid conclusions. Kennedy's vice president, Lyndon B. Johnson, took over Kennedy's role as president. Johnson pushed housing and employment programs through Congress by saying they were what Kennedy had wanted.

Read the clues about John F. Kennedy.
Then complete the puzzle using the word list on the next page.

⭐ *Across* ⭐

1. Kennedy created the _____ Corps.
3. Kennedy's initials
4. Kennedy demanded these weapons be removed from Cuba.
6. Name of Kennedy's killer
8. Kennedy approved an invasion of Cuba's Bay of ____.

9. Kennedy's political party
11. Cuban leader

★ *Down* ★

2. Term for killer of an important person
3. Vice president under Kennedy
5. Fanciful name given to Kennedy's brief "reign"
7. City where Kennedy was killed
10. Kennedy was riding in an open one when he was shot
11. Caribbean island which brought trouble for Kennedy
12. Number of children Kennedy had

Word List

ASSASSIN	CASTRO	JFK	PEACE
CAMELOT	CUBA	JOHNSON	PIGS
CAR	DALLAS	MISSILES	TWO
	DEMOCRAT	OSWALD	

Disney's Empire

In 1928, a black-and-white cartoon character known as Mickey Mouse appeared on American film screens. His squeaky voice belonged to Walt Disney, pioneer of film animation (using many drawings or paintings to make a picture appear to move). Little did anyone know that Walt Disney would become the emperor of an entertainment kingdom.

Disney's first films were cartoons that ran before the feature film in theaters. In 1937, the first full-length animated feature film was produced by Disney's studios, Snow White and the Seven Dwarfs. It was a hit, followed by many others including Pinocchio, Fantasia, Dumbo, and Bambi. In the 1950s, the Disney studios began producing live action films such as Treasure Island, and creating television series, including Davy Crockett and The Mickey Mouse Club. Disney's works were aimed at children, presenting fantasy that left out the darker side of life and sentimentalized old stories and fairy tales. The visual appeal of the animation, combined with humor and music, made his work popular with people of all ages.

The Disney impact increased when the amusement park Disneyland opened in Southern California in 1955. The Disney businesses continued after the death of Walt Disney in 1966, creating the huge Disney World park in Florida, followed by EuroDisney near Paris. At the parks, technology and theater arts combine to give the visitor the sense of being in the environment of Disney films. The basic rides were familiar, but the feeling was new.

In the 1970s, Disney studios began producing more animated feature films that depended on computer animation for background and movement. They combined these computer aids with the old hand-painting animation techniques that always made Disney features especially appealing. By the end of the twentieth century, the Disney company was a corporate giant. Its ever-expanding products have become symbols of America around the world.

Read the clues about Disney's empire.
Then complete the puzzle using the word list on the next page.

★ Across ★

1. Machine used to create animation beginning in the 1970s

2. Two letter abbreviation of the state where Disneyland is
3. Name of an early Disney film about a boy whose nose grew when he lied
5. Disney creations are familiar symbols _____ wide.
8. Name of Disney's park near Paris: _____ Disney
9. The process of creating a moving picture from many drawings or paintings
10. Medium for which several Disney series were created
11. Disney World is located in this state

★ *Down* ★

1. Disney's core audience
2. Term for an animated short film
4. Quality that makes people smile; common in Disney productions
6. Long film; Snow White was the first animated one
7. Disney's first name

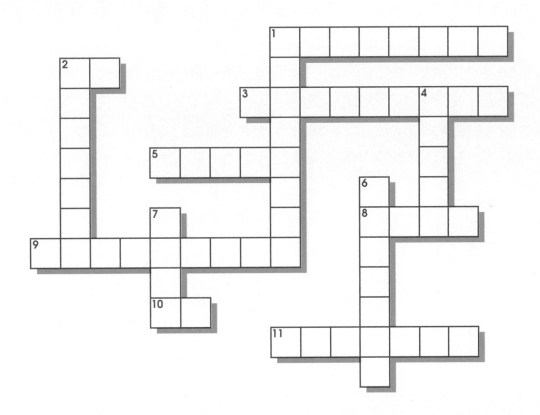

Word List

ANIMATION	**COMPUTER**	**FLORIDA**	**TV**
CA	**EURO**	**HUMOR**	**WALT**
CARTOON	**FEATURE**	**PINOCCHIO**	**WORLD**
CHILDREN			

The Vietnam War

Americans fought in the Vietnam War between 1965 and 1973. The struggle was a long and hard one that divided the nation bitterly.

Vietnam is a long, narrow country located in southeast Asia. By the 1960s, an international agreement had divided the country into two parts: the Communist North, and the non-Communist South. The United States government was afraid that the North and its ally, China, would take over the South and then go on to conquer other nearby countries. In order to stop this "domino" effect, the U.S. sent advisors to help the South Vietnamese army. However, the advisors seemed to do little good; this was partly because the South Vietnamese government was corrupt.

When Lyndon Johnson became president, he wanted to finish the job in Vietnam. He decided the only way to do this was to send in American troops. He needed the approval of Congress and the people, though. He announced that two American ships had been attacked by North Vietnam in the Vietnamese Tonkin Gulf. Congress quickly approved sending troops, unaware that the ships had been illegally aiding the South Vietnamese army.

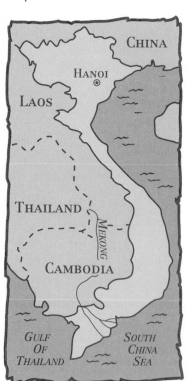

As young Americans were drafted into the army, antiwar protests began. The protests increased year by year, and reached a peak in 1970 when the U.S. invaded Cambodia to chase enemy troops. U.S. soldiers were frustrated as they fought enemies who often disappeared in the hot, humid jungle. Anyone, even women and children, might be hostile. Sometimes soldiers shot Vietnamese civilians with little justification. U.S. soldiers continued to die without any progress being made. Finally, President Nixon said he would "Vietnamize" the war, which meant replacing American troops with South Vietnamese troops. Two years after the last Americans left, the North won the war.

Vietnam is now a U.S. trading partner.

Read the sentences about the Vietnam War.
Then complete the sentences by filling in each blank.
Use the word list if you need help.

★ The temperature in Vietnam is usually _____.

★ President Johnson convinced _____ to pass a
war resolution.

★ Big protests followed the U.S. invasion of _____,
a neighbor of Vietnam.

★ Johnson said peaceful American ships were fired upon in the

_____ Gulf.

★ Vietnam is located in _____.

★ Vietnam's large Communist ally is _____.

★ Nixon coined the term _____ for replacing U.S.
troops with Vietnamese ones.

★ Today, the exchange of goods, or _____, occurs
between the U.S. and Vietnam.

★ Soldiers, as well as _____, were sometimes
dangerous in Vietnam.

★ _____ Vietnam allied with the U.S. in the war.

Word List

Asia	China	hot	trade
Cambodia	civilians	South	Vietnamization
	Congress	Tonkin	

The Civil Rights Movement

Slavery ended with the Civil War, but laws and customs—especially in the South—made African Americans unequal citizens in the U.S. Beginning in 1954, a movement for civil rights changed attitudes across the nation.

The movement was triggered by a Supreme Court decision, Brown v. Board of Education, which declared separate schools for white and black students illegal. From Central High School in Little Rock, Arkansas, to the University of Mississippi, black students faced the dangers of violence and protests during desegregation.

In 1955, Rosa Parks of Montgomery, Alabama became a heroine of the civil rights movement. She refused to give up her seat on a city bus to a white man. Her arrest led black leaders to urge others not to use the bus system. This boycott, led by Dr. Martin Luther King, proved successful. Though Black leader Malcolm X argued that African Americans should separate themselves from white society, Dr. King continued to urge cooperation and peace among all people. Martin Luther King was assassinated in 1958.

During the Civil Rights Movement, students led lunch counter "sit-ins," where African Americans refused to leave "whites only" counters until they were served. Black and white "freedom riders" took buses across the South to desegregate public facilities. Groups set out to register black citizens to vote. They met opposition and sometimes violence, but when the public saw the violence on national television, feeling grew in favor of change. Congress passed the Civil Rights Act of 1964 and the Voting Rights Act of 1965, which guaranteed federal protection of rights as never before.

Both the NAACP and CORE were active in promoting civil rights.

Use the word list to help you find the words about the
Civil Rights Movement that are hidden in the block on the next page.
Some of the words are hidden backward or diagonally.

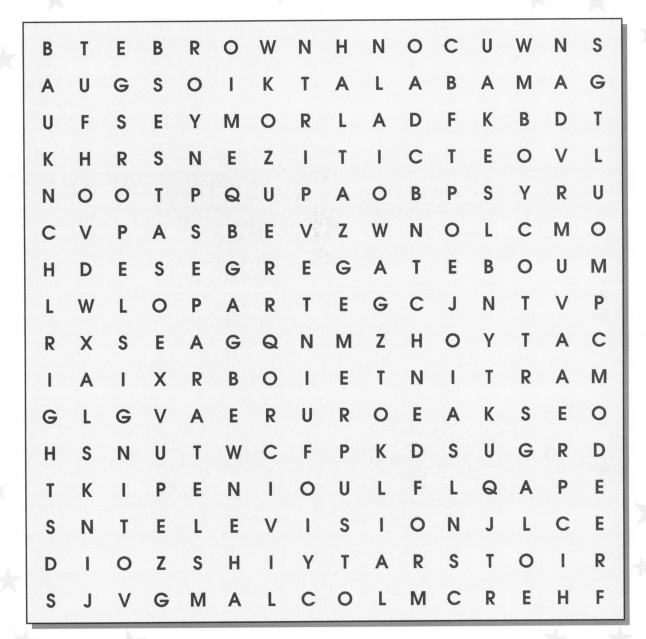

```
B  T  E  B  R  O  W  N  H  N  O  C  U  W  N  S
A  U  G  S  O  I  K  T  A  L  A  B  A  M  A  G
U  F  S  E  Y  M  O  R  L  A  D  F  K  B  D  T
K  H  R  S  N  E  Z  I  T  I  C  T  E  O  V  L
N  O  O  T  P  Q  U  P  A  O  B  P  S  Y  R  U
C  V  P  A  S  B  E  V  Z  W  N  O  L  C  M  O
H  D  E  S  E  G  R  E  G  A  T  E  B  O  U  M
L  W  L  O  P  A  R  T  E  G  C  J  N  T  V  P
R  X  S  E  A  G  Q  N  M  Z  H  O  Y  T  A  C
I  A  I  X  R  B  O  I  E  T  N  I  T  R  A  M
G  L  G  V  A  E  R  U  R  O  E  A  K  S  E  O
H  S  N  U  T  W  C  F  P  K  D  S  U  G  R  D
T  K  I  P  E  N  I  O  U  L  F  L  Q  A  P  E
S  N  T  E  L  E  V  I  S  I  O  N  J  L  C  E
D  I  O  Z  S  H  I  Y  T  A  R  S  T  O  I  R
S  J  V  G  M  A  L  C  O  L  M  C  R  E  H  F
```

Word List

ALABAMA	CIVIL	MARTIN	SEPARATE
BOYCOTT	CORE	NAACP	SIT
BROWN	DESEGREGATE	PARKS	SUPREME
BUS	FREEDOM	RIGHTS	TELEVISION
CITIZENS	MALCOLM	RIOTS	VOTING

Martin Luther King

Martin Luther King was born the son of a preacher in Atlanta, Georgia. He was well educated, with a doctorate from Boston University. His very first job as a pastor was at a Montgomery, Alabama, Baptist church. He had been there less than a year when he was elected to head the bus boycott aimed at ending bus segregation laws. That successful campaign launched Dr. King's career as a civil rights leader. He favored nonviolent civil disobedience, a method he had learned from the works of Mahatma Ghandi, the great leader from India. Ghandi taught that people were

Coretta Scott King kept Martin's ideas and work going after his death.

right to nonviolently disobey laws that were wrong. The publicity gained from such disobedience could then help change public opinion and put an end to bad laws.

In 1960, King returned to Atlanta to become co-pastor with his father at Ebenezer Baptist Church. He headed the Southern Christian Leadership Conference (SCLC), a group of ministers working for civil rights. He led several civil rights campaigns, including the March on Washington of 1963. There, he gave his most famous speech that begins with the words "I have a dream..." His address told of his great hope that one day racial prejudice would play no part in American society.

On a march for voter registration from Selma to Montgomery in 1965, King's people were attacked and beat back by police. Americans all over the nation were shocked, and many times the original number of people that began the march assembled to finish it.

In 1968, King determined that economic improvement was as necessary to African Americans as civil rights. In the midst of planning a large poor people's march on Washington, he flew to Memphis to support a sanitation workers' strike. There he was assassinated. Investigations afterward did not find that the killer, James Earl Ray, was working with others. Though King was dead, his dream lived on.

Read the clues about Martin Luther King.
Then complete the puzzle using the word list on the next page.

★ *Across* ★

2. King tried to sway this kind of opinion with well-publicized actions
4. Not obeying; King favored this approach when no one was harmed
7. Mrs. King's first name
10. Two letter abbreviation of the state where King was born
11. Two letter abbreviation of the state where King led a march from Selma to Montgomery
12. Name of the city in which King first served as a pastor

13. Both King and his father held this job
14. Initials of the group of pro-civil rights ministers King headed

★ Down ★

1. Indian leader whose writings inspired Martin Luther King
3. Organized refusal to buy or use certain goods or services; used against the Montgomery bus system
5. This date in King's life is a federal holiday
6. King's famous speech begins, "I have a _____."
8. City where King led several civil rights campaigns
9. City where King was shot

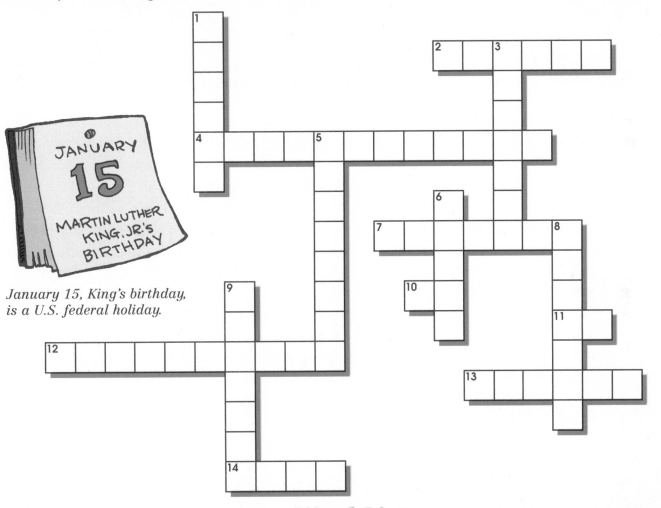

January 15, King's birthday, is a U.S. federal holiday.

Word List

AL	BOYCOTT	GA	PASTOR
ATLANTA	CORETTA	GHANDI	PUBLIC
BIRTHDAY	DISOBEDIENCE	MEMPHIS	SCLC
	DREAM	MONTGOMERY	

Changes for Women

At the end of World War II, many women who had been working in defense industries were happy to go home. Homemaking was considered right for women who could afford not to work in the 1950s. In the next decade, though, a major change in attitudes began with the publication of Betty Friedan's book, The Feminine Mystique. Friedan pointed out that many women wanted to do more than raise a family and keep house. In the late 1960s, Friedan and others founded the National Organization for Women (NOW) to increase and support women's rights at home and in the workplace. Some conservative women opposed this movement, saying traditional life was best.

Women found a "glass ceiling" of prejudice that kept them from some top jobs.

In 1972, the Supreme Court, in the case of Roe v. Wade, ended the ban most states had placed on abortion. Many women felt the ruling protected their personal right to choose. They also felt that legal abortion was safer because it could be regulated. Other people opposed abortion because they thought it was morally wrong. The debate continues through the new millennium.

In the 1970s, the women's movement focused on an Equal Rights Amendment (ERA) to the Constitution, which said no person's rights could be denied because of his or her sex. The amendment failed to pass by a narrow margin. In the meantime, publications like Gloria Steinem's Ms. Magazine, and debate nationwide had awakened many Americans to the need for equal treatment of women.

The women's movement gave girls more choice of what to wear to school.

Taking a job became the normal thing for most women. More women entered Congress and gained other offices. Sandra Day O'Connor became the first woman Supreme Court Justice, and Geraldine Ferraro the first female major party vice-presidential candidate. Although women are still seeking better childcare, equal pay for equal work, and more opportunities in work and education, much progress had been made.

Use the word list to help you find the words about
changes for women that are hidden in the block on the next page.
Some of the words are hidden backward or diagonally.

```
Q N S X O R G F R I E D A N E T
H S T R A D I T I O N A L M P W
B E Y U D E A L B R O D X U Z O
R M R L M P Q K F A M I L Y A C
E O I D F W B L E L W P E I I O
D H G J Z S T E I N E M G C J N
C R H E S Y Y C S T N L F H S N
M T T V A O W O L Y I A I O C O
V S S U P R E M E O U U C O R R
H B K N T A U R I F B Q L S X U
C O N S E R V A T I V E L E L Q
U W G O E R K D S N J Z O N I V
D E B A T E C T W O R K T O O R
M I R D R F E X N G N A J E L W
A S O M U M O E C R G B K H R T
G L A S S J R S T N A P F L Z A
```

Word List

CHILD	ERA	HOME	ROE
CHOOSE	FAMILY	NOW	STEINEM
CONSERVATIVE	FERRARO	OCONNOR	SUPREME
DEBATE	FRIEDAN	PANTS	TRADITIONAL
EQUAL	GLASS	RIGHTS	WORK

Earth Day and the Environmental Movement

April 22 is Earth Day, a time when many Americans think about the health of the earth and help it by planting, recycling, cleaning, and more. There was no Earth Day when the twentieth century began, but at that time the first environmental movement was under way. President Theodore Roosevelt and like-minded naturalists such as John Muir were trying to save

Recycling increased in the 1970s.

the last grand patches of wilderness in the nation. Building, lumbering, and mining were threatening to destroy these lands. Some especially beautiful areas were made into national parks; others became national forests or designated areas where resources were managed by the government.

Decades later, a second environmental movement began. It was in response to the fact that human acts were again threatening the land. Rachel Carson first pointed it out in her book, Silent Spring, in 1962. She said pesticides like DDT and other chemicals and wastes were harming plants and animals. Her book was followed by others that exposed more threats to the environment, including human population growth; waste of disappearing natural resources like oil; and pollution of the air, land, and water by careless people and industries. Beginning in 1969, a series of laws was passed to help keep the environment clean. The Environmental Protection Agency (EPA) was created to enforce these laws in 1970, the year of the first Earth Day. Then, as now, industries and environmentalists sometimes clashed over how much protection was needed—and what the cost would be.

At the end of the twentieth century, Americans began to see that the big environmental problems, including global warming, acid rain, and loss of resources were really world problems. It would take cooperation among many nations and groups to address these global environmental issues.

**Read the clues about Earth Day and the Environmental Movement.
Then complete the puzzle using the word list on the next page.**

★ *Across* ★

1. Another word for contamination
4. Rachel Carson warned about this pesticide
7. Term for people intent on improving the health of the natural world
9. Month of Earth Day

11. Saving things so the material of which they are made can be used again; this increased in the 1970s
13. Individuals and _____ cause most pollution.
14. Many trees have been protected in national _____.

★ *Down* ★

2. Industry that can destroy forests if replanting is not done
3. A resource people are using up, especially in automobiles
5. These large plants are vital to keeping the air clean.
6. Initials of the Environmental Protection Agency
8. John ____ was a naturalist early in the century.
10. First name of the President Roosevelt who first worked to save wilderness land
12. The EPA enforces environmental ____.

Trees help keep the air clean.

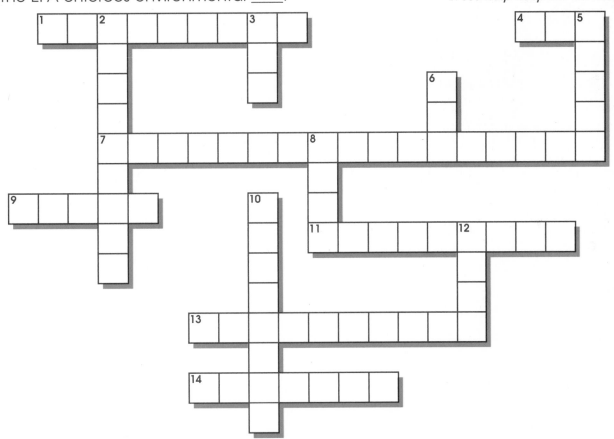

Word List

APRIL	EPA	LUMBERING	RECYCLING
DDT	FORESTS	MUIR	THEODORE
ENVIRONMENTALISTS	INDUSTRIES	OIL	TREES
	LAWS	POLLUTION	

Cesar Chavez

Cesar Chavez was a labor organizer and spokesman for Mexican Americans. Chavez was born in 1929 in Arizona, but his family was forced to move westward like many others because of the Depression and the Dust Bowl. His family ended up in California, working as migrant laborers in fields and orchards. Young Cesar attended over 30 different elementary schools as his family followed the harvests.

Growing up in migrant camps, Chavez saw how bad conditions were for the workers—especially for the many ethnically Mexican, Spanish-speaking people. Some were citizens, and some were recent or illegal immigrants. These farm workers were poorly paid and often badly treated or misunderstood because they were Hispanic (people from ethnic groups that traditionally speak Spanish).

Labor unions were helping workers gain better wages and conditions in many industries. Cesar Chavez decided to try with his own people. He faced almost impossible odds. Not only were growers strongly opposed to unions, but farm workers themselves were always on the move and often feared authorities like the government. In 1970, after Chavez's years of struggle, California grape growers agreed to recognize the United Farm Workers Union. Chavez declared it was not the money that was important, but the "dignity." During the 1970s and 1980s, Chavez organized national boycotts in which he asked consumers not to buy lettuce, wine, or grapes until growers made conditions safer for those who labored on the farms.

Mexican Americans are part of the larger Hispanic minority in America. At the close of the twentieth century, Hispanics were the least wealthy Americans. However, Hispanic incomes and education have been improving, and elements of Hispanic culture such as music and foods have entered the mainstream. The Bilingual Education Act of 1968 allowed many Spanish-speaking Americans to be taught in Spanish for the first time.

Use the word list to help you find the words about
Cesar Chavez that are hidden in the block on the next page.
Some of the words are hidden backward or diagonally.

```
I J G D V D L A B O R E R S A I
Z U A K C I R H N L Y U O K D M
O N T E L G G U R T S W E I Q M
H I S P A N I C S D L E I F N I
L O M E X I C A N J C I M T V G
A N E C O T H M K S D R E J B R
Q S W P C Y F R P Y H T G Y D A
U W A G E S C M I G R A N T I N
S Y X M B C A L I F O R N I A T
T P L H J C S A E H S I N A P S
T E G T H U I L L O N P X E G W
O S P O K E S M A N F M R U J N
C L T L A N L E T T U C E D F C
Y O C I T I Z E N S E C D F O W
O K S V P D R E Z I N A G R O R
B I L I N G U A L Q U A B H S H
```

Word List

BILINGUAL	DIGNITY	LETTUCE	SPOKESMAN
BOYCOTTS	FIELDS	MEXICAN	STRUGGLE
CALIFORNIA	HISPANIC	MIGRANT	UFW
CAMPS	IMMIGRANTS	ORGANIZER	UNIONS
CITIZENS	LABORERS	SPANISH	WAGES

Into Outer Space

The United States first sent ships into outer space as a result of the Cold War rivalry with the Soviet Union. Both nations were working on rocket ships as an outgrowth of rocketry research begun by Germany during World War II. The U.S. was shocked, though, when the Soviets sent Sputnik, the first satellite, into orbit in 1957. Sputnik inspired work that allowed the first American satellite, Explorer, to be launched just four months later. The government also began a program of stronger science education, and founded an agency to overlook its space exploration—the National Aeronautics and Space Administration, or NASA.

In spite of these efforts, the Soviet Union remained "ahead," when Yuri Gagarin became the first man in space in 1961. American Alan Shepard went up less than a month later. Americans at home followed the fortunes of the first space pilots, called "astronauts," with excitement. Rocket launches from Florida's Cape Canaveral (later called the Kennedy Space Center) were shown on television.

The U.S. space program achieved a triumph in 1969. Neil Armstrong became the first man to step onto the moon, and said, "That's one small step for a man, one giant leap for mankind." After the moon landings, the reusable space shuttle was developed to save money and provide an outer space laboratory. Astronaut Sally Ride became the first woman in space aboard the shuttle. The worst disaster in NASA history occurred in 1986, when the space shuttle Challenger exploded with six astronauts and schoolteacher Christa McAuliffe aboard.

By the end of the century, the U.S. had launched many useful satellites, providing communications around the world, and had sent unmanned probes to explore the planets and the galaxy. With the Cold War at an end, the U.S. alone could plan the next steps for humans in outer space.

Read the clues about space exploration.
Then complete the puzzle using the word list on the next page.

★ Across ★

2. The first man on the moon
4. Initials of the agency that oversees U.S. space exploration
6. The first man to go into outer space
7. A reusable space ship with wings for flying
8. The second phrase of the first sentence spoken on the moon: "...one giant ____ for mankind"

10. The first woman in space
11. Name of the first satellite in outer space
12. Research in this field made reaching outer space possible.

★ Down ★

1. Original name of the cape where rockets are launched for outer space
3. Course of a ship or satellite around a planet
5. Name of the Florida space center today
6. An astronaut who returned to space over 30 years after his first trip
7. The first American in outer space
9. Term for an unmanned space exploring machine

Word List

ARMSTRONG	GLENN	ORBIT	SHEPARD
CANAVERAL	KENNEDY	PROBE	SHUTTLE
GAGARIN	LEAP	RIDE	SPUTNIK
	NASA	ROCKETRY	

The Computer Revolution

The first computers were based on the efforts of mathematicians and inventors dating back to the 1600s. By the 1940s, the first general-purpose electronic computer was available for sale. The machine took up many rooms' worth of floor space and used 1800 vacuum tubes. The invention of the transistor allowed for removal of the vacuum tubes, so that computers could be much smaller. By the late 1960s, many large businesses depended on computers.

The first personal computer (PC), called Altair, was created in 1975. Two college students, Bill Gates and Paul Allen, founded Microsoft Corporation to make programs for the Altair. By the end of the twentieth century, Gates was the richest man in the nation. Another company, Apple Computers, founded by Steve Jobs, introduced its own PC and programs, followed by IBM. In time, the IBM type of PC became the most popular and used the Windows system "software" developed by Microsoft.

Another great advance in computer use began in 1969, when a network of computers was first developed by scientific researchers. This "Internet" grew, and became even more useful with the addition of the "World Wide Web," a system of networked Internet sites connected by mechanisms called "hyperlinks." A computer user could click on a hyperlink to move quickly to a related site. By the year 2000, about half of all U.S. households and most businesses had computers connected to the Internet, were communicating via e-mail (electronic mail), and were using Internet sites to shop "online." The impact of the computer revolution has been compared to that of the automobile on work and daily life.

Read the clues about the Computer Revolution.
Then complete the puzzle using the word list on the next page.

★ *Across* ★

2. Mail sent electronically by computers
6. With Bill Gates, he founded Microsoft.
7. Name of the earliest computer to be sold
8. Invention of this part allowed early computers to be smaller.

New Technology for a New World

11. World Wide _____
12. Co-founder of Microsoft and richest American at century's end

★ *Down* ★

1. A common computer operating program
3. Company that developed the Windows software system
4. Name of the first personal computer
5. Ordering from Internet sites is called shopping _____.
9. Computer company that rivals IBM-type PCs
10. Vacuum _____ made the earliest computers big.

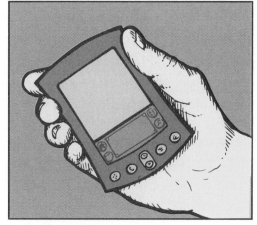

Computers have become much smaller and portable.

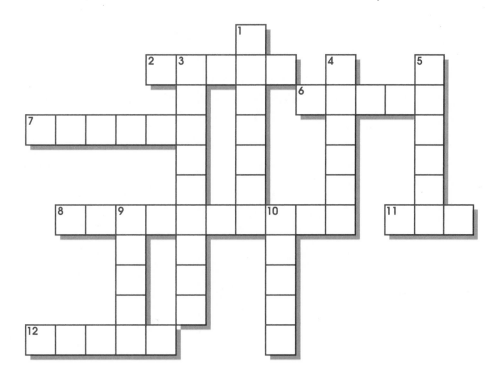

Word List

ALLEN	EMAIL	ONLINE	UNIVAC
ALTAIR	GATES	TRANSISTOR	WEB
APPLE	MICROSOFT	TUBES	WINDOWS

America in the Global Economy

The United States has always traded with other countries. However, a big change began when multinational companies first became powerful. Multinational companies are companies with large operations in several countries. After the 1960s, many multinationals with U.S. headquarters began manufacturing in foreign countries where the least expensive labor could be found. For this reason, and because of ongoing replacement of workers with machines, many factories in the U.S. closed. This resulted in the so-called Rust Belt—abandoned aging plants across the Midwest and the East.

Many of those who lost their jobs in factories gained new jobs in the 1970s or 1980s in the services industry. The services sector of the economy includes jobs in health care, education, entertainment, food, and other areas. Because service sector jobs do not typically pay as much as unionized factory jobs, this change helped propel many women into the workplace as families tried to keep up their standard of living.

In the last 20 years of the twentieth century, the computer revolution stimulated the American economy and helped make possible even more global trade.

At the end of the twentieth century, European countries had united to form a stronger trading unit, the European Community. The U.S. also helped create one continent-wide economy by joining Canada and Mexico in the North American Free Trade Agreement (NAFTA). A trend toward ever-larger multinational companies continued. However, some people worried that while global trade and business boomed, the companies were without controls. The gap between rich and poor individuals and countries was growing. A series of protests against world trade powers including the World Trade Organization (WTO) and the International Monetary Fund (IMF) began in Seattle in 1999.

**Read the clues about America and the global economy.
Then complete the puzzle using the word list on the next page.**

★ Across ★

5. Term for companies that have large operations in more than one country
6. _____ products, such as corn and soybeans, are major U.S. exports.

7. Economic area of businesses that serve people instead of making things: education, tourism, health care, etc.
9. Buying and selling
11. Opposite of imports; includes farm products and computer software for the U.S.

★ *Down* ★

1. Initials of a global trade organization
2. Initials of the free trade agreement signed by North American countries
3. When services jobs replaced industrial jobs, more of this group went to work.
4. Country that joined the U.S. and Mexico in a continental trade agreement
5. Central U.S. region, hard hit by losses of industry in the 1970s
8. City where demonstrations took place against the World Trade Organization at the end of the century
10. Initials of the European civil and trade community

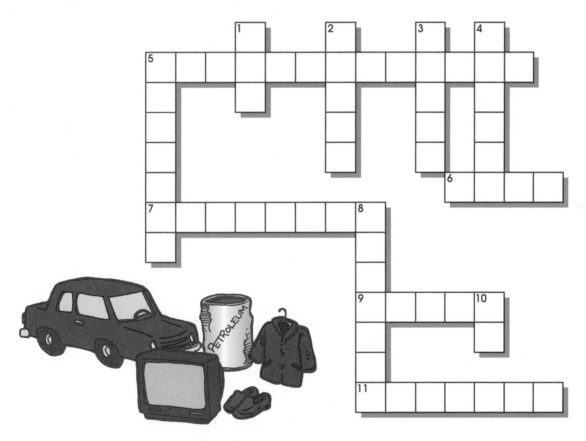

Word List

CANADA	FARM	NAFTA	TRADE
EC	MIDWEST	SEATTLE	WOMEN
EXPORTS	MULTINATIONAL	SERVICES	WTO

"Little" Wars and Terrorism

After the Vietnam War and the cooling of Cold War tensions, it seemed that the nation might not have to face war again for a long time. Conflicts around the world sometimes seemed to require an American role.

The largest American war of the last part of the century was the brief Persian Gulf War of 1991. Iraq, led by Saddam Hussein, invaded the tiny neighboring country of Kuwait. President George Bush wanted to protect world oil supplies in the region, so he sent U.S. troops to nearby Saudi Arabia. He then formed an alliance with Arab and other nations to force Iraq back. With U.N. approval, the mostly American armed forces quickly defeated the Iraqis. A long period of dispute followed over whether or not Iraq was destroying arms as it had agreed to do.

Slobodan Milosevic led Serbian attackers in Kosovo.

Other conflicts arose after 1992 when ethnic groups of the former Yugoslavia attacked one another. As part of the North Atlantic Treaty Organization (NATO), the U.S. helped make peace in Bosnia-Herzegovina and sent most of the troops that made up a peacekeeping force there. In 1999, ethnic war engulfed Kosovo, another former Yugoslav area. The U.S. sent aircraft to bomb the attacking Serbs. Finally, the war ended and peacekeeping troops from NATO were placed there.

Beginning in the 1970s, terrorists found they could pursue their goals even with only a few followers. The worst terrorist incident occurred in 1979, when Iranian revolutionaries took U.S. diplomats hostage in Teheran, the capital of Iran. America's might and advanced weapons were useless in trying to get the hostages back. They were not returned until the beginning of 1981.

Read the sentences about wars and terrorism.
Then complete the sentences by filling in each blank.
Use the word list if you need help.

★ Bush helped form an _____ to fight the Persian Gulf War.

★ The hostage crisis of 1979 took place in _____.

★ Parts of _____ fell into ethnic conflict in the late century.

★ This former Yugoslav area, _____, is where the U.S. bombed attacking Serbs in 1999.

★ People kidnapped and kept for political reasons are called

_____.

★ The U.S. went to war against Iraq in the _____ Gulf.

★ People who use terror to gain political ends are called

_____.

★ The initials of the international organization that fought and enforced the peace

in the former Yugoslavia are _____.

★ Saddam Hussein said he had destroyed _____, but the U.S. disagreed.

★ Iraq's invasion of _____ set off the Gulf War.

Word List

alliance	hostages	Kuwait	terrorists
arms	Iran	NATO	Yugoslavia
	Kosovo	Persian	

Genetic Engineering

Genes are tiny units of heredity located within every living thing. In 1953, scientists discovered the structure of DNA, the acid that contains genes in a pattern. However, not until the 1970s were scientists able to isolate and change individual genes, a process called genetic engineering. The first genetically engineered product to be approved by the Food and Drug Administration (FDA) was insulin. People with diabetes use insulin to help their bodies process sugars normally.

By the 1980s, genetic engineers were producing plants and animals with special qualities. The first patent on a genetically engineered plant was for corn with greater

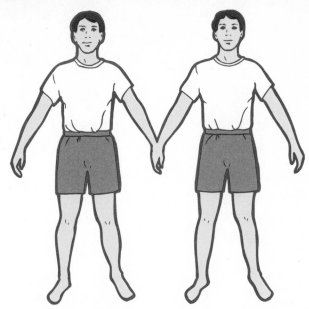

At century's end, the Human Genome Project mapped all human genes.

nutritional value. The first similar patent for an animal went to a mouse intended for use in cancer research. These two patents suggest the possible benefits of genetic engineering. By the end of the twentieth century, most corn and soybeans in the United States were grown from seed that had been genetically engineered to resist diseases and pests. In Europe and elsewhere, people objected to these changes in foods, because they were afraid the foods might be unsafe to eat or pose unknown dangers to the environment.

In 1996, British biologist Ian Wilmut and his colleagues produced the first animal clone, a creature genetically identical to its one "parent." The cloning of the sheep, known as "Dolly," showed it might be possible to create greatly improved herds of animals cloned from chosen individuals. Dolly also unleashed debate about the possibility of eventual human cloning. Meanwhile, advances in testing allowed scientists to match DNA even in old human samples. As a result, some accused killers were found to be innocent; the right fathers were matched to their children; and even tracing ancient human ancestry was possible.

Read the clues about genetic engineering.
Then complete the puzzle using the word list on the next page.

★ Across ★

2. Term for the total of human genes
3. Initials of the agency which must approve new foods and drugs
5. Just the same; describes a clone and its parent

New Technology for a New World

9. Continent which refused some genetically engineered products
10. Dolly aroused debate about this kind of possible cloning.
11. Dolly was the first of this category of animal to be cloned.
12. Nation where the sheep was cloned

★ *Down* ★

1. The first genetic engineering patent went to a form of this vegetable.
4. Genetic engineering can protect plants against pests and _____.
5. The first genetically engineered drug
6. A creature artificially created from genetic material of one parent
7. The biologist who cloned a sheep
8. Name of the first cloned sheep

Dolly the sheep was the first clone of a mammal.

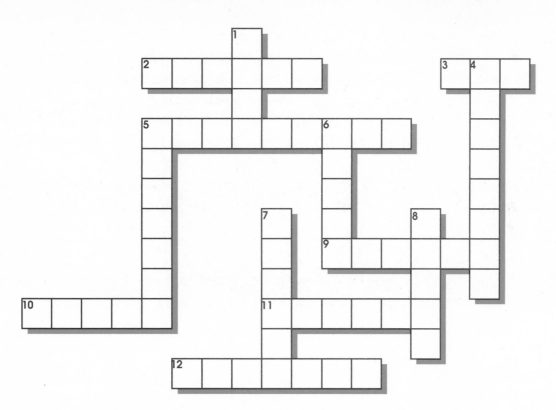

Word List

BRITAIN	**DOLLY**	**GENOME**	**INSULIN**
CLONE	**EUROPE**	**HUMAN**	**MAMMAL**
CORN	**FDA**	**IDENTICAL**	**WILMUT**
DISEASES			

Twenty-First Century Predictions

The year 2000 brought the twentieth century to an end, and began both a new century and a new millennium (thousand-year period). It is hard to imagine what might happen in America over the next thousand years, but we can guess at some events of the twenty-first century based on trends at the end of the twentieth.

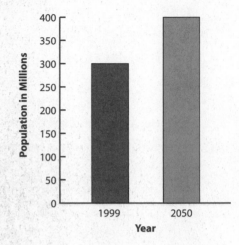

Certainly, there will be more Americans. The additional population may add to suburban sprawl, but perhaps it is more likely (considering the high price of gasoline) that people will return to city centers. A trend toward this "new urbanism" began in the 1990s.

Many in the added population will be elderly—the 16% aged 60 or over in 1999 will become 25% by 2050. This aging of the "baby boom" generation born after World War II will affect employment opportunities. There will be still more jobs in the rapidly growing health care field in order to meet the needs of aging citizens. Tourism and leisure may provide the most jobs of all, as retirees look for ways to spend their free time.

Technology is bound to play an even bigger role in people's lives. Miniature computers may be attached to nearly everything we use or wear. Wireless communications will keep Americans connected wherever they are. Many people will not distinguish between being at work and being at leisure. Not surprisingly, the second-highest job category, after tourism and leisure, will be information technology.

America's role in the world may be less powerful than it was at the end of the twentieth century. Greater economic strength may give Europe and especially China more weight in international affairs. However, the United States will most likely continue to be a world leader in space exploration.

Read the clues about twenty-first century predictions. Then complete the puzzle using the word list on the next page.

★ Across ★

3. Kind of mobile phones and devices likely in future
8. Computer related technology is called _____ technology
10. This kind of care will provide more jobs.
12. The U.S. will still lead the way in ____ space.

★ Down ★

1. Term for a thousand years; a new one began in 2000
2. Economic strength may give this continent more world power.

4. An aging population will put strain on _____ Security.
5. Asian country that may take a lead in international affairs
6. The price of this may help end suburban sprawl.
7. Flow of people from this may reverse in the future
9. Overflowing rivers; natural disasters that may be caused by global warming
11. In the future, fewer people will distinguish between leisure and this.

Global warming may cause more weather disasters like floods.

Word List

CHINA	FLOODS	INFORMATION	SOCIAL
CITY	GASOLINE	MILLENIUM	WIRELESS
EUROPE	HEALTH	OUTER	WORK

The New Millennium

The year 2000 arrived amidst a multitude of festivities around the world. The celebration in Times Square was the biggest New Year's party ever. In attendance were over 1 million partygoers donned in brightly colored wigs and hats who were soon covered in 3,500 pounds of confetti! The celebration also featured the traditional New Year's Rockin' Eve with host Dick Clark, and a new "ball" covered in Waterford crystal. Security was very tight for the event, and there were no incidents to speak of.

At a New Year's celebration in Hawaii, citizens enjoyed traditional Hawaiian music while they watched an electric pineapple climb to the sky. In Chicago, the celebration along the lakefront featured fireworks and the music of blues great Buddy Guy. Our country's capitol featured then President Clinton speaking on the stairs of the Lincoln Memorial, which was illuminated by fireworks. Ceremonies in Washington D.C. also featured the Marine Corps Band and the Millennium Choir.

In other parts of the world, a variety of celebrations ensued. Citizens of Australia enjoyed brilliant fireworks that lit skies above Sydney Harbor. In Rome, crowds gathered to listen to Pope John Paul II as he gave his traditional blessing in St. Peter's Square. London's celebration featured 16 barges loaded with fireworks that created an enormous fireworks display, and turned the River Thames into a "River of Flame." The Eiffel Tower took center stage in Paris as it was lit from bottom to top during the countdown to midnight. In Cairo, the ancient pyramids of Giza were set aglow with floodlights, lasers, and fireworks.

The year 2000 was preceded by massive concerns about the "Y2K bug," a problem that would cause computers to malfunction. Early computers represented years in only two digits, rather than four. Therefore, older computers read the year 2000 as the year 1900 or 0, causing errors in calculations. Everyone expected the worst—crashing computers, paralyzed businesses—upon the arrival of the year 2000, but there were few problems. People had prepared thoroughly by replacing older computers and by installing updated software.

New Technology for a New World

Words about the new millenium have been scrambled.
Rearrange the letters and write the correct word on each line.
Use the word list if you need help.

SABELNICEROT

_____

SEMTI QESRAU

_____

TINFEOCT

_____

SFKIRROEW

_____

LOWDR

_____

FFLIEE ROWTE

_____

OWNDCNUOT

_____

GBU

_____

MPOETSRCU

_____

ANEPELPPI

_____

NEYDYS

_____

SHEAMT

_____

Word List

BUG	**CONFETTI**	**FIREWORKS**	**THAMES**
CELEBRATIONS	**COUNTDOWN**	**PINEAPPLE**	**TIMES SQUARE**
COMPUTERS	**EIFFEL TOWER**	**SYDNEY**	**WORLD**

September 11, 2001

On September 11, 2001, four American airliners were hijacked by terrorists. Two of the planes were deliberately crashed into the World Trade Center Towers in New York City. The third plane crashed into the Pentagon in Washington, D.C., and the fourth plane crashed in a field in western Pennsylvania. Heroic passengers on this plane are believed to have taken action against the terrorists on board, diverting the plane from hitting another target, such as the White House.

New York skyline...before September 11, 2001

Firefighters and police officers rushed to the scene of the World Trade Center in a mass effort to save victims. When the towers collapsed, several hundred firefighters and police officers were killed, along with several thousand people who were at work in the towers.

American citizens immediately took action—many rushed to donate blood. Doctors and nurses stood waiting outside of hospital emergency rooms ready to care for the wounded. Rescue workers and specially trained dogs spent days searching the rubble at "Ground Zero" for survivors. Many corporations donated resources and money. Volunteers helped provide food and water to the rescue workers. Children across the country helped to raise money for the American Red Cross. And, in a show of solidarity, U.S. citizens displayed the American flag on their houses, their cars, their clothing, and anywhere else they possibly could. The country felt united in the tragedy and was determined to show that such acts could not diminish American strength and pride.

President George W. Bush, New York City mayor, Rudolph Giuliani, and other leaders came forward immediately to assure the American public that their government was doing everything possible to keep its citizens safe. Leaders from countries around the world came forward, too, to show their grief and support for America.

Osama bin Laden, the leader of the al-Qaeda terrorist group based in Afghanistan, is believed to be responsible for the attacks. Bin Laden and the terrorists disapprove of the American way of life, and the World Trade Center Towers represented American power and wealth. As a result of this tragic day, President Bush declared a war on terrorism and made it clear that acts of violence and terror would not be tolerated.

American History from 1900 to the Present—Topics to Explore

You have read only a brief history of the events and people that influenced America's development in the twentieth century. Below, you will find a list of more topics related to American History from 1900 to the Present. Choose some topics from the list, or think of other subjects on your own, that you would like to learn more about. Use the following pages to take notes and create your own activities.

Other Topics in American History from 1900 to the Present:

- The Vietnam Veterans' Memorial

- The Harlem Renaissance

- Charles Lindbergh, aviator

- NAACP—National Association for the Advancement of Colored People

- Mary McLeod Bethune, educator and civil rights activist

- ACLU—American Civil Liberties Union

- Woody Guthrie, folk singer and songwriter

- The League of Nations

- Sandra Day O'Connor, first woman Supreme Court Justice

- Steve Jobs, founder, Apple Computers

Notes Page

Choose one of the topics from page 137, or think of a topic on your own, and write about what you know in the space below. Research your chosen topic further, using the library or the Internet to help you find information. Take lots of notes, as you will use these notes to create your own activity on the next page.

★ NOTES ★

Create Your Own Activity

Use this page to create your own activity based on the notes you took on the previous page. Share your activity with a friend.

Notes Page

Choose one of the topics from page 137, or think of a topic on your own, and write about what you know in the space below. Research your chosen topic further, using the library or the Internet to help you find information. Take lots of notes, as you will use these notes to create your own activity on the next page.

★ NOTES ★

Create Your Own Activity

Use this page to create your own activity based on the notes you took on the previous page. Share your activity with a friend.

Notes Page

Choose one of the topics from page 137, or think of a topic on your own, and write about what you know in the space below. Research your chosen topic further, using the library or the Internet to help you find information. Take lots of notes, as you will use these notes to create your own activity on the next page.

★ NOTES ★

Create Your Own Activity

Use this page to create your own activity based on the notes you took on the previous page. Share your activity with a friend.

American History Ticktacktoe

For 2 or more players

A quick and easy game that tests American History knowledge!

How to play:

★ If there are more than two players, divide the players evenly into teams.

★ Cut out the markers on page 149, then have each player or team pick either the stars or flags as their markers.

★ Tear out the quiz card pages on pages 151-155 and cut out the cards. Divide them, giving half of the cards to each player or team.

★ Tear out the ticktacktoe game grid on page 147 and lay it out in front of both players or teams, within easy reach.

★ One player or team draws a card from their stack and reads a question to the other player or team. If the player or team answers correctly, that player or team places a marker on the game grid in one of the open squares. If the question is answered incorrectly, play moves to the other player or team.

★ Play continues until one of the players or teams has three of its markers in a row, diagonally, up and down, or across. If all of the squares are full with no ticktacktoes, the game is considered a tie and a new game begins.

★ If desired, score may be kept on a separate sheet of paper.

American History Ticktacktoe Grid

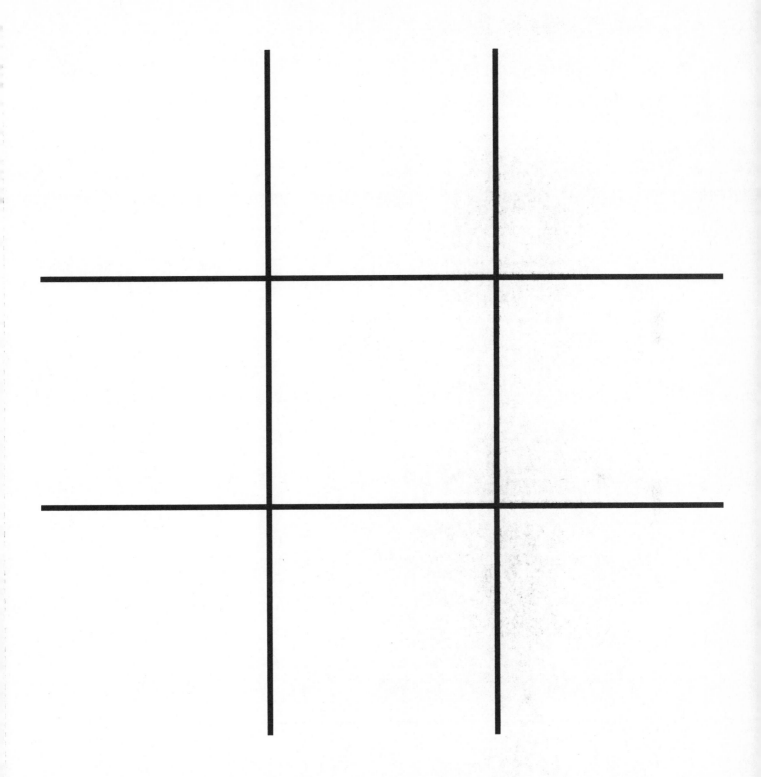

Game Pieces

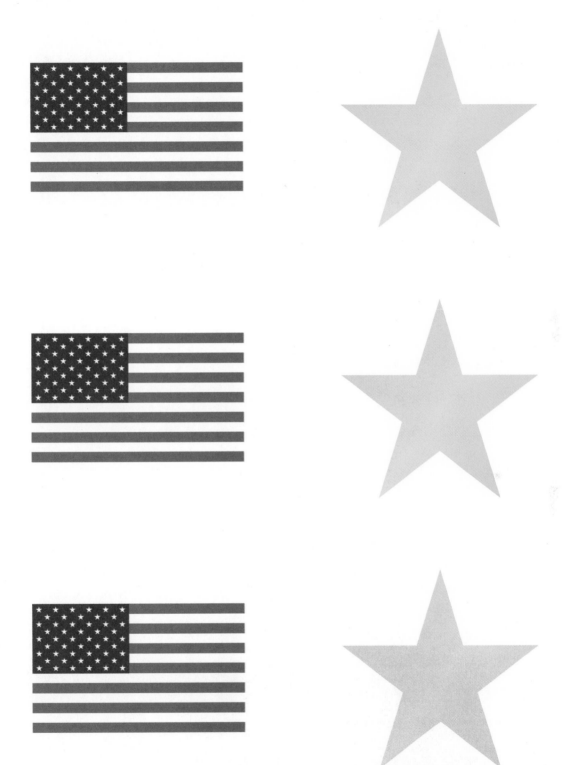

American History Trivia Questions

Q: Who was the first president of the United States? **A:** George Washington	**Q:** Who wrote the first draft of the Declaration of Independence? **A:** Thomas Jefferson
Q: Who gave Christopher Columbus the royal backing he needed to sail to Asia? **A:** Ferdinand and Isabella of Spain	**Q:** Who was Commander in Chief of the Continental Army during the Revolutionary War? **A:** George Washington
Q: Who founded Plymouth colony? **A:** The Pilgrims	**Q:** Who is sometimes called the father of the Constitution? **A:** James Madison
Q: What is the oldest European-founded city in the United States? **A:** St. Augustine, Florida	**Q:** Who explored the Louisiana Territory and beyond? **A:** Lewis and Clark
Q: What Native American helped to teach the Pilgrims how to survive? **A:** Squanto	**Q:** What was the nickname for covered wagons? **A:** "Prairie schooners"
Q: Who was the leader of the secret Colonial society called the Sons of Liberty? **A:** Samuel Adams	**Q:** What was the nickname for people who rushed to California to look for gold in the mid 1800s? **A:** "Forty-niners"
Q: What was the name of the German soldiers recruited by King George of England during the Revolutionary War? **A:** Hessians	**Q:** Who invented the cotton gin? **A:** Eli Whitney

American History Trivia Questions

Q: Who led the abolitionist movement to end slavery in the United States?

A: Frederick Douglass

Q: For whom was the "teddy bear" named?

A: Theodore Roosevelt

Q: What kind of house was Abraham Lincoln born in?

A: A log cabin.

Q: Who used the "assembly line" method to manufacture cars?

A: Henry Ford

Q: Who was the president of the Confederacy?

A: Jefferson Davis

Q: Where did Orville and Wilbur Wright make their first successful flight?

A: Kitty Hawk, North Carolina

Q: What was the name of the agency established to help former slaves?

A: The Freedmen's Bureau

Q: What kind of music are Louis Armstrong and Bessie Smith famous for?

A: Jazz

Q: Where and when was the first Women's Rights Convention held?

A: In Seneca Falls, New York in 1848

Q: What does "Black Tuesday" refer to?

A: The day the stock market crashed on October 24, 1929

Q: What was the Cherokee Indians' devastating journey to Oklahoma called?

A: The Trail of Tears

Q: What happened on December 7, 1941?

A: There was an attack on Pearl Harbor in Hawaii by the Japanese

Q: Who was known as the Wizard of Menlo Park?

A: Thomas Edison

Q: Who was known as the King of Rock 'n' Roll?

A: Elvis Presley

American History Trivia Questions

Q: Who founded the Peace Corps? A: John F. Kennedy	Q: For what is Neil Armstrong famous? A: He was the first man to step on the moon.
Q: Which was war was fought between 1965 and 1973? A: The Vietnam War	Q: What company developed the "Windows" software system? A: Microsoft
Q: In 1955, who refused to give up her seat in a city bus to a white man? A: Rosa Parks	Q: What does NAFTA stand for? A: North American Free Trade Agreement
Q: What are the first words of Martin Luther King's most famous speech? A: "I have a dream…"	Q: What was the first genetically engineered product to be approved by the Food and Drug Administration (FDA)? A: Insulin
Q: What does NOW stand for? A: National Organization for Women	Q: What was the nickname for the year 2000? A: Y2K
Q: What do we celebrate on April 22? A: Earth Day	Q: What was the first clone of a mammal and what was its name? A: sheep, Dolly
Q: Who was a famous labor organizer and spokesman for Mexican Americans? A: Cesar Chavez	Q: What do the letters UNIVAC stand for? A: Universal Automatic Computer

Section 3
U.S. PRESIDENTS

Do you know which president nearly doubled the size of the United States? Who was the first president to speak Spanish well? Which one kept an alligator for a pet? This section will help you review these and many other interesting and fun facts about the lives and accomplishments of the presidents of the United States, from George Washington to the very latest person in the White House.

You can use the activities in this section to review a president's term in office or to learn about a president that you may not know much about. These activities are meant to be a fun way for you to remember names and facts about the nation's leaders. Of course, not all of their biographies or the history surrounding their presidencies could be included; instead these activities are meant to stir your curiosity and encourage you to find out more.

To complete each activity, you will need to read and understand the reading selection, as well as locate information in illustrations that may accompany each reading passage or activity. You can also find an appropriate word in the alphabetical list of words provided with most of the activities as another helpful tool in completing each activity.

If you have already learned about the topic that is featured, you may want to challenge yourself to complete as much of the activity as you can without reading the introduction, looking at the illustrations, or using the word lists.

Some of the reading selections and activities focus on just one president, and some cover two or three. The presidents are arranged in chronological order, but you can work on the activities in any order you choose. If you would like to learn more about a particular president or want to learn more about the presidency in general, you may wish to do some research on your own and create your own activities—complete with clues and/or word lists. We have included extra pages at the end of this section with suggestions for topics to explore.

Section 3
U.S. PRESIDENTS
Table of Contents

George Washington (1732-1799)

George Washington was born on a Virginia farm. He was given a primary education, then, as a young man, worked as a surveyor measuring land. When his half-brother died, Washington inherited his land and a home, Mount Vernon. Tall and strong, he liked outdoor work and the army. He became an officer in the Virginia militia and fought to push the French out of the upper Ohio River valley. In fighting at Fort Duquesne (now Pittsburgh, Pennsylvania), Washington learned Indian techniques and battle strategies.

**George Washington
1st President
Party: Federalist
Term: 1789-1797**

By the end of the French and Indian War, Washington was a well-known officer. The Continental Congress asked him to become commander in chief of the Continental army in the Revolutionary War. Outnumbered by the enemy, the army never had enough supplies and were not as well trained as the British. Washington trained the army, gave them discipline, and kept up their hopes. Even in the winter of 1777-1778, when he and his men were nearly starving and freezing at Valley Forge, Washington refused to give up. His wife, Martha, joined him there and helped nurse sick soldiers. Training continued through the winter. In June 1778, the army followed Washington to a victory over the British in Monmouth, New Jersey. It was such determination, along with luck and good allies, that allowed Washington and his army to win the war.

After the Revolution, Washington tried to retire to Mount Vernon. But he was called back to become chairman of the Constitutional Convention—the gathering of delegates responsible for creating a fresh plan of government for the United States. When this plan, the Constitution, was approved, he was elected the first president of the United States and served two terms. As president, Washington helped unite the new country. He listened to arguments from all sides, then steered a middle course. He was so well known for his strength and fairness that foreign countries were willing to accept and trade with the new nation. There is little wonder that Congress decided to name the new capital city in the District of Columbia after him.

It is a myth that George Washington's false teeth were made out of wood. They were made from other teeth— those of humans and animals—and also from tusks!

Read the sentences about George Washington and his presidency.
Then complete the sentences by filling in each blank.
Use the word list if you need help.

★ Washington fought for the British against the Indians and this country:

_____.

★ Washington's home colony, or state, was _____.

★ Washington was _____ of the Constitutional
Convention.

★ Alexander _____ served as Secretary of the
Treasury under Washington.

★ The Whiskey Rebellion was a result of farmers refusing to pay a federal

_____.

★ Washington served as a _____ during the
Revolutionary War.

★ Washington retired to his home, Mount _____,
after his presidency.

★ Washington worked to keep the nation _____,
or free from alliances that might result in war.

★ Thomas Jefferson was Washington's Secretary of

_____.

★ Washington married a young widow named _____.

Word List

Chairman	general	neutral	Vernon
France	Hamilton	State	Virginia
	Martha	tax	

John Adams *(1735-1826)*

John Adams
2nd President
Party: Federalist
Term: 1797-1801

His enemies called him "His Rotundity" and laughed at his stuck-up manners. Yet John Adams worked hard all his life to shape and serve the nation he loved.

Adams grew up on a Massachusetts farm. He was educated at Harvard University and became a lawyer. As a young man, Adams took on the difficult task of defending the British soldiers who fired into a mob of colonists in the Boston Massacre. He entered the Massachusetts legislature and was caught up in the fight against Britain for colonial rights. Adams was an important member of the Continental Congress, and after urging Thomas Jefferson to write the first draft of the Declaration of Independence, Adams continued to play an important role in the making of that historic document. He spent several years in Europe, working as a diplomat for the new United States.

Because of his political career, Adams was often separated from his wife, Abigail. They wrote to each other frequently. "Remember the ladies," Abigail once wrote, "and be more generous and favorable to them than your ancestors!"

Soon after Adams returned from Europe, he was elected vice president under George Washington. He disliked the job much of the time because he had so little power. After eight years, though, he was in a position to be elected president.

The presidency proved to be hard for Adams. His toughest job was maintaining peace with France. He managed to do so, in part, by creating a navy that would threaten anyone planning to attack an American ship. However, keeping the peace did not help Adams's political career. Alexander Hamilton and other members of the Federalist Party had wanted to fight France. They withdrew their support for Adams and he lost the election in 1800.

John and Abigail Adams enjoyed a long retirement in Massachusetts. Adams' favorite activity was reading. "You will never be alone with a poet in your pocket," he declared. As a very old man, he was overjoyed when his son John Quincy Adams became president.

Read the clues about John Adams and his presidency.
Then complete the puzzle using the word list on the next page.

★ *Across* ★

3. First name of Adams's wife
4. Adams's biggest challenge was keeping the peace with this country.
6. Adams liked to keep the work of this kind of writer in his pocket.
7. Adams worked with Jefferson on the Declaration of _____.

8. Adams grew up on one in the countryside.
9. Adams served as a member of this government body in the Massachusetts colony.
11. As a lawyer, Adams defended the British soldiers involved in the Boston _____.

★ *Down* ★

1. Adams's home colony or state
2. Adams's profession
4. Party that withdrew support for Adams after one term
5. Adams was the first president to live in the _____ House in Washington, D.C.
10. Number of years Adams served as vice president

Adams was the first president to live in the White House.

Word List

ABIGAIL	FEDERALIST	LAWYER	MASSACRE
EIGHT	FRANCE	LEGISLATURE	POET
FARM	INDEPENDENCE	MASSACHUSETTS	WHITE

Thomas Jefferson *(1743-1826)*

Thomas Jefferson was born on a prosperous plantation in Virginia. Jefferson's accomplishments—in and out of politics—are amazing! He mastered many languages and was an expert on plants and crops, music, fine food, and Indian artifacts. He was trained in the law. Jefferson designed his own home, called Monticello, and the buildings at the University of Virginia, which he also founded. He created money for the United States and invented the swivel chair, among other things.

Thomas Jefferson
3rd President
Party: Democratic-Republican
Terms: 1801-1809

At age twenty-six, Jefferson became a member of the colonial legislature of Virginia. Although he did not fight in the Revolutionary War, Jefferson was an important member of the Continental Congress. He was the chief author of the Declaration of Independence. After the war, he wrote a statute, or law, of religious freedom for Virginia. He was a U.S. ambassador, or minister, to France when the Constitution was written, but he returned to serve in the first cabinet as President Washington's secretary of state. After serving as John Adams's vice president, Jefferson was elected president.

Jefferson headed the new Democratic Republican Party, an earlier form of today's Democratic Party. Jefferson and his party thought that the national government should be small and not interfere in private affairs. As president, Jefferson spent little money and cut the budgets of the army and navy.

Although Jefferson thought the government should stay within the bounds set by the Constitution, he could not resist buying the Louisiana Territory from France for the bargain price of $15 million. With the Louisiana Purchase, Jefferson nearly doubled the size of the United States.

After eight years in office, Jefferson retired to Monticello. On July 4, 1826, the fiftieth anniversary of the Declaration of Independence, Jefferson (and his old colleague John Adams) died.

Read the clues about Thomas Jefferson and his presidency.
Then complete the puzzle using the word list on the next page.

★ *Across* ★

3. Jefferson founded the Democratic _____ Party.
5. Jefferson reduced spending for this fighting force.
8. Jefferson died _____ years after the Declaration of Independence was written.
9. President for whom Jefferson served as vice president
11. Jefferson made a good deal for the Louisiana _____.
12. Jefferson's home

Down

1. Jefferson was chief author of the _____ of Independence.
2. Jefferson was a U.S. _____ in France when the Constitution was written.
4. Jefferson's family business
6. Jefferson invented a form of this for the nation.
7. Jefferson was trained in this field.
10. Jefferson wrote an important Virginia law to protect the religious kind of this.
13. Number of terms Jefferson served as president

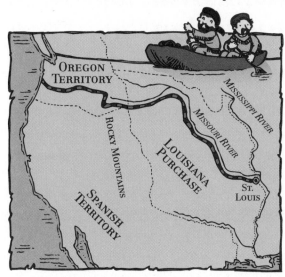

The Lewis and Clark Expedition

President Jefferson sent Meriwether Lewis and William Clark to explore the Louisiana Territory after its purchase.

Word List

ADAMS	FIFTY	MONEY	PURCHASE
AMBASSADOR	FREEDOM	MONTICELLO	REPUBLICAN
ARMY	LAW	PLANTATION	TWO
DECLARATION			

James Madison *(1751-1836)*, James Monroe *(1758-1831)*, and John Quincy Adams *(1767-1848)*

James Madison and James Monroe were the last leaders of the American Revolution to become presidents. John Quincy Adams, son of the nation's second president, represented a new generation.

James Madison helped create the U.S. Constitution. His notes on the secret debates over how to shape the U.S. government are an invaluable part of American history. In addition, Madison wrote the Bill of Rights, the first ten amendments to the Constitution.

Thomas Jefferson appointed Madison secretary of state (Monroe and John Quincy Adams later held the same job for different presidents). France and Britain were already at war, and the Democratic Republican Party wanted the nation to join France in the fight. After he was elected president, Madison declared war against Britain. In 1814, the British attacked Washington, D.C., burning the Executive Mansion (later called the White House) and other buildings, and forcing members of the government to flee for a time. In spite of the turmoil, Madison's life in Washington was a social success, thanks mostly to his wife, Dolley, who loved hosting parties. The War of 1812 ended in 1815 and inspired "The Star-Spangled Banner," a song that became the national anthem.

James Monroe received some credit for postwar contentment. One newspaper nicknamed his time in office the "era of good feeling." During Monroe's administration, the United States acquired Florida from Spain. Spain and other European countries later threatened to retake their former colonies in Central and South America. Monroe issued the Monroe Doctrine, a document warning the countries of Europe not to create colonies in the Americas.

As a member of Monroe's cabinet, John Quincy Adams helped create the Monroe Doctrine and acquire Florida. However, Adams did not accomplish much during his time

James Madison
4th President
Party: Democratic-Republican
Terms: 1809-1817

James Monroe
5th President
Party: Democratic-Republican
Terms: 1817-1825

John Quincy Adams
6th President
Party: Democratic-Republican
Term: 1825-1829

in office, because the majority of representatives in Congress were politically opposed to him. President Adams went swimming in the Potomac River every morning when the weather was good. He also kept an alligator as a pet! John Quincy Adams was not elected to a second term as president, but he did serve as a congressman after he left office. In that position, he worked against slavery and for people's rights and helped found the Smithsonian Institute in Washington, D.C.

Words about James Madison, James Monroe, and John Quincy Adams and their presidencies have been scrambled. Rearrange the letters and write the correct word on each line. Use the word list if you need help.

CERFAN

_____

TRMINDATIINOSA

_____

SERGNOCS

_____

ELODLY IMODNAS

_____

EROMNO RTCNEIDO

_____

NISAMOTSNIH

_____

ULOVTRINEO

_____

TGWSOHNIAN

_____

MPTOOCA

_____

RILDAFO

_____

TOSUTIOCINNT

_____

HITEW SHEOU

_____

Word List

ADMINISTRATION	DOLLEY MADISON	MONROE DOCTRINE	SMITHSONIAN
CONGRESS	FLORIDA	POTOMAC	WASHINGTON
CONSTITUTION	FRANCE	REVOLUTION	WHITE HOUSE

Andrew Jackson (1767-1845)

Andrew Jackson
7th President
Party: Democratic
Terms: 1829-1837

They called him "Old Hickory" because he was so tough. Andrew Jackson was born in a log cabin along the border of North and South Carolina and barely learned to read. At the age of thirteen, he became a messenger for the militia in the Revolutionary War and was captured by the British. When he refused to clean a British officer's boots, the man slashed Jackson's hand with a sword. The scar remained for life—and so did Jackson's fighting spirit. He fought Indians along the frontier and had become a general in the U.S. Army by the War of 1812. Old Hickory led American troops to victory over the British in the battle of New Orleans, and became famous for it nationwide. It did not seem to matter that the war had actually ended before the battle took place, as news of the peace had not arrived in time.

Jackson's supporters wanted him to be president after Monroe, but Jackson lost to John Quincy Adams when the close election had to be decided in the House of Representatives. Four years later, Jackson won. His wife, Rachel, died just before Jackson took office. His frontier followers showed up to celebrate his inauguration. The crowd muddied White House furniture, broke glasses, and overturned the punch. Refined Americans were horrified, but Jackson's friends called him the first "people's president."

In office, Jackson insisted he was there to represent the people, not to go along with Congress. He was the first president to veto many bills. He pushed for what he wanted, such as the removal of Indian tribes from the eastern United States in the 1830s. He also strengthened the hand of the federal government against the states. When South Carolina refused to obey a tariff law (a tax on imported goods), he was prepared to use force—until the state agreed to a compromise. After two terms, Jackson retired to Tennessee, as popular as when he was elected.

Read the clues about Andrew Jackson and his presidency.
Then complete the puzzle using the word list on the next page.

★ Across ★

4. Jackson defeated the British at the battle of New _____.
5. Jackson fought in more than one of these.
6. Ceremony at the beginning of a presidency; Jackson's was riotous
9. Age at which Jackson served as messenger for the Revolutionary militia
11. Jackson forced Indian tribes from this part of the United States to move west of the Mississippi.
12. Jackson made officials in South _____ obey a federal tariff law.

14. Jackson was the first president to use this power often.

★ *Down* ★

1. As a young man, Jackson fought these people.
2. Jackson was born in this kind of house.
3. Tax on imported goods, which South Carolina did not want to pay
7. Job Jackson had as a boy during the Revolutionary War
8. Rank Jackson attained in the U.S. Army
10. Uneducated, Jackson could barely do this.
13. First word in Jackson's nickname

Jackson fought more than one duel during his lifetime.

Word List

CABIN	EASTERN	MESSENGER	TARIFF
CAROLINA	GENERAL	OLD	THIRTEEN
DUEL	INAUGURATION	ORLEANS	VETO
	INDIANS	READ	

Martin Van Buren (1782-1862), William H. Harrison (1773-1841), and John Tyler (1790-1862)

Martin Van Buren was the first president to be born an American citizen (presidents before him were born British citizens), yet he spoke Dutch at home! That's because his family was part of the old Dutch settlement of Kinderhook, New York.

Van Buren was a good politician. He was able to "ride Andrew Jackson's coattails," rising from vice president during Jackson's second term to president in 1837. Van Buren's election campaign was the first in which rallies, sing-alongs, and slogans played an important role.

Martin Van Buren
8th President
Party: Democratic
Term: 1837-1841

Van Buren ran into big trouble once he became president. The country was plunged into an economic depression. Too many people had borrowed money to buy land, expecting the value of land to rise. When it did not, they lost money. Banks and businesses closed, and many workers lost their jobs. Even though the depression was caused mostly by overspeculation and a natural economic downturn, it hurt the president's image. Van Buren was defeated after his first term by William Henry Harrison.

Harrison was an Ohio general, famous for winning the battle against Chief Tecumseh at the Tippecanoe River. Known as "Old Tippecanoe," Harrison ran for president with vice presidential candidate John Tyler. Harrison became ill while giving his inauguration speech in cold weather. It was the longest inauguration speech in American history—one hour and forty-five minutes! Afterward, Harrison said, "I am ill, very ill." He died one month after his inauguration.

William H. Harrison
9th President
Party: Whig
Term: 1841-1841

Subsequently, John Tyler became president. Although Tyler was a Whig, as Harrison had been, he did not agree with most of the party's policies. The Whigs favored central government, while Tyler wanted the states to have more rights. He vetoed his own party's bills, including one that would create a national bank. However, just three days before he left office, Tyler did sign a bill to make Texas a part of the United States.

John Tyler
10th President
Party: Whig
Term: 1841-1845

Read the sentences about Martin Van Buren, William H. Harrison, and John Tyler and their presidencies. Then complete the sentences by filling in each blank. Use the word list if you need help.

★ Van Buren was _____ in Andrew Jackson's administration.

★ _____ was the site of the battle from which Harrison got his nickname.

★ Harrison was president for one _____.

★ Van Buren spoke _____ at home.

★ After his inauguration, Harrison admitted he was

_____.

★ Tyler opposed the creation of a _____ bank.

★ The nation faced this economic problem while Van Buren was in office:

_____.

★ Snappy sayings, or _____, were an important part of Van Buren's campaign.

★ Van Buren lost for a second term because he could not improve the state of the

_____.

★ _____ was the Indian chief who was defeated by Harrison at Tippecanoe.

Tyler introduced the polka to people at White House parties.

Word List

depression	economy	national	Tippecanoe
Dutch	ill	slogans	Vice President
	month	Tecumseh	

James Polk (1795-1849), Zachary Taylor (1784-1850), and Millard Fillmore (1800-1874)

James Polk was chosen by the Democrats partly because no one knew him well enough to be his enemy. He was the first dark-horse, or unlikely to win, presidential candidate. No alcohol was allowed in the White House during Polk's administration. He is said to have preferred water instead.

James Polk
11th President
Party: Democratic
Term: 1845-1849

By the mid-1800's, American pioneers wanted to move west freely, but Mexico and Britain still claimed some of the land. Polk helped arrange an agreement with Britain to divide the Oregon Territory into two sections, one of which would become part of Canada. However, he could not pry California away from Mexico. In fact, the United States and Mexico were still disputing about the recently annexed Texas. Polk sent U.S. troops to Mexico, where they were attacked by Mexican forces. American troops easily defeated the Mexican army, and Polk arranged to pay Mexico for land that would one day become part of California, Nevada, Utah, Arizona, New Mexico, and Wyoming.

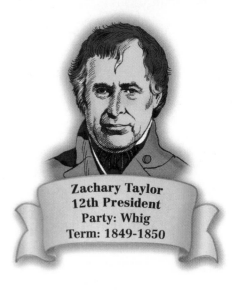

Zachary Taylor
12th President
Party: Whig
Term: 1849-1850

Polk retired after only one term and died soon after he left office. Polk's political rivals, the Whigs, nominated the army general whom Polk had sent to Mexico. His name was Zachary Taylor, also known as "Old Rough and Ready." Taylor did not have any political experience before entering office. Taylor brought his horse, Old Whitey, to the White House, where it grazed on the lawn. He focused on the major issue of the day—whether California and New Mexico would ban slavery when they entered the Union. The Southern states were afraid this would upset the balance of states and threatened to leave the Union. Taylor favored slavery, but he told Congress that he would lead an army against the Southern states if they tried to destroy the Union.

On July 4, 1850, President Taylor fell ill with stomach distress. He died five days later of cholera. Vice President Millard Fillmore, from New York, became president.

Millard Fillmore
13th President
Party: Whig
Term: 1850-1853

Fillmore was opposed to slavery, but he wanted to preserve the Union. He approved the Compromise of 1850, which had been proposed by Congress to relieve tensions between the North and the South. Among other things, the agreement allowed California to enter the Union as a free state, without slavery. It also set forth the Fugitive Slave Law, which required every state to allow the arrest and return of runaway slaves. Many Northerners were upset because this "compromise" seemed to favor slavery. Some Southerners were distressed that the federal government was now passing legislation on slavery rather than leaving it up to the states.

Words about James Polk, Zachary Taylor, and Millard Fillmore and their presidencies have been scrambled. Rearrange the letters and write the correct word on each line. Use the word list if you need help.

PISOMEMOCR

_____

AANDCA

_____

ONINU

_____

LVAEYSR

_____

SEWT

_____

WIGSH

_____

MICEOX

_____

RANELEG

_____

STAEMOCRD

_____

EREF

_____

RAYLOT

_____

RIFONALCIA

_____

Word List

CALIFORNIA	DEMOCRATS	MEXICO	UNION
CANADA	FREE	SLAVERY	WEST
COMPROMISE	GENERAL	TAYLOR	WHIGS

Franklin Pierce (1804-1869) and James Buchanan (1791-1868)

**Franklin Pierce
14th President
Party: Democratic
Term: 1853-1857**

Franklin Pierce, a handsome New Hampshire lawyer and politician, was not well known when he was elected president. If he seemed unhappy at times, people remembered that all three of his sons had died—the last one just before his inauguration.

As president, Pierce tried to get more land for the United States. He was unable to buy Cuba from Spain or take over Hawaii. However, in 1853, Pierce made the Gadsden Purchase, buying land from Mexico that today forms the Southern part of Arizona and New Mexico.

Pierce felt that each new state should decide for itself whether or not to have slavery. He signed the Kansas-Nebraska Act, overriding the 1820 Missouri Compromise, which outlawed slavery in the Northern part of the nation. When it became clear that the settlers in Kansas would decide whether or not to allow slavery in the new state, people on both sides of the issue rushed in. Violence resulted and the territory was nicknamed "Bleeding Kansas."

**James Buchanan
15th President
Party: Democratic
Term: 1857-1861**

The Democratic Party did not want to nominate Pierce again. They chose James Buchanan, who had not been involved in the Kansas-Nebraska Act or its violent aftermath. Buchanan was afraid the Southern states would leave the Union, so he tried to keep both sides satisfied. He supported the Supreme Court's decision in the Dred Scott case, which said that slaves and their descendents had no rights and suggested that the federal government could not stop any state or territory from having slavery. Many Americans were furious at the decision. Then Buchanan split his own party by asking Congress to accept Kansas as a slave state. Congress did not accept that plan, and Kansas remained a territory.

Buchanan is the only U.S. president who never married. His niece, Harriet Lane, acted as hostess while Buchanan was in the White House. Buchanan was not nominated by his party again. In 1860, Abraham Lincoln, of the antislavery Republican Party, was elected. In the last months of Buchanan's term, before Lincoln took office, states began to secede from the Union.

Read the clues about Franklin Pierce and James Buchanan and their presidencies. Then complete the puzzle using the word list on the next page.

★ Across ★

2. Lincoln belonged to this political party, which opposed slavery.

4. Buchanan asked Congress to accept Kansas as this kind of state.
6. Both Pierce and Buchanan belonged to this political party.
8. Pierce was the first president to celebrate this holiday with a tree in the White House.
9. Pierce's purchase of land in the Southwest was called the _____ Purchase.
10. People rushed into this territory to decide if it would be a free or slave state.
11. Buchanan sided with the decision in the Dred _____ case.

★ *Down* ★

1. Land bought in the Gadsden Purchase became part of _____ Mexico.
3. Adjective used to describe the violent Kansas territory
4. Buchanan feared the Southern states would do this.
5. The Missouri Compromise of 1820 outlawed slavery in this area of the nation.
7. Adjective describing Pierce's looks
8. Island in the Caribbean that Pierce wanted to acquire.

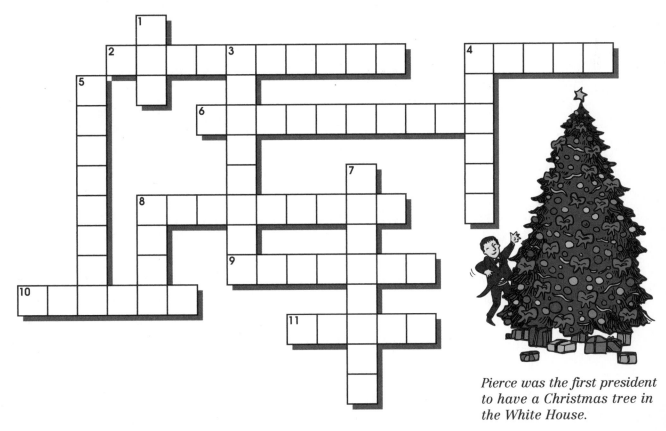

Pierce was the first president to have a Christmas tree in the White House.

Word List

BLEEDING	GADSDEN	NEW	SCOTT
CHRISTMAS	HANDSOME	NORTHERN	SECEDE
CUBA	KANSAS	REPUBLICAN	SLAVE
DEMOCRATIC			

Abraham Lincoln *(1809-1865)*

Abraham Lincoln was born in a Kentucky log cabin and grew up on the frontier in Indiana and Illinois. Young Abe loved to read and often borrowed books that he read at night by firelight.

**Abraham Lincoln
16th President
Party: Republican
Term: 1861-1865**

As a young man, Lincoln studied law on his own. He married Mary Todd, a woman some people believe had a bad temper, in 1842. He was elected to the Illinois state legislature, and then to the House of Representatives. He argued that slavery should not be allowed in new territories, although it was acceptable in the existing ones. When Lincoln ran for the U.S. Senate, he challenged his rival, Democrat Stephen A. Douglas, to a series of debates. Although he lost the election, the Lincoln-Douglas debates made Lincoln famous. People appreciated his homespun wit and wisdom. Two years later, he was elected president. Lincoln, and the antislavery Republican Party, wanted to preserve the Union, but the Southern states had already started to secede. Soon after Lincoln took office, Southerners fired on federal troops at Fort Sumter, South Carolina, and the Civil War began.

Lincoln faced enormous challenges as president during this time. The war became long and drawn out. On January 1, 1863, Lincoln issued the Emancipation Proclamation, freeing the slaves in the rebelling states. Lincoln worried greatly about the suffering of the nation's people during the war. During his famous Gettysburg Address in Pennsylvania, Lincoln asked Americans to continue fighting for freedom and democracy so that the soldiers would not have to die in vain. Lincoln walked the streets of the capital and the halls of the War Department late at night, grieving and thinking. After trying many other generals, Lincoln finally put Ulysses S. Grant in charge of the Union army.

Lincoln was reelected as the war drew to an end. He urged Congress to restore the nation as soon as rebel states promised their loyalty. "Blood cannot restore blood," he said, "and government should not act for revenge." Lincoln's plans for the future were cut short. He was shot at Ford's Theater in Washington, D.C., by John Wilkes Booth, a bitter Southerner seeking his own revenge.

**Read the clues about Abraham Lincoln and his presidency.
Then complete the puzzle using the word list on the next page.**

★ *Across* ★

1. Congressman Lincoln was known for opposing slavery in these places.
5. Last name of the person with whom Lincoln debated when he ran for Senate
8. Lincoln's _____ Proclamation declared an end to slavery in the Confederate states.

9. Kind of animal Jack, a pet in the Lincoln household, was
10. Lincoln's profession before he entered politics
11. The kind of city Washington, D.C., is; where Lincoln walked the streets worrying
12. Lincoln said, "Blood cannot restore _____."

★ *Down* ★

1. Lincoln's wife's maiden name
2. Kind of building; where Lincoln was assassinated
3. Last state Lincoln lived in before he became president
4. The Lincoln-Douglas debates were part of a campaign for this kind of seat.
6. Lincoln tried out several of these before he settled on Grant.
7. Pennsylvania battleground where Lincoln gave a famous address

Lincoln, shown here in his famous stovepipe hat, kept a pet turkey named Jack. The bird had been rescued from becoming a Thanksgiving dinner.

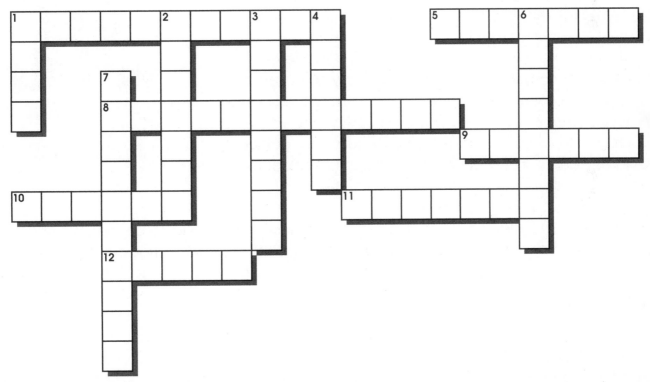

Word List

BLOOD	GENERALS	LAWYER	THEATER
CAPITAL	GETTYSBURG	SENATE	TODD
DOUGLAS	ILLINOIS	TERRITORIES	TURKEY
EMANCIPATION			

Andrew Johnson *(1808-1875)* and Ulysses S. Grant *(1822-1885)*

**Andrew Johnson
17th President
Party: Democratic
Term: 1865-1869**

Andrew Johnson and Ulysses S. Grant, two very different presidents, oversaw the aftermath of the Civil War.

Johnson grew up without schooling in North Carolina. His sixteen-year-old bride helped him learn to write. A strong speaker, he took various governmental positions, from city council to the U.S. Senate. During the Civil War, he was the only Southerner who did not leave the Senate. He explained that he was against Lincoln, "but still I love my country." For Lincoln's second term, the Republican Party invited Johnson to run as his vice president, creating a "unity" ticket between the North and the South.

As president, Johnson wanted to follow Lincoln's ideas for a lenient Reconstruction program, treating the former rebel states kindly while rebuilding after the war. Radical Republicans in Congress favored harsher treatment. They became angry after Johnson vetoed several of their bills, and they tried to get rid of him. He was impeached (formally accused of a crime) for dismissing his Secretary of War without the Senate's permission. The Senate tried Johnson and was one vote short of finding him guilty. Then, in 1867, the Republicans gained a two-thirds majority in Congress, which meant they could overturn Johnson's vetoes. Congress and the army took control of Reconstruction of the South.

**Ulysses S. Grant
18th President
Party: Republican
Terms: 1869-1877**

In the next presidential election, General Ulysses S. Grant, a hero of the Civil War, was elected. Grant, the son of Jesse and Hannah Simpson Grant, was originally named Hiram Ulysses, but his family called him Ulysses or 'Lyss. He decided to adopt the name Ulysses S. Grant after a clerical error was made listing his name as Ulysses Simpson at West Point. Grant was certainly at his best as general. Lincoln once said of him, "I can't spare this man. He fights." As president, though, Grant did not do as well. He had no political experience before taking office. Reconstruction of the South did not go smoothly. White Southerners resented Reconstruction, and secret groups such as the Ku Klux Klan terrorized African Americans. Although Grant was an honest man, his administration was marked by one scandal after another. Grant decided not to run for a third term.

Read the clues about Andrew Johnson and Ulysses S. Grant and their presidencies. Then complete the puzzle using the word list on the next page.

1850s—1900s

★ Across ★

1. To formally accuse a president of a crime
4. Johnson was impeached (but not convicted) for dismissing the secretary of this department without Congress's permission.
7. Federal program intended to rebuild the South after the Civil War
10. Kind of book Grant wrote
11. Grant was popular as a war _____.
12. Johnson used this to stop the radical Republicans.

★ Down ★

2. Johnson grew up in North _____.
3. Speech-maker; Johnson was a good one
4. Johnson's wife helped teach him to do this.
5. After impeachment charges were made, Johnson was tried by this group.
6. Grant's presidency was mired in these, which gave him a bad name.
8. Johnson was opposed to Lincoln but still had this for his country.
9. Kind of ticket created with Northerner Lincoln for president and Southerner Johnson for vice president

Grant finished writing his memoirs a month before he died.

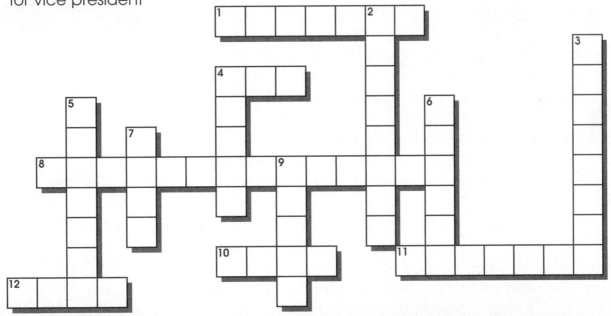

Word List

CAROLINA	MEMOIRS	SENATE	VETO
HERO	RECONSTRUCTION	SPEAKER	WAR
IMPEACH	SCANDALS	UNITY	WRITE
LOVE			

Rutherford B. Hayes (1822-1893), James A. Garfield (1831-1881), and Chester A. Arthur (1829-1886)

Rutherford B. Hayes almost did not become president. He lost the vote of the electors (the representatives who elect the president) to Democratic candidate Samuel J. Tilden. However, the Republican Party challenged the voting results in three Southern states, as well as Oregon. The decision might have resulted in a deadlock if it had gone to Congress, which was made up of a Democratic House and a Republican Senate, but the Republicans and Democrats struck a deal. The questionable votes would go to Hayes, making him president, but he would have to pull the army troops out of the South and end Reconstruction. That is how Hayes became president. In the South, white Democrats took control and received little interference from the federal government for a long time.

Hayes entered the presidency with a solid reputation. He had been a Civil War general and governor of Ohio. Hayes and his wife, nicknamed, "Lemonade Lucy" because she banned alcohol in the White House, were religious and honest. Hayes made every effort to live by his motto: "He serves his party best who serves his country best."

Like Hayes, James A. Garfield was a Republican from Ohio and an officer in the Civil War. He served seventeen years in Congress before he was elected president. Garfield was the first president to be fluent in Spanish. His vice president, Chester Arthur, was from a Republican group called the "Stalwarts." Garfield had been president for less than seven months when he was assassinated. A mentally disturbed man named Charles J. Guiteau, who cried, "I am a Stalwart; now Arthur is president!" Although it was later shown that Guiteau was not acting as part of a conspiracy for the Stalwarts, Chester Arthur entered the presidency with a cloud over his head. Some people thought the Stalwarts would stop at nothing to get what they wanted.

Arthur was opposed to reform, but he did back a new civil service law, changing the way people got federal

Rutherford B. Hayes
19th President
Party: Republican
Term: 1877-1881

James A. Garfield
20th President
Party: Republican
Term: 1881-1881

Chester A. Arthur
21st President
Party: Republican
Term: 1881-1885

government jobs. He also improved the navy and the postal system. He had such a large wardrobe—including eighty pairs of pants!—that people called him "Elegant Arthur."

Read the sentences about Rutherford B. Hayes, James A. Garfield, and Chester A. Arthur. Then complete the sentences by filling in each blank. Use the word list if you need help.

★ The U.S. _____ system was improved by Arthur.

★ Hayes was a _____ in Ohio.

★ Garfield served seventeen years in _____ before he was elected president.

★ Garfield was fluent in _____.

★ Arthur improved this fighting force: the _____.

★ Arthur helped reform _____ jobs.

★ Garfield was killed in the seventh _____ of his presidency.

★ _____ are the representatives who elect the president.

★ The civil _____ is the system of government jobs.

★ Arthur had eighty pairs of _____.

Word List

Congress	government	Navy	service
Electors	governor	pants	Spanish
	month	postal	

Grover Cleveland (1837-1908)

At the end of Grover Cleveland's first term, his wife told the White House servants to take care of things while she and her husband were gone. They'd be sure to return, she said, in four years! It turned out to be true—Grover Cleveland was the only president to serve a term, be out a term, and then serve a second term.

Cleveland was known as an honest reformer. He cleaned up government as Buffalo's mayor, then as governor of New York. In 1884, Cleveland ran for president as a Democrat, receiving extra support from a reform-minded group of Republicans called the "mugwumps."

Grover Cleveland
22nd & 24th President
Party: Democratic
Terms: 1885-1889
1893-1897

In office, Cleveland enforced the Pendleton Civil Service Act, which had been signed by President Arthur. Thousands of jobs once given out as political favors were made available to the public. Cleveland made the railroads give back land they had claimed illegally. He vetoed bills that would have given pensions to Civil War veterans who had not been wounded. Cleveland wanted a low tariff, but he was unable to achieve this.

In 1888, Cleveland ran for reelection against Benjamin Harrison. It was a tight race, but Cleveland lost. Four years later, Cleveland rode a large vote into office again, defeating Harrison this time. Soon afterward, the panic of 1893 led to a major economic depression. Cleveland tried to change the U.S. treasury system but was unable to improve the situation and received a lot of the blame for the country's economic troubles. Earlier, in 1892, Cleveland sent federal troops to end the Pullman railroad strike in Chicago. Although that move was favored by businesses, it angered union workers.

Although Cleveland was not always popular, his oldest daughter, Ruth, was so well liked that she had a candy bar named after her. Baby Ruth bars are still sold in stores today.

An illustration of Cleveland's White House wedding to his much younger wife, Frances

Use the word list to help you find the words about
Grover Cleveland and his presidency that are hidden in the block below.
Some of the words are hidden backward or diagonally.

```
A K H O D E P P R E S S I O N R
O M C G U R O S B H L P A U Y E
R T O A O J O B S A E J P O G E
T H W C P V S N C R I O E W N L
A Q K I R S E I M R S T N D J E
R U W H N M L R Q I D H S A R C
C G I C V R T X N S F F I R A T
O S Z L U E D B P O N I O Q O I
M D A E F T B M U N R S N P S O
E A R P Y O U G N Z F F S V C N
D O O E V W F H I L M M V S T E
G R Y B G T F K O X H E Y A K Y
C L A U I R A R N F T O M I J R
K I M Z P L L C B O U H R B U S
X A W R E F O R M E R T D H Q X
T R E A S U R Y S Y S T E M V N
```

Word List

BUFFALO	GOVERNOR	PENSIONS	RUTH	TWO TERMS
CHICAGO	HARRISON	RAILROADS	STRIKE	UNION
DEMOCRAT	JOBS	REELECTION	TARIFF	VETO
DEPRESSION	MAYOR	REFORMER	TREASURY	
	MUGWUMPS		SYSTEM	

Benjamin Harrison (1833-1901) and William McKinley (1843-1901)

Benjamin Harrison
23rd President
Party: Republican
Term: 1889-1893

Benjamin Harrison was an Indiana lawyer, an officer in the Civil War, and a senator. When he ran against Grover Cleveland for president, he got votes largely because his name was so well known. His grandfather, William Henry Harrison, had been president many years earlier. Harrison also had the backing of business leaders who wanted a high tariff, or tax, on imported goods. Harrison signed the McKinley Tariff Act, written by House member and future president William McKinley. The new tariff raised prices and increased profits for U.S. manufacturers. People with less money, such as farmers, laborers, and especially America's flood of new immigrants, were unhappy with the high prices. They also wanted better wages and working conditions. At the end of Harrison's term, President Cleveland was voted back in to office.

William McKinley
25th President
Party: Republican
Term: 1897-1901

Although McKinley supported a high tariff, he was voted into office because the economy had worsened during Cleveland's second term. McKinley had been a lawyer, a congressman, and governor of Ohio. As a presidential candidate, McKinley received support from the powerful business and financial leaders in the Republican Party, who feared his opponent, William Jennings Bryan, would upset the economy by changing the basis of U.S. money from gold to silver.

The Spanish-American War marked McKinley's first term. American newspapers published sensational stories about Cuba's fight for independence from Spain, urging the United States to help free Cuba. This "yellow journalism" was only partly true, but it convinced many people that the United States should act. After the United States became involved in the Spanish-American War, Cuba won its independence, and the United States gained control of the Philippines, Puerto Rico, and Guam. McKinley later accepted Hawaii as a U.S. territory and divided the Samoan Islands with Germany. Only seven months into his second term, McKinley was assassinated by Leon Czolgosz, an anarchist who was disturbed by social injustice.

Words about Benjamin Harrison and William McKinley and their presidencies have been scrambled. Rearrange the letters and write the correct word on each line. Use the word list if you need help.

CRANHASTI

_____

NOSERTA

_____

VERSLI

_____

ROGERVON

_____

FARIFT

_____

SCTRANFEMUAUR

_____

MAUG

_____

YREALW

_____

BACU

_____

AIHAIW

_____

CEMOONY

_____

CARBILUNEP

_____

Harrison's nickname was "Little Ben."

Word List

ANARCHIST	GOVERNOR	LAWYER	SENATOR
CUBA	GUAM	MANUFACTURERS	SILVER
ECONOMY	HAWAII	REPUBLICAN	TARIFF

Theodore Roosevelt (1858-1919)

As a child, Theodore Roosevelt was so sick with asthma and other illnesses that he had to be tutored at home instead of going to school. When he was thirteen, he began an exercise program and eventually became strong and energetic. His enthusiasm for fresh air and exercise lasted the rest of his life.

Theodore Roosevelt
26th President
Party: Republican
Term: 1901-1909

Born well off, Roosevelt went to Harvard University, then held a number of government positions. He worked as a rancher in the Dakota Territory for two years after his mother and his first wife died. He worked in President McKinley's administration during the Spanish-American War before deciding to join the fight himself. After the war, Roosevelt was elected governor of New York.

Roosevelt became vice president during McKinley's second term. He was made president when McKinley was assassinated in 1901. Roosevelt was just forty-two years old at the time, making him the youngest president in U.S. history.

During his two terms as president, Roosevelt accomplished a lot. He believed people should have a fair, or "square," deal. He tried to break up large business groups that controlled prices, called "trusts." He also managed to raise wages for coal miners. He supported the Pure Food and Drug Act and the Meat Inspection Act, raising standards for food and medicine. He received the Nobel Peace Prize for his role as mediator in the Russo-Japanese War. He built up the navy and encouraged the building of the Panama Canal on the isthmus of Panama. Roosevelt said it was best to "speak softly and carry a big stick."

Roosevelt also supported the creation of many national parks and forests. Once, while on a hunting trip, Roosevelt refused to shoot a bear cub. A toy maker created the first "Teddy Bear" in honor of Roosevelt.

The White House was a lively place while Roosevelt was in office. He always made time to play with his six adventurous and fun-loving children.

Read the clues about Theodore Roosevelt and his presidency.
Then complete the puzzle using the word list on the next page.

★ Across ★

3. Roosevelt worked for laws that would preserve the wilderness in national parks and _____.
4. Term for the kind of deal Roosevelt promised voters
7. Healthy activity that Roosevelt favored
9. Roosevelt fought in the _____-American War.

10. Some players of this game were members of the Rough Riders.
11. Narrow land between bodies of water; the Panama Canal was built across one
12. Territory where Roosevelt ranched for two years

★ *Down* ★

1. Large business combinations that Roosevelt tried to break up
2. Roosevelt was elected to this position after the Spanish-American War.
5. Number of children Roosevelt had
6. Health problem Roosevelt experienced as a child
8. Roosevelt said, "Speak softly and carry a big _____."

Roosevelt formed the Rough Riders, a cavalry regiment, with friends including cowboys from the west and polo players from the east.

Word List

ASTHMA	FORESTS	POLO	SQUARE
DAKOTA	GOVERNOR	SIX	STICK
EXERCISE	ISTHMUS	SPANISH	TRUSTS

William H. Taft (1857-1930)

William H. Taft grew up in Cincinnati, Ohio. His family called him "Big Lug" because of his size—he was six feet tall and weighed as much as 330 pounds. However, Taft was athletic. He liked to play tennis and dance, and even learned to surf in Waikiki.

Taft was an Ohio state court judge before he became governor of the Philippines, which were recently gained through the Spanish-American War. Taft improved conditions all around and gave the people of the Philippines limited self-government. In 1904, he returned to the United States to become President Roosevelt's Secretary of War. Roosevelt wanted Taft to succeed him as president when he retired, and Taft easily won the election.

William H. Taft
27th President
Party: Republican
Term: 1909-1913

Soon after taking office, Taft found out that being president was difficult and often "lonesome." Many people, including Theodore Roosevelt, thought Taft acted too conservatively, but he did his best to carry out the policies Roosevelt had set in place. Taft's administration attempted to break up ninety trusts, or business combinations, which was even more than Roosevelt had targeted while president. Taft supported the establishment of a federal income tax, which was charged according to the amount a person earned.

Taft favored "dollar diplomacy," which meant using trade and investments to influence other countries. He even sent troops to Central America to protect American property and lives. Some people believed that the U.S. Army was under control of American business.

The Republicans nominated Taft for a second term. Theodore Roosevelt, unhappy with the job Taft was doing, decided to run for president again and formed his own political party to do so. As a result, the Republican vote was split and the election went to the Democratic candidate, Woodrow Wilson.

Taft was glad to leave the White House. He was later appointed Chief Justice of the Supreme Court, a job he had wanted all his life.

Read the clues about William H. Taft and his presidency.
Then complete the puzzle using the word list on the next page.

★ Across ★

2. Taft became Chief _____ of the Supreme Court.
6. Taft acted as governor of these islands.
7. Taft favored this kind of tax.
9. Nickname for Taft's diplomacy based on monetary incentives
10. Taft had to have an extra-large one put in the White House.

11. Last name of the Democrat who defeated Taft after one term
12. Court Taft last worked in

★ *Down* ★

1. Taft's home city
3. Taft's description of the presidency
4. Number of business trusts Taft's administration tried to break up
5. Taft sent troops to this part of the Americas.
8. Taft's job before he became governor of the Philippines

Taft, who was a big man, had an extra-large tub installed in the White House.

Word List

BATHTUB	**DOLLAR**	**JUSTICE**	**PHILIPPINES**
CENTRAL	**INCOME**	**LONESOME**	**SUPREME**
CINCINNATI	**JUDGE**	**NINETY**	**WILSON**

Woodrow Wilson (1856-1924)

Woodrow Wilson was one of the most learned presidents. He was a professor at and president of Princeton University before he was elected governor of New Jersey. Just two years later, he became president, largely because the opposing vote was split between Theodore Roosevelt and William Taft.

**Woodrow Wilson
28th President
Party: Democratic
Term: 1913-1921**

Wilson felt that Congress represented special regions and interests but the president should "look out for the general interests of the whole country." He worked for a lower tariff, or tax on imported goods, which angered some manufacturers but lowered prices for most Americans. He established the Federal Reserve System to regulate the nation's banks and money supply. He supported laws that would improve conditions for workers, including one that restricted railroad workers to eight-hour workdays.

Wilson is most famous for his role as a leader in World War I. He tried hard to keep the nation out of the war, until German submarines began attacking American ships. Once the United States entered the war, the tide turned against Germany. Wilson named "Fourteen Points" he thought were needed to create a lasting peace once the war was over. The most important one was the formation of the League of Nations, where countries could meet to resolve disputes instead of going to war. The Treaty of Versailles contained some of the points Wilson had proposed, but he was forced to compromise on several issues.

At home, though, Wilson could not get the Senate to agree to the treaty. They were afraid the League of Nations would reduce the power of the United States. Wilson became ill during a trip to rally public support for the treaty. Soon afterward, he suffered a stroke and did not appear publicly for months. His wife, Edith, took messages to him and announced his decisions. Some historians believe that Edith may actually have been making the decisions herself. The treaty was never approved by the Senate.

During World War I, President Wilson used sheep to mow the White House lawn instead of men who could help the war effort.

Words about Woodrow Wilson and his presidency
have been scrambled. Rearrange the letters and write the correct
word on each line. Use the word list if you need help.

★ ★

★ EAPEC

_____

★ AETRYT

_____

★ TINCREONP

_____

★ MRAGEN

_____

★ REWOP

_____

★ SNBKA

_____

★ SOREPOSRF

_____

★ CISIDENOS

_____

★ SDIPTUES

_____

★ NOTREEUF

_____

★ NETASE

_____

★ OKRSWRE

_____

★ ★

Word List

BANKS	FOURTEEN	POWER	SENATE
DECISIONS	GERMAN	PRINCETON	TREATY
DISPUTES	PEACE	PROFESSOR	WORKERS

Warren G. Harding (1865-1923) and Calvin Coolidge (1872-1933)

Warren G. Harding and Calvin Coolidge, two very different men, took office as president and vice president in 1921. Harding was tall, handsome, and likeable, but he had spent most of his time as a senator doing favors for friends back home in Ohio. Coolidge was a strict, conservative New Englander. He became famous when, as a governor of Massachusetts, he broke up a Boston police strike by calling in the National Guard. "There is no right to strike against the public safety," he declared, "by anyone, anywhere, any time."

Warren G. Harding
29th President
Party: Republican
Term: 1921-1923

Harding probably won the presidency because he promised a return to "normalcy" after World War I. He was opposed to the League of Nations, but he called for the Washington Disarmament Conference. There, the United States and other nations agreed to reduce the size of their navies.

Harding preferred gambling, drinking, and playing golf to work. He gave friends from Ohio jobs in Washington, D.C. Many of them were without ability; others were careless of their duties. The press called them the "Ohio Gang." Three years into his term, Harding died suddenly, probably from a heart attack. After Harding's death, many scandals

Calvin Coolidge
30th President
Party: Republican
Term: 1923-1929

became known publicly, including the Teapot Dome scandal in which the secretary of the interior was found guilty of accepting over $3 million in bribes to rent government land to oil drillers.

Coolidge spoke so little he was called "Silent Cal."

Calvin Coolidge was an honest president. He made government more efficient and economical. He did not believe government should interfere in private business, even though people seemed to be gambling on the stock market. "The business of America is business," he declared. Coolidge served the remainder of Harding's term plus one of his own. He retired a few months before the stock market crashed in 1929, leading to the worst economic depression in U.S. history.

Use the word list to help you find the words about Warren G. Harding and Calvin Coolidge and their presidencies that are hidden in the block below. Some of the words are hidden backward or diagonally.

```
L  E  V  I  T  A  V  R  E  S  N  O  C  D  T  R
A  E  P  T  E  A  P  O  T  D  O  M  E  G  E  I
P  L  A  N  A  T  I  O  N  A  L  G  U  A  R  D
S  Y  X  G  I  D  H  T  M  O  K  T  I  G  J  B
N  O  S  H  U  P  R  E  K  I  R  T  S  N  O  U
O  H  I  O  Y  E  P  T  C  N  E  C  P  A  M  S
I  C  L  S  R  C  O  O  L  I  D  G  E  G  R  I
S  P  E  K  H  S  Y  F  B  U  Z  N  Y  O  U  N
S  R  N  G  O  V  E  R  N  O  R  I  V  I  M  E
E  E  T  G  A  B  N  X  J  A  E  W  R  H  E  S
R  S  E  N  A  T  O  R  G  K  T  J  F  O  U  S
P  I  K  I  E  M  Z  L  I  B  R  I  B  E  S  F
E  D  Q  D  N  O  R  M  A  L  C  Y  O  D  I  Q
D  E  G  R  V  T  E  G  J  F  N  P  L  N  L  U
A  N  M  A  S  S  A  C  H  U  S  E  T  T  S  W
U  T  M  H  S  T  O  C  K  M  A  R  K  E  T  B
```

Word List

BRIBES	GOVERNOR	NAVY	SENATOR
BUSINESS	HARDING	NORMALCY	SILENT
CONSERVATIVE	LEAGUE OF NATIONS	OHIO	STOCK MARKET
COOLIDGE	MASSACHUSETTS	OHIO GANG	STRIKE
DEPRESSION	NATIONAL GUARD	PRESIDENT	TEAPOT DOME

Herbert C. Hoover (1874-1964)

Herbert C. Hoover
31st President
Party: Republican
Term: 1929-1933

Herbert Hoover was perhaps most remarkable for all the things he did when he was not president. By profession, he was a mining engineer, educated in the first class at Stanford University in California. As a young man, he managed mines all over the world and became very wealthy. Hoover was living in London when World War I began, and he organized a committee to help his fellow Americans get home from Europe. Soon he was heading the Commission for Relief in Belgium, which helped distribute aid in war-torn Europe.

President Wilson took advantage of Hoover's experience, making him the wartime U.S. food administrator, responsible for getting Americans to save food so more would be available for the troops. Then, after World War I, Hoover headed a council to distribute food to the hungry in Europe.

By this time, Hoover was so well known that President Harding named him secretary of commerce. He did so much for the country that people called him "Undersecretary of Everything Else." Hoover was untouched by the scandals of Harding's administration.

In 1928, Hoover was elected president—his first elective office. Just seven months into his presidency, the Great Depression struck. About a quarter of all Americans were out of work; many were homeless and hungry. Hoover increased government loans to banks and businesses and supported some public works projects, but he did not think it was right for government to give aid to poor people or create jobs with borrowed money. He was afraid that would destroy the individual American's drive to succeed. Although he had not created the conditions that led to the economic troubles, Hoover was blamed for the depression. At the end of his term, he was defeated in a landslide.

Hoover continued to help others after he left office. In 1946, President Truman made Hoover chairman of the Famine Emergency Commission in Europe. He later worked on two different commissions to help make government more efficient.

Read the clues about Herbert C. Hoover and his presidency.
Then complete the puzzle using the word list on the next page.

★ *Across* ★

3. Hoover headed Belgium's Commission for _____.
4. Word used for camps of the poor and unemployed during the depression
5. Term for a big election win
6. Mass hunger; Hoover helped fight this in Europe
8. Hoover trained for this profession in college.

10. University Hoover attended

★ *Down* ★

1. As secretary of commerce, Hoover was called "_____ of Everything Else."
2. The last commissions Hoover served on were supposed to make government more_____.
5. British city where Hoover lived for a time
7. As a young man, Hoover managed these.
9. Help; given out by many Hoover-led groups
11. Number of terms Hoover served

The tent and shack cities of the unemployed during the Great Depression were called "Hoovervilles."

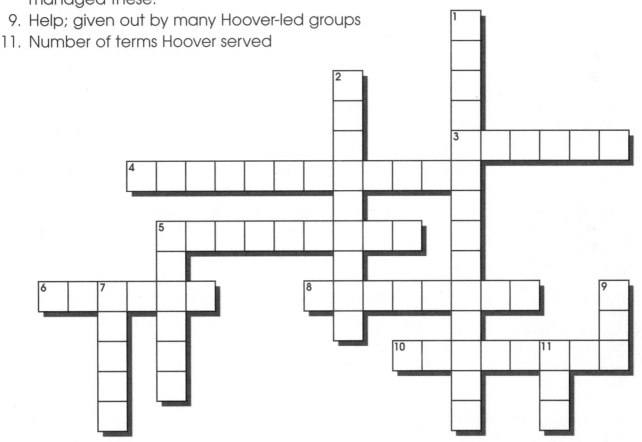

═ *Word List* ═

AID	**FAMINE**	**LONDON**	**RELIEF**
EFFICIENT	**HOOVERVILLES**	**MINES**	**STANFORD**
ENGINEER	**LANDSLIDE**	**ONE**	**UNDERSECRETARY**

Franklin D. Roosevelt *(1882-1945)*

Franklin D. Roosevelt
32nd President
Party: Democratic
Terms: 1933-1945

Franklin Delano Roosevelt, often called "FDR," was born into a wealthy and well-connected family. In fact, he was related to eleven former American presidents. He was also distantly related to the woman he married. Trained in the law, FDR served in the New York State Senate before President Wilson made him assistant secretary of the navy.

At age 39, FDR contracted polio, which left his legs paralyzed. For the rest of his life, he wore leg braces and used crutches or a wheelchair. He ran for governor of New York in 1928. When the Great Depression struck, he took measures to help suffering people in his state.

The Democrats nominated Roosevelt for president in 1932. He offered Americans the New Deal, promising that the government would do much more to relieve suffering and end the depression. In the so-called "First Hundred Days" of his presidency, FDR put through a storm of new laws. He temporarily closed banks to end panic withdrawals, then reopened them with federal help and deposit insurance. Later, he fought for laws that laid a foundation of security for Americans, creating Social Security, unemployment insurance, and federal aid to dependent children. FDR's radio talks, called "fireside chats," gave people new confidence. "The only thing we have to fear is fear itself," Roosevelt said.

FDR would have done even more to control business and industry, but the Supreme Court blocked some of his measures. In 1937, he tried to enlarge the size of the Court in order to appoint judges who would agree with him, but the plan failed.

The nation appreciated FDR's strong leadership during World War II. He died at the start of his last term in 1945. Roosevelt was elected to four terms—no other president had been elected to more than two terms! Congress later passed a law limiting presidents to two consecutive terms in office.

Eleanor Roosevelt, one of the greatest first ladies, worked hard to achieve equality for people of all races and wrote the Universal Declaration of Human Rights.

Use the word list to help you find the words about
Franklin D. Roosevelt and his presidency that are hidden in the block
below. Some of the words are hidden backward or diagonally.

```
A  M  Y  J  O  S  Y  R  A  T  E  R  C  E  S  L
P  N  J  F  E  P  O  A  N  S  M  Z  T  M  A  G
A  U  N  E  M  P  L  O  Y  M  E  N  T  W  N  D
R  P  L  A  M  H  A  S  J  E  L  B  Q  R  H  D
E  L  E  R  L  Y  F  W  R  M  E  E  U  F  K  G
P  O  L  I  O  S  D  I  O  E  A  I  H  I  U  S
H  E  R  T  O  G  O  V  E  R  N  O  R  R  E  P
P  B  A  N  K  S  C  S  L  P  O  Y  D  E  N  I
H  L  T  A  Y  L  P  F  O  U  R  I  F  S  A  C
L  M  L  D  X  I  L  I  P  S  G  Q  D  I  V  R
E  N  K  E  R  A  U  G  E  C  A  L  N  D  Y  U
L  U  P  R  E  J  W  Z  D  X  L  O  R  E  R  T
E  M  I  D  T  Y  T  I  R  U  C  E  S  F  A  C
V  L  W  N  L  S  E  R  R  I  F  G  V  I  Z  H
E  E  T  U  W  A  V  R  D  N  G  D  K  O  N  B
N  W  G  H  H  U  M  A  N  Y  E  N  R  A  C  E
```

Word List

BANKS	FEAR	HUNDRED	RACE
CRUTCH	FIRESIDE	LAW	SECRETARY
ELEANOR	FOUR	NAVY	SECURITY
ELEVEN	GOVERNOR	NEW DEAL	SUPREME
FDR	HUMAN	POLIO	UNEMPLOYMENT

Harry S. Truman *(1884-1972)*

Harry S. Truman had served only eight-two days as vice president when Franklin Roosevelt's death pushed him into the presidency. As a young man, Truman was not able to afford to go to college, but he had read every book in the Independence, Missouri, library by the time he was fifteen. He entered politics as a county official, then was elected senator. Roosevelt chose Truman to be his running mate for 1944 because his last vice president was seen to be too liberal.

Harry S. Truman
33rd President
Party: Democratic
Terms: 1945-1953

Truman proved to be an energetic president who did not hesitate to attack his critics. In his first term, Truman tried to pass new civil rights laws and expand Social Security, but Congress refused to cooperate. Truman's greatest challenges came from abroad, however. World War II came to an end in Europe soon after he took office, but the war continued in the Pacific. Truman decided to use the newly developed atomic bomb on the Japanese. It is estimated that more than 130,000 people were killed in the atomic explosions at Hiroshima and Nagasaki. Historians still argue over whether or not the bombing was needed to end the war and therefore save lives that might have been lost in an invasion of Japan.

At the end of the war, Truman put through the Marshall Plan, a vast aid program for Europe. He also came to Berlin's aid when the Soviets threatened to take control of it in 1948. With roads closed, he ordered planes to carry supplies to the parts of the city that were controlled by the United States and its allies. The airlift succeeded, and the Soviets opened the city again.

During his second term, Truman focused much of his attention on the Korean War. In 1950, communist North Korea invaded South Korea. Truman sent troops to Korea, then asked for backing from the United Nations, an international organization that had been formed in 1945. Truman was very concerned about stopping the spread of communism.

Truman's wife and daughter were so much a part of his life that White House staff called them "the Three Musketeers." His wife, Bess, often gave him valued advice, and Truman called her "the Boss."

Bess "The Boss" Truman.

Words about Harry S. Truman and his presidency have
been scrambled. Rearrange the letters and write the correct
word on each line. Use the word list if you need help.

FILATIR

_____

MOICTA

_____

ICOSLA CUTRYESI

_____

ETESMSKURE

_____

MARHHOISI

_____

LIBNER

_____

DNINEPEECNDE

_____

MUSMCOMIN

_____

HLARAMSL APLN

_____

TINDEU SITONNA

_____

TENASOR

_____

EKAOR

_____

Word List

AIRLIFT	COMMUNISM	KOREA	SENATOR
ATOMIC	HIROSHIMA	MARSHALL PLAN	SOCIAL SECURITY
BERLIN	INDEPENDENCE	MUSKETEERS	UNITED NATIONS

Dwight D. Eisenhower *(1890-1969)*

"I like Ike!" was Dwight D. Eisenhower's campaign slogan, and it was what people said about him all his life.

**Dwight D. Eisenhower
34th President
Party: Republican
Terms: 1953-1961**

Eisenhower grew up in Abilene, Kansas. He attended West Point military academy and became a career officer. At the beginning of World War II, he was asked to command the War Plans Division of the War Department. His global strategy and early plan for the invasion of France were so good that President Roosevelt put him in charge of the U.S. Army in Europe. Soon he was heading the Allied forces there, coordinating armies and officers from six different countries. By the end of the war, Eisenhower, who had many good ideas and got along well with people, was an international hero. Both political parties wanted him to be their presidential candidate, but he didn't commit until 1952, when he decided to run as a Republican.

Eisenhower declared that he had already taken part in war and, as president, wanted to make peace. After his inauguration, Eisenhower helped arrange a peace agreement between North and South Korea, ending the Korean War. Like Truman, Eisenhower worried about communism spreading to more countries. He put forth the Eisenhower Doctrine, which said that any country in the Middle East threatened by communists could ask for U.S. aid. He sent troops to Lebanon when they were requested. Eisenhower also tried to deal directly with Soviet communist leaders in summit talks, although these stopped for a time when an American U-2 spy plane was shot down over the Soviet Union.

At home, in a time of prosperity, Eisenhower did little to change the policies set by Presidents Roosevelt and Truman. He enforced existing civil rights laws, sending federal troops to make sure African American students could attend school in Little Rock, Arkansas, in 1957. He helped initiate the interstate highway system. And Eisenhower warned the nation that American arms-makers were combining with the armed forces in a "military-industrial complex" that was dangerous and expensive for the nation.

**Read the clues about Dwight D. Eisenhower and his presidency.
Then complete the puzzle using the word list on the next page.**

★ *Across* ★

1. Eisenhower's nickname
4. Eisenhower worried about the spread of this political belief system.
7. Eisenhower's hometown
9. Eisenhower said that, as president, he wanted to make _____.
10. Eisenhower renamed the presidential retreat _____ David after his grandson.

11. The Eisenhower _____ said Middle East countries threatened by communism could get U.S. aid.

★ *Down* ★

1. Kind of highway system Eisenhower helped start
2. Eisenhower met with leaders of the Soviet Union in this kind of meeting.
3. Continent where Eisenhower served as chief of the armed forces
5. Both political parties wanted Eisenhower to be their _____ after the war.
6. Asian country where Eisenhower helped to make peace
8. Eisenhower sent troops to this Middle Eastern country.
9. Second word in the name of the military academy Eisenhower attended
10. Eisenhower sent federal troops to Little Rock to enforce _____ rights laws.

Eisenhower painting at Camp David, the presidential retreat formerly called "Shangri-La," which he renamed for his grandson David

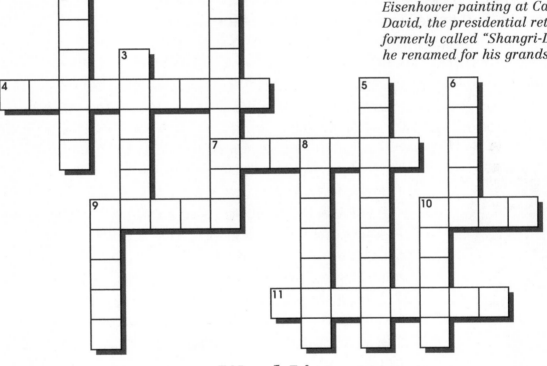

Word List

ABILENE	CIVIL	IKE	PEACE
CAMP	COMMUNISM	INTERSTATE	POINT
CANDIDATE	DOCTRINE	KOREA	SUMMIT
	EUROPE	LEBANON	

John F. Kennedy (1917-1963)

John F. Kennedy started life with many advantages. He was good looking and wealthy. In fact, he was the first president since George Washington to turn down his salary (he donated it to charities instead). He was also from a large, close family. His brothers and sisters helped him throughout his political career. And Kennedy was a talented thinker and writer. His book, *Profiles in Courage*, about courageous senators in history, won a Pulitzer Prize in 1957.

John F. Kennedy
35th President
Party: Democratic
Term: 1961-1963

Jack, as he was known to friends and family, went to Harvard, served in the navy during World War II, and became a congressman and then a senator for his home state of Massachusetts. Finally, in 1960, Kennedy was able to achieve his most important goal—the presidency. Kennedy's strong speaking ability helped him win the first televised debates between presidential candidates.

As president, Kennedy started the Peace Corps, which sent American volunteers to serve in poor or underdeveloped countries. His Alliance for Progress was meant to strengthen ties and trade among the nations of the Americas.

In 1961, Kennedy supported an attack on communist Cuba. The Bay of Pigs invasion was an embarrassing failure. The next year, however, Cuba was the scene of a Kennedy policy triumph. Aerial pictures showed that the Soviets were placing missiles in Cuba. President Kennedy told the Soviets to remove the missiles or risk war. After one tense week, Soviet leader Nikita Khrushchev withdrew the missiles. In 1963, tensions eased a little when Kennedy signed a treaty with Britain, France, and the Soviet Union to stop nuclear testing in the atmosphere, underwater, and in outer space.

At home, Kennedy favored strong civil rights laws and worked hard for desegregation in schools. However, it is hard to know what more Kennedy might have accomplished; he was assassinated after only a few years in office. On November 22, 1963, Kennedy was shot during a parade in Dallas, Texas. The alleged assassin, Lee Harvey Oswald, was killed soon afterward, so the public may never know exactly why or how Kennedy was assassinated.

The years Kennedy spent in the White House with Jackie, Caroline, and John Jr. were compared to King Arthur's Camelot, a time of great happiness that was cut short by tragedy.

Words about John F. Kennedy and his presidency have been scrambled. Rearrange the letters and write the correct word on each line. Use the word list if you need help.

MASGCNRONSE

_____

VRKHSCHEHU

_____

THACSEMASTSUS

_____

DRAHRVA

_____

YBA FO GPIS

_____

BESEATD

_____

ITREGNSEEDOAG

_____

SALADL

_____

AMELTOC

_____

LASWOD

_____

CEPAE PORSC

_____

TILUPRZE

_____

Word List

BAY OF PIGS	DALLAS	HARVARD	OSWALD
CAMELOT	DEBATES	KHRUSHCHEV	PEACE CORPS
CONGRESSMAN	DESEGREGATION	MASSACHUSETTS	PULITZER

Lyndon B. Johnson (1908-1973)

Lyndon B. Johnson grew up in Johnson City, a small town named after his grandfather. Johnson's father and both his grandfathers had served in the Texas state legislature. Maybe that is why, when Lyndon was born, his father rode a horse around town shouting that a future U.S. senator had just come into the world.

Johnson taught high school briefly before he entered the House of Representatives and then the Senate. By 1955, he was majority leader (leader of the Democrats) in the Senate. Johnson tried to get his party's presidential nomination in 1960 but agreed to run as vice president when Kennedy was chosen. Johnson became president when Kennedy was assassinated and was easily elected in his own right in 1964.

As Americans mourned Kennedy, Johnson got certain laws through Congress that Kennedy had wanted. He managed to pass several major civil rights laws, including ones protecting the right of African Americans to vote and forbidding employers from discriminating against people on the basis of race or sex. Johnson also got Congress to pass laws to improve housing, provide Medicare for elderly people without health insurance, and protect the environment. He was aiming, he said, for a "Great Society" in which all people would be able to take part and prosper.

However, Johnson's dreams were thwarted. The new civil rights laws did not bring equality and jobs to all poor inner city African Americans. Frustrations increased and some cities were torn apart by riots. Meanwhile, young men were being drafted to fight

in Vietnam. The war there, begun slowly in Eisenhower's day, escalated under Johnson as the United States, with South Vietnam, struggled against communist North Vietnam. Antiwar feelings grew stronger in the United States. In 1968, Johnson shocked the nation by saying he would not run for the presidency again. At the end of his term, he returned to Texas.

Johnson and his family all had similar names: Lyndon Baines, Lady Bird, Lynda Bird, and Luci Baines.

Use the word list to help you find the words about
Lyndon B. Johnson and his presidency that are hidden in the block below.
Some of the words are hidden backward or diagonally.

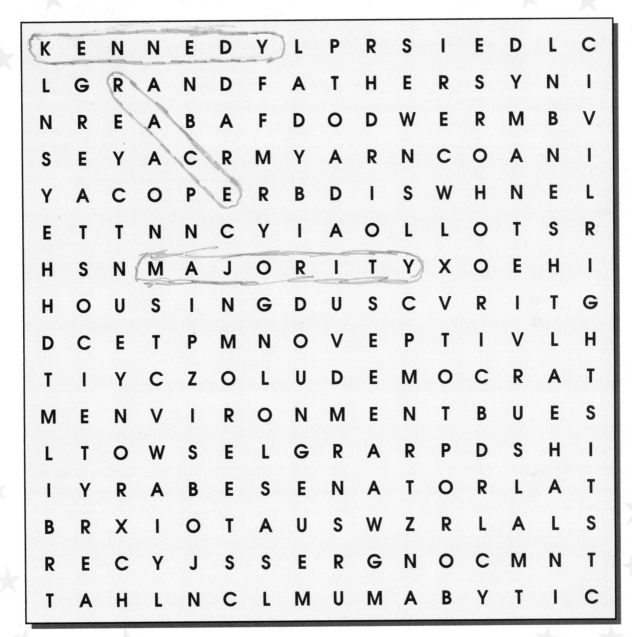

K E N N E D Y L P R S I E D L C
L G R A N D F A T H E R S Y N I
N R E A B A F D O D W E R M B V
S E Y A C R M Y A R N C O A N I
Y A C O P E R B D I S W H N E L
E T T N N C Y I A O L L O T S R
H S N M A J O R I T Y X O E H I
H O U S I N G D U S C V R I T G
D C E T P M N O V E P T I V L H
T I Y C Z O L U D E M O C R A T
M E N V I R O N M E N T B U E S
L T O W S E L G R A R P D S H I
I Y R A B E S E N A T O R L A T
B R X I O T A U S W Z R L A L S
R E C Y J S S E R G N O C M N T
T A H L N C L M U M A B Y T I C

Word List

CITY	GRANDFATHERS	JOBS	RIOTS
CIVIL RIGHTS	GREAT SOCIETY	KENNEDY	SENATOR
CONGRESS	HEALTH	LADY BIRD	TEXAS
DEMOCRAT	HORSE	MAJORITY	VIETNAM
ENVIRONMENT	HOUSING	RACE	VOTE

Richard M. Nixon (1913-1994)

"I am not a crook," Richard M. Nixon insisted when people accused him of lying. But it turned out that he was guilty of one of the worst presidential scandals in history, known as "Watergate."

Nixon's accomplishments before Watergate form a long list. As a young senator from California, he was picked to be Dwight Eisenhower's vice president. In that position, Nixon traveled the world on diplomatic missions. He lost a close presidential election to John F. Kennedy, then lost another election for California governor. He told the press that they wouldn't "have Nixon to kick around any more," but Nixon never gave up easily. Within six years, he had been elected president.

**Richard M. Nixon
37th President
Party: Republican
Term: 1969-1974**

President Nixon's first priority was ending the war in Vietnam. He began a program, which he called "Vietnamization" of the war. American soldiers were slowly brought home as the bombing of North Vietnam was intensified and South Vietnamese soldiers were given training. Finally, Nixon got a cease-fire agreement signed with North Vietnam and pulled the last Americans out of the region. However, the North and South continued to fight until 1975, when the North won.

Nixon helped arrange a cease-fire between Israel and its Arab neighbors, Egypt and Syria. He was the first president to visit communist China. Back home, he tackled rising prices with federal wage and price controls—a daring move.

In 1972, Nixon was easily reelected, but during the campaign five agents of CREEP, the Committee to Re-Elect the President, were caught burglarizing the Democratic National Committee headquarters at the Watergate apartment complex in Washington, D.C. Nixon claimed he knew nothing about the theft of important records, but the scandal grew as the Senate Watergate Committee took evidence in televised hearings. The turning point came when the Supreme Court ordered Nixon to turn over tape recordings he had made. The tapes proved he had lied and covered up illegal actions. Nixon resigned on August 9, 1974. He was pardoned by the new president, Gerald Ford, soon afterward.

**Read the clues about Richard M. Nixon and his presidency.
Then complete the puzzle using the word list on the next page.**

★ Across ★

2. Last name of president who pardoned Nixon
6. Acronym (initials) for the Committee to Re-Elect the President
7. Nixon's term for turning over the war to Vietnam
9. Part of Vietnam that won the war

10. Nixon staff members stole records from this political party.
11. Kind of missions Nixon made abroad for Eisenhower
13. Nixon helped arrange a cease-fire between Israel and Syria and _____.

★ *Down* ★

1. Nixon was the first president to visit this communist country.
3. Nixon decided to do this when evidence showed he was guilty.
4. Nixon's home state
5. Term used for the Nixon scandal
6. Nixon daringly placed these on wages and prices to keep them down.
8. Court that ordered Nixon to turn in his tapes
12. Nixon said, "I am not a _____."

Nixon gave a famous speech in which he denied taking gifts in return for favors, and stated that he was going to keep Checkers, a dog he had been given.

Word List

CALIFORNIA	**CREEP**	**EGYPT**	**SUPREME**
CHINA	**CROOK**	**FORD**	**VIETNAMIZATION**
CONTROLS	**DEMOCRATIC**	**NORTH**	**WATERGATE**
	DIPLOMATIC	**RESIGN**	

Gerald R. Ford *(1913-)* and
James (Jimmy) E. Carter, Jr. *(1924-)*

**Gerald R. Ford
38th President
Party: Republican
Term: 1974-1977**

Gerald R. Ford of Michigan was minority leader (leader of the Republicans) in the House of Representatives when Richard Nixon asked him to replace Spiro Agnew as vice president. Agnew had resigned after being accused of income tax cheating and accepting bribes. Nixon wanted a man with a reputation for honesty, and he got one. The Senate and the House approved Nixon's choice, as is called for in the Twenty-fifth Amendment to the Constitution.

When Nixon resigned because of the Watergate scandal, Ford became president. Ford was the first person to take this office without ever having been elected president or vice president. Soon after he became president, Ford gave Nixon a full pardon, absolving him of any crimes he may have committed. This move angered many people and damaged Ford's chances in the next presidential election.

In 1976, newcomer Jimmy Carter was elected. James Earl Carter, who preferred to be called Jimmy from childhood on, sold peanuts while growing up in Plains, Georgia. Carter had been governor of Georgia for one term but had no national government experience. Carter had high ideals and a relaxed, personable leadership style. He supported human rights around the world and pushed for environmental protection and arms control.

**James (Jimmy) E. Carter, Jr.
39th President
Party: Democratic
Term: 1977-1981**

Carter's greatest success in foreign policy was the signing of the 1979 Camp David Accords, which brought peace between Israel and Egypt. He also arranged for Panama to receive control of the Panama Canal in 1999. Just before the last year of Carter's presidency, Americans at the U.S. embassy in Tehran were taken hostage by a group of Iranian revolutionaries. The hostages were not released until the day Carter left office. The prolonged hostage crisis, along with a limping economy, caused Carter to lose his bid for a second term.

Jimmy Carter has continued to do diplomatic work since retiring from office. He has helped supervise free elections around the world and worked to provide housing for the poor in the United States.

James Earl Carter; a country boy, was known as Jimmy from childhood on.

Words about Gerald R. Ford and Jimmy Carter and their presidencies have been scrambled. Rearrange the letters and write the correct word on each line. Use the word list if you need help.

NAODRP

_____

SNUOGHI

_____

STEPNUA

_____

AERGGIO

_____

NAHMU STIGRH

_____

YLPCIO

_____

WEANG

_____

IARELS

_____

ROGNOREV

_____

MAAPNA

_____

ATGSEOSH

_____

DEEAMNNTM

_____

Word List

AGNEW	GOVERNOR	HUMAN RIGHTS	PARDON
AMENDMENT	HOSTAGES	ISRAEL	PEANUTS
GEORGIA	HOUSING	PANAMA	POLICY

Ronald Reagan *(1911-)*

Ronald Reagan grew up in Illinois. While working as a radio sportscaster in Iowa, Reagan traveled to California. There, he took a Hollywood screen test and soon began making movies. He became a famous actor, working in films for nearly twenty-eight years. During the 1950's, he worked as a spokesman for General Electric, hosting a television show and giving speeches.

**Ronald Reagan
40th President
Party: Republican
Terms: 1981-1989**

California Republicans noticed Reagan and asked him to run for governor. During his two terms as governor, Reagan cut down the number of people on welfare. He criticized university students who were protesting and cut funds for higher education.

Reagan was elected president in 1980, winning such popularity with his speeches that the press called him "the Great Communicator." He cut taxes while increasing defense spending, which led to a record-high national debt. He urged Congress to support anticommunist movements in Nicaragua, Angola, and elsewhere around the world. In 1983, he sent U.S. troops to overthrow the government of the tiny island of Grenada. Although Reagan built up arms, he also met with Soviet leader Gorbachev in a series of summit meetings, easing relations with the Soviet Union.

Scandal struck Reagan's administration when it was revealed that U.S. officials had sold arms to Iranian kidnappers in exchange for American hostages being held in Lebanon. In addition, profits from the arms sales had gone to the Nicaraguan "contras," a group of people who were rebelling against their government, in spite of Congress's decision not to support the contras. Reagan had pledged never to negotiate with terrorists. Reagan claimed he had nothing to do with the Iran-contra affair, but many people on his staff were involved.

At the end of Reagan's second term, the economy was strong. Despite the earlier scandal, Reagan left office as one of the most popular presidents of the century. A few years later, Reagan announced that he had been diagnosed with Alzheimer's disease, an incurable illness that leads to loss of memory.

**Read the clues about Ronald Reagan and his presidency.
Then complete the puzzle using the word list on the next page.**

★ *Across* ★

1. Last name of Reagan's press secretary, paralyzed by shots aimed at the president
4. This improved in the second half of Reagan's presidency.
6. Reagan held summit meetings with this Soviet leader.
9. Reagan once gave speeches for _____ Electric.

10. Reagan's favorite candy
13. The contras were in this country.
14. While governor of California, Reagan spoke against this group of people.

★ Down ★

2. Money owed; Reagan increased this for the nation
3. Alzheimer's disease causes loss of this.
5. Reagan was called "the Great _____."
7. In California, Reagan cut down on this aid to the needy.
8. Reagan increased spending on this.
11. The Iran-contra affair centered on profits gained from selling these.
12. Term for a rebel fighting against the Nicaraguan government

Reagan's press secretary, Jim Brady, was paralyzed in an assassination attempt on the president. From his wheelchair, Brady works tirelessly for gun control.

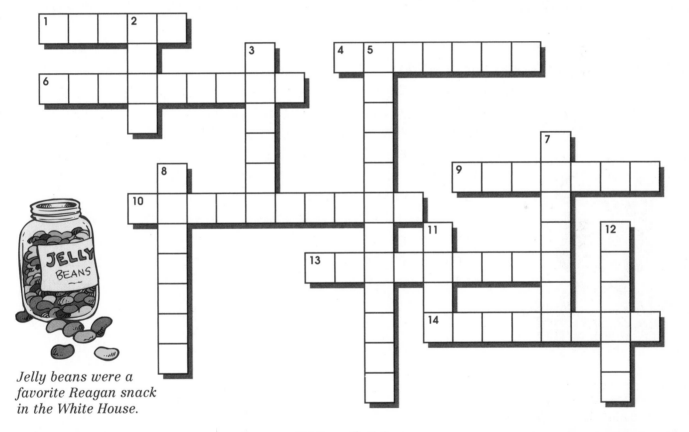

Jelly beans were a favorite Reagan snack in the White House.

Word List

ARMS	CONTRA	GENERAL	NICARAGUA
BRADY	DEBT	GORBACHEV	STUDENTS
COMMUNICATOR	DEFENSE	JELLY BEANS	WELFARE
	ECONOMY	MEMORY	

George Bush *(1924-)*

"Read my lips: no new taxes!" That's what George Bush promised when he was running for president. He was a Republican through and through, and he thought government should do less, not more.

Bush grew up in a wealthy Connecticut family. After a stint as a navy pilot during World War II and studying law at Yale University, he moved to Texas to enter the booming oil business. He made a small fortune there and was elected to the House of Representatives. Presidents Nixon and Ford gave him a series of important jobs: ambassador to the United Nations, chair of the Republican National Committee, chief of the U.S. Liaison Office in China, and director of the Central Intelligence Agency. Then, in 1981, he became Ronald Reagan's vice president. After two terms, he was easily elected as Reagan's successor to the presidency.

George Bush
41st President
Party: Republican
Terms: 1989-1993

As president, Bush had to deal with a Democratic Congress. He signed a budget bill that reduced the amount the government had to borrow, but the bill also increased taxes, contrary to Bush's promise. The president had better luck in foreign affairs. The old Soviet Union was crumbling, a change that some people said was due to the triumph of American-style free enterprise. In the Persian Gulf, Iraqi leader Saddam Hussein tried to take over the tiny, oil-rich nation of Kuwait. Bush organized allies and sent troops to turn him back. The war was over quickly, with few lives lost.

The popularity Bush enjoyed at the end of the Gulf War faded as the economy drooped. Bush did not have any workable solutions to the problem of high unemployment. He lost the next election, leaving office after only one term.

Barbara Bush marked her years as First Lady with a strong commitment to literacy.

Millie, the White House dog, is credited with writing a popular book actually written by her owner, Barbara Bush.

Words about George Bush and his presidency
have been scrambled. Rearrange the letters and write the correct
word on each line. Use the word list if you need help.

SPIL

_____

LOI

_____

SETXA

_____

LEAY

_____

AROMBADSSA

_____

RAABBAR

_____

TOLPI

_____

NURPLICAEB

_____

TUIWKA

_____

TUOLNNPYEEMM

_____

STAXE

_____

MOOCNYE

_____

Word List

AMBASSADOR	KUWAIT	PILOT	TEXAS
BARBARA	LIPS	REPUBLICAN	UNEMPLOYMENT
ECONOMY	OIL	TAXES	YALE

William Jefferson Clinton (1946-)

William Jefferson Clinton, often called Bill, spent most of his childhood in Hot Springs, Arkansas, where he did well in school and learned to play the saxophone for fun. Clinton graduated from Georgetown University, attended Oxford University as a Rhodes scholar, and received a degree from Yale Law School before returning to Arkansas. There, he taught law and won his first election, as state attorney general. He then became governor on and off for several terms before he ran for president as a Democrat.

William Jefferson Clinton
42nd President
Party: Democratic
Terms: 1993-2001

Clinton won the presidential election partly because he favored a center path between traditional Republican and Democratic ideas. In his first term, Clinton pushed for NAFTA—the North American Free Trade Agreement—which linked Mexico, Canada, and the United States, allowing companies and products to move freely across borders. Many Republicans favored this agreement, while some traditional Democrats did not.

Bill Clinton's health-care reform program did not pass through Congress. Clinton was criticized for placing his wife, Hillary, in charge of the effort. In 1996, Clinton signed an important welfare reform bill, which required people on welfare to seek work. And by the middle of his second term, there was a federal surplus—the first in a generation.

In foreign affairs, Clinton's attention turned to the former Yugoslavia, where ethnic groups clashed. In 1995, following a peace agreement, Clinton sent U.S. troops to Bosnia to keep the peace. Later, Serbs attacked ethnic Albanians in the neighboring province of Kosovo. This time, Clinton argued for a bombing campaign to stop Serb leader Slovodan Milosevic. The bombing succeeded, but many lives were lost. Clinton also played an important part in the Middle East peace agreement made between Israel and the Palestinians in 1993.

Clinton, no stranger to scandal, may be best remembered as the second president to be impeached, or formally accused of a crime. He was charged with lying under oath about his inappropriate relationship with a White House aide, Monica Lewinsky. At the Senate trial, Clinton was found not guilty of "high crimes and misdemeanors," in the language of the Constitution. Clinton apologized to the nation and returned to his job.

Hillary Clinton, one of the most active First Ladies in U.S. history, became the first woman senator from New York and the only First Lady to win public office.

Read the clues about Bill Clinton and his presidency. Then complete the puzzle using the word list on the next page.

★ Across ★

1. First name of Clinton's wife

3. Clinton served in this position just before he became president.
6. Clinton was found not guilty of "high crimes and _____."
7. Last name of Serb leader who tried to take over Kosovo
8. Clinton's formal first name
9. Clinton had hoped to reform the way people pay for this type of care.
10. Province where the United States and its allies stopped a Serb takeover

★ *Down* ★

2. Major conflicts occurred in Bosnia and Kosovo, located within this former country.
4. Initials for the North American Free Trade Agreement
5. Clinton taught this in Arkansas.
6. Clinton hosted the _____ East peace agreement between Israel and the Palestinians.
7. First name of White House aide involved in scandal with Clinton
8. Under Clinton's law, people who get welfare money must now seek this.

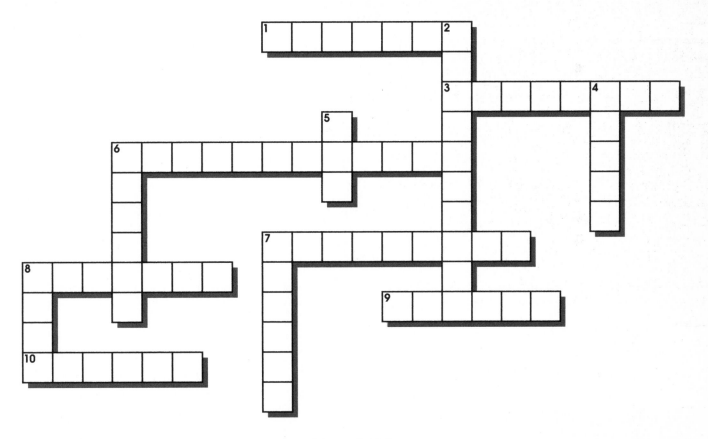

Word List

GOVERNOR	**LAW**	**MISDEMEANORS**	**WILLIAM**
HEALTH	**MIDDLE**	**MONICA**	**WORK**
HILLARY	**MILOSEVIC**	**NAFTA**	**YUGOSLAVIA**
KOSOVO			

George W. Bush (1946-)

George W. Bush
43rd President
Party: Republican
Term: 2001-

George Walker Bush was born on July 6, 1946 in New Haven, Connecticut. He spent most of his childhood in Texas, where his father, George Herbert Walker Bush became involved in the oil business. Bush graduated from Yale University and received his M.B.A. at Harvard University. He also served as an airman in the Texas Air National Guard.

Bush's father campaigned for president in the 1988 election. The young Bush assisted his father with the campaign, and his father won the election. After the election, George W. Bush and his wife, Laura, and daughters, Jenna and Barbara, settled in Dallas, Texas. Bush also worked in the oil business and was a managing general partner of the Texas Rangers baseball team.

After an unsuccessful run for congress in the late 1970's, Bush returned to politics and became governor of Texas in 1994. He was re-elected as governor in 1998 by a wide margin. He received national attention because of his policies, which included large tax cuts, educational reforms, and increased school funding. Even though Bush was criticized for not focusing more on racial issues, poverty, and environmental issues, he was already being touted as a possible presidential candidate.

Following in his father's footsteps, Bush won the nomination for the Republican party's presidential candidate in 1999. He ran against Democratic candidate, Vice President Al Gore. The election of 2000 was one of the closest races in U.S. history. The outcome took weeks to determine—the winner of Florida was in dispute. The vote was extremely close in Florida, and election officials demanded a machine recount. When the machine recount declared Bush to have more votes, Gore asked for a manual recount. Finally, five weeks after the election, the U.S. Supreme Court put an end to the recounts. Although Gore won the popular vote, Bush received Florida's electoral votes and became the 43rd president of the United States on January 20, 2001.

Bush began his presidential career by focusing on tax cuts, education reform, and issues that he had concentrated on during his campaign. But, on September 11, 2001, Bush and the American nation turned their attention to a far more critical situation. Four commercial airliners were hijacked by terrorists and were intentionally crashed into the World Trade Center Towers and the Pentagon. Thousands of people were killed in the worst terrorist attack in United States history. Less than a month later, the U.S. began military strikes against Afghanistan, the country believed to be home to terrorist parties responsible for the attacks.

Use the word list to help you find the words about
George W. Bush and his presidency that are hidden in the block below.
Some of the words are hidden backward or diagonally.

```
L I O G W A L K E R O G D R T M
A O N C N A C I L B U P E R B A
R E H T A F O L M R C T T A A K
L A R O T C E L E T Z C D R S S
T A R E P U I N O C L R S N E T
C A N E G L N P A O A H A N B N
E C F N A J O C F U T D C J A U
L J J P C R I G G R R S Y P L O
E A P B E D T L H T O S A W L C
X V E K R S A R A C N R D X S E
B L I J N N C W N D R L G H E R
P H H F O M U A I B E A W E S T
B E A I R E D W S A V M R S M B
S L T D S R E H T T O O K U D X
D A F L O R I D A F G S T M A J
N Y F L O Y R P N A S K D T H L
```

Word List

AFGHANISTAN	FATHER	LAURA	REPUBLICAN
BASEBALL	FIVE	MBA	TAX
COURT	FLORIDA	NATIONAL GUARD	TEXAS
EDUCATION	GORE	OIL	WALKER
ELECTORAL	GOVERNOR	RECOUNT	YALE

U.S. Presidents—Topics to Explore

You have read only a brief summary about the men that shaped America's political history from its beginnings to the present. Below, you will find a list of more topics related to U.S. presidents and the government. Choose some topics from the list, or think of other subjects on your own, that you would like to learn more about. Use the following pages to take notes and create your own activities.

Other Topics About U.S. Presidents and the Government:

- The White House
- Congress
- First Ladies
- The Supreme Court
- Political campaigns
- How a bill becomes a law
- The Capitol
- Presidential elections and the Electoral College
- The President's Cabinet members
- Amendments to the Constitution

Notes Page

Choose one of the topics from page 219, or think of a topic on your own, and write about what you know in the space below. Research your chosen topic further, using the library or the Internet to help you find information. Take lots of notes, as you will use these notes to create your own activity on the next page.

★ NOTES ★

Create Your Own Activity

Use this page to create your own activity based on the notes you took on the previous page. Share your activity with a friend.

Notes Page

Choose one of the topics from page 219, or think of a topic on your own, and write about what you know in the space below. Research your chosen topic further, using the library or the Internet to help you find information. Take lots of notes, as you will use these notes to create your own activity on the next page.

★ NOTES ★

Create Your Own Activity

Use this page to create your own activity based on the notes you took on the previous page. Share your activity with a friend.

Notes Page

Choose one of the topics from page 219, or think of a topic on your own, and write about what you know in the space below. Research your chosen topic further, using the library or the Internet to help you find information. Take lots of notes, as you will use these notes to create your own activity on the next page.

★ NOTES ★

Create Your Own Activity

Use this page to create your own activity based on the notes you took on the previous page. Share your activity with a friend.

Presidential Time Line

Write the names of these early nineteenth century presidents on the lines below each picture. Then, put them in the correct order by numbering the pictures from 1 to 4.

★ ＿   # ★ ＿   # ★ ＿   # ★ ＿

_____   _____   _____   _____

| 1800 | 1825 | 1850 | 1875 | 1900 |

19TH CENTURY

Write the names of these late nineteenth century presidents on the lines below each picture. Then, put them in the correct order by numbering the pictures from 1 to 4.

★ ＿   # ★ ＿   # ★ ＿   # ★ ＿

_____   _____   _____   _____

| 1800 | 1825 | 1850 | 1875 | 1900 |

19TH CENTURY

Presidential Time Line

Write the names of these early twentieth century presidents on the lines below each picture. Then, put them in the correct order by numbering the pictures from 1 to 4.

Write the names of these late twentieth century presidents on the lines below each picture. Then, put them in the correct order by numbering the pictures from 1 to 4.

Presidential Compare and Contrast

Write the name of each president under his picture.

_____ _____ _____ _____

19TH CENTURY   1900   1950   2000

1800   1850   1900   20TH CENTURY

Name the presidents pictured above that match these statements. You may need to research some of the statements to write the name of the correct president.

We were born in Ohio. _____

I served as governor of a state. _____

Our vice presidents became presidents after us. _____

_____

The three of us were in office on the first day of a new century. _____

_____

I was born in the eighteenth century but died in the nineteenth. _____

I was born in the nineteenth century but died in the twentieth._____

We were both assassinated while in office. _____

_____

We both have the same first name._____

Presidential Compare and Contrast

Write the name of each president under his picture.

_____ _____ _____ _____

19TH CENTURY

1900   1950   2000

1800   1850   1900

20TH CENTURY

Name the presidents pictured above that match these statements. You may need to research some of the statements to write the name of the correct president.

★ We were both born in New York. _____

★ The two of us served as governors of states. _____

_____

★ We both served as vice president. _____

★ The three of us were in office during times of economic trouble. _____

_____

★ The three of us served only one term each. _____

_____

★ We were both elected as Republicans. _____

_____

★ We were both elected as Democrats. _____

Presidents and Wars

Write the name of each president under his picture. Then, draw a line to the name of the war with which he is most closely associated. You may need to research the wars in order to match each war to the correct president.

19TH CENTURY   1900   1950   2000

1800   1850   1900   20TH CENTURY

_____

_____

_____

Revolutionary War
War of 1812
Civil War
Spanish-American War
World War I
World War II
Vietnam War
Persian Gulf War

_____

_____

_____

_____

_____

Who's Who

Write the name of each president under his picture. Then, draw a line to another name by which each president was known. You may need to research the presidents in more detail to match each name to the correct president.

19TH CENTURY

1800   1850   1900

1900   1950   2000

20TH CENTURY

Old Rough and Ready
Old Buck
Hero of Appomattox
Old Hickory
Little Magician
Ike
FDR
William Jefferson Blythe III

_____   _____   _____

_____   _____   _____

_____   _____   _____

Slogans and Quotations

Write the name of each president under his picture. Then, draw a line to the slogan or quotation with which he is associated. You may need to research the presidents in more detail to match each slogan or quotation to the correct president.

19TH CENTURY   1900   1950   2000

1800   1850   1900   20TH CENTURY

_____   _____   _____

"He serves his party best who serves his country best."

"First in war, first in peace, first in the hearts of his countrymen."

"Remember the Maine."

"Ask not what your country can do for you…"

"A house divided against itself cannot stand."

"… the world must be made safe for democracy."

_____   _____   _____

Presidents and Important Events

Write the name of each president under his picture. Then, draw a line to match each president with an important event with which he is associated. You may need to research the events in order to match each event to the correct president.

19TH CENTURY   1900   1950   2000

1800   1850   1900   20TH CENTURY

_____   _____

The end of slavery
The end of Reconstruction
The end of the Cold War
The end of World War II
The Watergate scandal
The Teapot Dome scandal
The Lewis and Clark Expedition
The founding of the League of Nations

_____   _____

_____   _____   _____

Presidents and Programs

Write the name of each president under his picture. Then, draw a line to match each president with an important program with which he is associated. You may need to research the programs in order to match each program to the correct president.

19TH CENTURY   20TH CENTURY
1800   1850   1900   1900   1950   2000

_____   _____   _____

14 Points

The New Deal

The Fair Deal

The Great Society

The Time of Good Feelings

The Full Dinner Pail

_____   _____   _____

Section 4
U.S. States

Did you know that ice-cream cones were first served in Missouri? Or that Minnesota has more lakes than any other state (over 10,000!)? Have you heard that Alaska is called the Last Frontier? This section will help you review these and many other fascinating facts about each of the 50 states.

The activities in this section are a practical and fun review of the 50 states. From the Aloha State (Hawaii) to the Last Frontier (Alaska), you'll discover tons of intriguing tidbits. You can use the activities to review information you already know about a state or to learn about a state that you don't know much about. Here is a fun way to learn that also reinforces what you are learning in school. You will also practice important skills like reading comprehension, vocabulary, and spelling.

To complete each activity, you will need to read and understand the reading selection, as well as locate information in illustrations or maps that may accompany each reading passage or activity. You can also find an appropriate word in the alphabetical list of words provided with most of the activities as another helpful tool in completing each activity.

If you have already learned about the topic that is featured, you may want to challenge yourself to complete as much of the activity as you can without reading the introduction, looking at the illustrations, or using the word lists.

Each passage focuses on one to three states, with an emphasis on geography and how people live in each state today. Capital cities and important historic sites are mentioned throughout. As you complete each activity, you will learn about each state's unique history and geography, as well as the important events that have helped shape the nation. You'll also learn about Washington, D.C., the capital of the United States. Of course, not every topic about the 50 states could be covered, but we have included those facts that are most interesting and enjoyable. If a topic you want to explore is not included, you may wish to do some research on your own and create your own activities—complete with clues and/or word lists. We have included extra pages at the end of this section with suggestions for topics to explore.

Section 4
U.S. STATES
Table of Contents

Hawaii

Aloha! That expression means "love" in Hawaiian, and it is used to say "hello" and "goodbye." The state of Hawaii is a group of islands located in the middle of the north Pacific Ocean. Many of the islands are so small that no one lives on them permanently.

The Hawaiian Islands were first settled by Polynesian people who traveled there from other Pacific islands. Before becoming a state, the islands had several kinds of governments. For over a hundred years, Polynesian monarchs ruled. Today, you can visit some of the palaces where they once lived. The last monarch, Queen Liliuokalani, was the author of the favorite Hawaiian song, "Aloha Oe," or "Farewell to Thee." In 1893, Hawaii became a republic with elected leaders. It was made a United States territory in 1900. In 1959, Hawaii became the fiftieth state.

Hawaii produces tropical crops, especially pineapples, sugar, and coffee. However, its biggest industry is tourism. People come for the warm air, the clean beaches, the beautiful landscape, and the good shopping. Like the visitors, Hawaii's people come from all over the world. No ethnic group is in the majority there.

The Hawaiian island with the biggest population is Oahu, where the capital, Honolulu, is located. Near Honolulu is Pearl Harbor. A Japanese attack on the U.S. naval base there thrust the United States into World War II.

The island of Hawaii is often called the Big Island because it is the largest in the state. There, at Hawaii Volcanoes National Park, you may be able to see active volcanoes spewing lava, superhot liquid rock from deep underground. In fact, all the state's islands were formed by cooled lava that turned into land. Popular tourist attractions on the island of Kauai include Mount Waialeale, which has the most rainy days on earth, and Waimea Canyon.

Read the clues about Hawaii.
Then complete the puzzle using the word list on the next page.

★ *Across* ★

4. Hawaii was one just before it became a state.
5. Capital of Hawaii
7. Name of the harbor attacked by Japan that caused the United States to enter World War II
9. The most populated island in the state of Hawaii
10. Hawaiian greeting
11. Hawaii lies in the middle of the north Pacific _____.

12. Nickname for the island of Hawaii—the _____ Island

★ Down ★

1. Name of Hawaii's last queen
2. Hawaii is famous for this fruit.
3. Hawaii's largest industry
4. The ones on Mauna Kea are the largest in the world.
6. Volcanic material that originally formed the islands
8. Hawaiian royalty lived in these.

Word List

ALOHA	LILIUOKALANI	PALACES	TELESCOPES
BIG	OAHU	PEARL	TERRITORY
HONOLULU	OCEAN	PINEAPPLE	TOURISM
LAVA			

Alaska

Alaska lies at the northwest tip of North America. It is separated from the main body of the United States by part of Canada. The state is so far north that much of it is continually covered with snow and ice. Yet Alaska is an enormously valuable state.

In the mid-1800's, Russia and the United States both wanted Alaska because of its position as a gateway between Asia and America—and because of its valuable fur trade. After the United States bought Alaska from Russia, gold was discovered. This discovery led to a gold rush and the founding of Juneau, which is now Alaska's capital. Alaska became a state just before Hawaii, in 1959. Nine years later, the most valuable resource of all was found at Prudhoe Bay, on the shore of the Arctic Ocean—oil. Today, oil is Alaska's greatest export. During the 1970's, people poured into the state to work in the new oil business. While the oil business still employs many Alaskans, the flood of new jobs has stopped.

Life in Alaska is ruled in many ways by the cold and rugged terrain. Although southern Alaska warms up enough to grow crops in summer, most of the state is full of glaciers, ice fields, and mountains. The highest peak in the United States, Mount McKinley, is in the Alaska Range. Although Alaska is about twice the size of Texas, it has a very small population. Alaska is often called the Last Frontier because so much of the land remains unsettled. Roads and railroads are used in Alaska, but boats and airplanes often reach towns more easily.

About 15 percent of Alaskans are Native Americans. Many important Native American traditions are still practiced, such as building temporary snow huts, or igloos, when on hunting trips. Their traditional dogsled travel has become a sport for all Alaskans. One of the most famous sled dog race champions is Susan Butcher. She helps organize the Iditarod race from Anchorage to Nome.

Read the clues about Alaska.
Then complete the puzzle using the word list on the next page.

★ *Across* ★

2. Moving masses of ice; there are many in Alaska
3. Name of Alaska's most famous sled dog race
6. Temporary round hut made of snow blocks
8. Country from which the United States bought Alaska
10. Alaska is about twice as big as this state.
11. Last name of a sled dog race champion
12. Country that lies between Alaska and the lower forty-eight states

★ Down ★

1. Name of the bay where oil was first discovered in Alaska
2. Mineral resource that caused a rush to Alaska
4. Form of transportation first used by Native Americans in Alaska and northern Canada
5. Percentage of Alaskans who are Native Americans
7. Alaska's most valuable export
8. Capital of Alaska

Alaska's flag shows the Big Dipper pointing to the North Star.

Word List

BUTCHER	GLACIERS	IGLOO	PRUDHOE
CANADA	GOLD	JUNEAU	RUSSIA
DOGSLED	IDITAROD	OIL	TEXAS
FIFTEEN			

California

California, here I come! That's what many people have said since 1848. Beginning with the discovery of gold in that year, newcomers from all over the United States and the world have made the Golden State their home. Today, California has the largest population of all the states in the union. Over 25 percent of Californians are Hispanic, and nearly 10 percent are Asian. California has acted as a gateway to the United States for these people or their ancestors. It is located northwest of Mexico and the rest of Spanish-speaking Central and South America, and east of Asia, which is across the Pacific Ocean.

You can find almost every kind of landscape in California. The state's long coast on the Pacific Ocean includes foggy redwood groves in the north and expansive, sunny beaches in the south. The Coast Ranges and the tall Sierra Nevada run through the state from north to south. Between these mountain ranges lies the warm, fertile Central Valley.

People may come to California because of its beauty, but they often stay because of the state's great resources. The cities of San Francisco, and Sacramento, now the state capital, grew during the gold rush. However, settlers soon found that the state's real treasure lay in the soil of the Central Valley. The fruits and vegetables that grow there year-round are sold throughout the nation. The huge Los Angeles metropolitan area is best known for Hollywood, where many American movies and television shows are made. Since the 1970's, another part of California has been in the spotlight: Silicon Valley, the area around the city of San Jose. Many computer companies are based there and have brought big changes to businesses and homes worldwide.

Californians do face one serious worry: the danger of earthquakes. But the threat of earthquakes is not enough to keep people from enjoying the unique California lifestyle.

Read the clues about California.
Then complete the puzzle using the word list on the next page.

★ *Across* ★

2. A shaking of the ground; a danger in California
5. Name of ranges of California hills and mountains near the sea
7. Movie capital of the United States
8. California has more of these than any other state.
11. Name of the valley where most fruits and vegetables grow in California
12. One of California's most valuable natural resources today

★ *Down* ★

1. Country bordering California to the southeast
3. Tree that grows along the foggy northern California coast
4. Name given to the valley where many computer makers work
6. California's tallest mountains—the _____ Nevada range
9. San _____ is the city at the center of Silicon Valley.
10. Resource that first brought many people to California

California's lovely lands inspired the great naturalist John Muir to argue for the creation of national parks in California. Today, Yosemite is one of California's eight national parks.

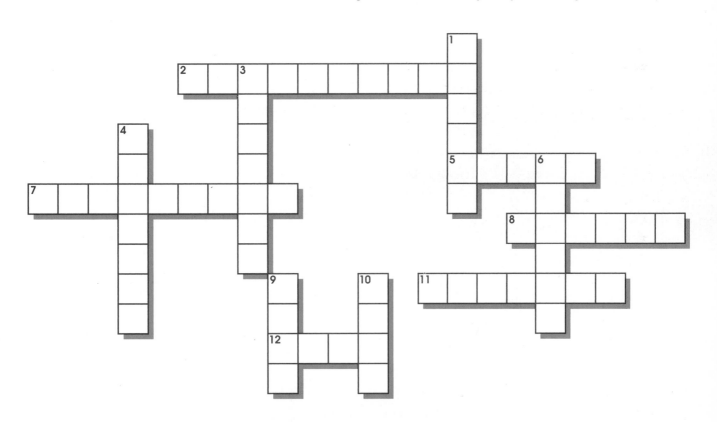

Word List

CENTRAL	GOLD	MEXICO	SIERRA
COAST	HOLLYWOOD	PEOPLE	SILICON
EARTHQUAKE	JOSE	REDWOOD	SOIL

Washington and Oregon

The beautiful volcanic Cascade Range runs through both Washington and Oregon from south to north. In 1980, Mount St. Helens in Washington erupted with huge clouds of smoke and soot, destroying houses and setting off mudslides. Most of the time, though, life is safe in the Pacific Northwest, and many people enjoy hiking and skiing on the tall mountains.

To the west of the Cascades, fertile valleys and a hilly coast get plenty of rain to water fruit and other crops. So much rain falls on Washington's Olympic Peninsula that an unusual rain forest grows there. Trees are so plentiful that Washington is called the Evergreen State, and Oregon leads the nation in producing lumber. East of the Cascades lies a high plateau where the climate is dry and temperatures are much higher in summer and lower in winter.

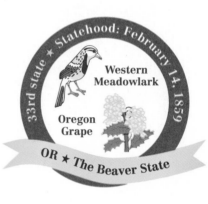

Between the two states flows the Columbia River. The Columbia once formed the last part of the Oregon Trail, which brought Western settlers to both states. Portland, the largest city in Oregon, lies at the mouth of the Columbia. Citizens of Portland have passed laws to ring their city with a "green belt" of parks in order to slow down the rapid spread of suburbs. Their goal is to make the central city a more attractive place to live and work, while saving farms and wildlands.

Oregonians are known for their concern for the environment—and for bringing government close to the people. In the early 1900's, they passed laws called the Oregon System that became a model for other states. The system included voting rights for women, more direct elections, and the right of citizens to vote directly on issues.

More people live in Washington than in Oregon, and many of those live in or near the Pacific Northwest's largest city, Seattle. In the Seattle area, aerospace and computer software industries are strong. The most famous person in Washington may be Bill Gates, the founder of the giant software company Microsoft.

Seattle, Washington is one of the most popular cities in the United States.

Mount Ranier in Washington

Use the word list to help you find the words about
Washington and Oregon that are hidden in the block below.
Some of the words are hidden backward or diagonally.

```
F H O S E G N A R E D A C S A C
V O R E G O N S Y S T E M U O P
B R I M O Y F E E W N O V A Y E
U E A S S G P D L A C Z S F I R
K G E N T R A I N J T T R V B A
V O T E H Z C L P M R T N O T W
A N J L M O X S C K E M L X N T
L T E E W R T D S Z E B I E E F
L R L H A R N U J F S N Q H M O
E A U T J A P M O U N T A I N S
Y I D S L B I B Y L G O D E R W
S L G T W I L D L A N D S L E U
Y X R N R E C A P S O R E A V A
C O L U M B I A R I V E R D O Q
P K A O T N T L E B N E E R G U
O L Y M P I C P E N I N S U L A
```

Word List

AEROSPACE	GREEN BELT	OREGON SYSTEM	SOFTWARE
CASCADE RANGE	MOUNT ST HELENS	OREGON TRAIL	TREES
COAST	MOUNTAINS	PORTLAND	VALLEYS
COLUMBIA RIVER	MUDSLIDES	RAIN	VOTE
GOVERNMENT	OLYMPIC PENINSULA	SEATTLE	WILDLANDS

Nevada and Utah

Nevada and Utah lie next to each other between the Sierra Nevada, on Nevada's western edge, and the Rocky Mountains, which take up the eastern half of Utah. Both states are high in altitude and have very dry, or arid, climates. The two states share an area called the Great Basin. This rocky, nearly treeless area is surrounded by mountains, but instead of a flat floor, it has ripples of ridges with valleys called "basins" between them. Streams from the mountains flow into the Great Basin only to disappear by evaporating or sinking. In northern Utah, the Great Salt Lake is all that remains of an ancient inland sea. To the south, rivers have carved the land into deep canyons and fantastic shapes.

These lands were not easy to settle, but many people settled in Nevada because of the Comstock Lode, a network of underground veins of gold and silver. That gold and silver helped the Union pay for the Civil War. The Comstock Lode was used up by the early 1900's, leaving ghost towns like Virginia City, which visitors can see today.

Utah was settled by Mormons. This religious group, led by Brigham Young, founded Salt Lake City, Utah's capital, on the edge of the Great Salt Lake. Utah remains about two-thirds Mormon. The headquarters of the church is an important place where many Americans can trace their family records. The Mormon Tabernacle Choir is also world-famous.

The people of Nevada and Utah have found ways to make a living in their harsh environment. Dams and irrigation have helped make farming and industry easier, especially in Utah. Tourists also come to Utah for winter skiing and for sightseeing in the canyon country of the south, where five national parks welcome visitors. Gambling is legal in Nevada. The casinos at Reno and Las Vegas, the two largest cities in Nevada, draw tourists from all over the United States. Nevada's capital, Carson City, is, however, a small city.

Devil's Garden in Arches National Park is one of the many unusual stone formations that can be found in Utah.

Words about Nevada and Utah have been scrambled.
Rearrange the letters and write the correct word on each line.
Use the word list if you need help.

RARIES VANEDA

_____

SAL GASEV

_____

STORUIST

_____

CYNOSAN

_____

NOUYG

_____

IGANIRVI CTYI

_____

VERSIL

_____

SABNI

_____

NIFRGMA

_____

LODG

_____

SACNOR TYIC

_____

SONMROM

_____

Word List

BASIN	FARMING	MORMONS	TOURISTS
CANYONS	GOLD	SIERRA NEVADA	VIRGINIA CITY
CARSON CITY	LAS VEGAS	SILVER	YOUNG

Idaho and Montana

ID ★ The Gem State

The Rocky Mountains rise high in the states of Idaho and Montana. The Continental Divide runs along the southern part of the border between the two states. There, you can tell if you are in Idaho if the streams run toward the west. If the streams are running eastward, you must be in Montana!

The mountains and foothills have yielded underground treasures in both states. Silver is especially plentiful in Idaho, home of the silver mine at Coeur d' Alene. Both gold and silver were found in Montana—though today, copper, zinc, and oil are among the most profitable minerals. Above ground, the mountains provide lumber and great slopes for skiing. Sun Valley, Idaho, is one of the area's famous winter resorts. In Glacier National Park in northern Montana, you can see beautiful views of the Rocky Mountains.

MT ★ The Treasure State

The land flattens out to the west in Idaho and to the east in Montana. The valley of Idaho's Snake River has proved perfect for the state's most famous crop—potatoes. Montana's high plains produce large crops of wheat. Farmers came to these states in large numbers when the Great Northern Railroad made easy transportation possible. Montana became a state in 1889, and Idaho became one in 1890. Although these states are two of the nation's largest, their populations are among the smallest. Their capitals—Boise, Idaho, and Helena, Montana,—are small cities.

Thousands of people in both states belong to Native American tribes, and many live on large reservations there. The Native American heritage of the region is rich. It includes such famous figures as Sacajawea, who helped guide Lewis and Clark across the Rockies, and Chief Joseph, one of the last great leaders of the Nez Percé.

Read the clues about Idaho and Montana.
Then complete the puzzle using the word list on the next page.

★ Across ★

2. Name of a national park in northern Montana
4. Capital of Idaho
5. Line in the Rocky Mountains that determines which way rivers flow—the Continental _____
6. Forest product of Idaho and Montana
9. Idaho's most famous vegetable
10. Name of the railroad that made Idaho and Montana easier to settle—the Great _____

11. First word in the name of the Idaho city where a large silver mine is located

★ *Down* ★

1. Valuable mineral found in both Idaho and Montana
2. Sacajawea acted as one for the Lewis and Clark expedition.
3. Area set aside for a Native American group; there are several in Idaho and Montana
4. Animal that used to roam on the high prairies
7. Idaho river surrounded by potato farms
8. Capital of Montana
9. The Nez _____ are a Native American tribe; Chief Joseph was once their tribal leader.

Buffalo once grew fat on prairie grass in Montana's high plains.

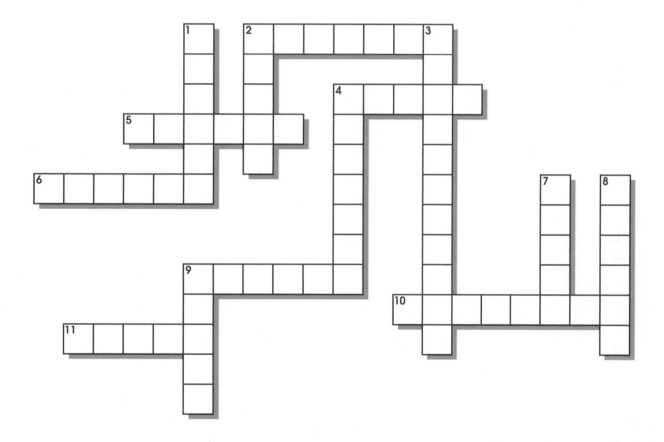

Word List

BOISE	DIVIDE	LUMBER	RESERVATION
BUFFALO	GLACIER	NORTHERN	SILVER
COEUR	GUIDE	PERCE	SNAKE
	HELENA	POTATO	

Wyoming and Colorado

Colorado has the highest average altitude in the Union, and Wyoming has the second highest. As in the other Rocky Mountain states, mining is an important industry. So is recreation. Wyoming includes the oldest American national park, Yellowstone. (Small portions of the park also falls in Montana and Idaho.) Some early pioneers passing through the region thought they must be near hell, because of Yellowstone's hot springs and geysers. Beautiful mountain scenery and good skiing can be had at many other parks and resorts, such as in Jackson Hole, Wyoming, and Aspen, Colorado.

Although the two states may seem similar, there are important differences. Wyoming has far fewer people—the population of Denver, Colorado, alone is greater than that of the whole state of Wyoming. On Wyoming's high, dry eastern plains that reach to the Rockies, ranching has long been a major way of life. It is said that there are two cows to every citizen in the state. Wyoming is also famous as the Equality State, because women in Wyoming Territory were the first in America to be allowed to vote, hold public office, and serve on juries. In the capital, Cheyenne, most people know the name of Ester Hobart Morris, a leader in the equality movement.

Denver, the capital of Colorado, is the business and cultural center for the entire Rocky Mountain region. One of the costs of Denver's continuing growth is smog. Even though the city sits at an altitude of a mile above sea level, the air is often polluted. Colorado Springs is another fast-growing city. It is home to the U.S. Air Force Academy and North American Aerospace Defense Command (NORAD). In the southwestern corner of Colorado, at Mesa Verde National Park, you can see the ancient cliff dwellings of the Anasazi, a Native American people who were skilled builders.

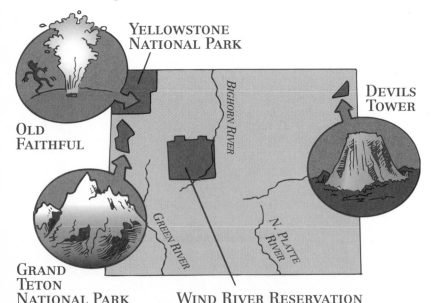

Wyoming's Wind River Reservation, almost as big as Yellowstone, is home to Shoshone and Arapaho people.

Mountain States

Read the sentences about Wyoming and Colorado.
Then complete each sentence by filling in each blank.
Use the word list if you need help.

★ _____ River is a large Native American reservation in central Wyoming.

★ Wyoming is home to _____ and Arapaho people.

★ Esther Hobart _____ sought equality for women in Wyoming Territory.

★ America's oldest national park, located in Wyoming, is

_____.

★ The Colorado town of _____ is famous as a ski resort.

★ The _____ were ancient Native American people who built cliff dwellings.

★ _____ has the highest average elevation in the United States.

★ Wyoming is known as the _____ State.

★ The U.S. _____ Force has an academy in Colorado Springs.

★ Wyoming has fewer _____ than Colorado.

Word List

Air	Aspen	Morris	Wind
Anasazi	Colorado	people	Yellowstone
	Equality	Shoshone	

Arizona and New Mexico

Arizona and New Mexico are located next to each other in the southwestern area of the United States. They share their southern borders with Mexico. In both states, you can find parts of the Rocky Mountains, high plains, and plateaus. In southwestern Arizona, the land dips lower into the Sonoran Desert.

People from nearly every Native American tribe on the continent come to New Mexico every year for the Intertribal Indian Ceremonial. New Mexico is a natural place for the gathering because this state and its neighbor, Arizona, include more than half the reservation land in the United States. At places like Chaco Canyon, New Mexico, you can still visit buildings created by native people hundreds of years before the arrival of Europeans. Today, many tribes continue traditions such as the Pueblo practice of building apartment-style structures of adobe bricks (made from clay mud mixed with straw). The Navajo reservation, located in northeast Arizona and part of New Mexico, is home to the nation's largest tribe. The Navajo farm and raise sheep. They practice traditional crafts including silversmithing and weaving. Discoveries of minerals on Navajo land have helped increase the tribe's income.

A significant part of the population in both states is of Mexican or Spanish heritage. The Spanish language and customs of both groups are an important part of life in cities like Santa Fe, the capital of New Mexico.

People come to Arizona and New Mexico for the dry, healthy air, and to find jobs in the growing economy of these and other warm-climate states in what is known as the Sun Belt. Arizona has had the most growth of the two states, especially in its two largest cities, Tucson and Phoenix, the capital. The natural beauty of the region is another draw. In northern Arizona, the Colorado River has carved out the spectacular Grand Canyon. Blooming deserts and New Mexico's Carlsbad Caverns present other kinds of beauty

**Read the clues about Arizona and New Mexico.
Then complete the puzzle using the word list on the next page.**

★ *Across* ★

3. Name of a New Mexico canyon with ancient Native American buildings
4. Nickname for the sunny region that includes New Mexico and Arizona
5. Language, other than English, that is an important part of culture in New Mexico and Arizona

10. First word of the name of the Native American ceremonial held yearly in New Mexico
11. Country bordering Arizona and New Mexico to the south
12. Tribe famous for building adobe housing
13. Largest Native American tribe in the United States

★ *Down* ★

1. New Mexico city that artist Georgia O'Keeffe helped make into an art center
2. Capital of Arizona
3. Name of famous caverns in New Mexico
6. The Sun Belt state with one of the fastest-growing populations in the nation
7. Animal raised by Navajo ranchers
8. Name of the canyon formed by the Colorado River
9. Name of the desert in southwest Arizona

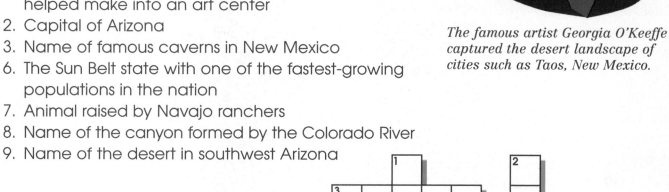

The famous artist Georgia O'Keeffe captured the desert landscape of cities such as Taos, New Mexico.

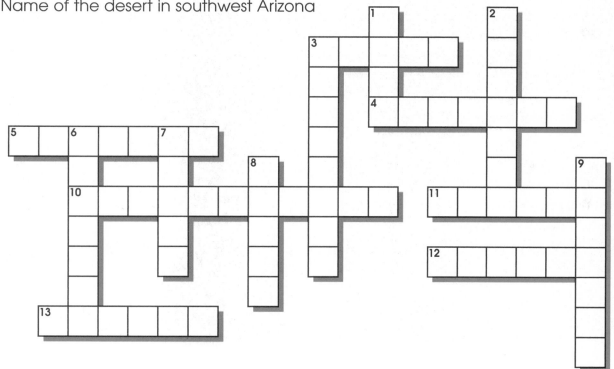

Word List

ARIZONA	**GRAND**	**PHOENIX**	**SPANISH**
CARLSBAD	**INTERTRIBAL**	**PUEBLO**	**SUN BELT**
CHACO	**MEXICO**	**SHEEP**	**TAOS**
	NAVAJO	**SONORAN**	

Texas and Oklahoma

Texas is bigger in area than any state except Alaska. Once, when Texas was part of Mexico, little moved on the vast plains that make up most of the state except cattle. Then American settlers rebelled to form their own "Lone Star" republic, and soon after, in 1845, joined the United States. People poured in to plant cotton—still the leading crop today—and to raise even more cattle. Then, in 1901, Texas's first big oil well, called Spindletop, began producing at a record rate.

Population has grown to suit the size and riches of the state. Texas is second in population only to California. Houston is the biggest city, located near the Gulf of Mexico. There, cotton is processed in mills, and oil is processed in refineries and chemical plants for easy shipping. Houston is also famous for its big, covered Astrodome stadium and for its space center. "Hello, Houston" has become a familiar phrase from astronauts on space missions. Dallas, in central Texas, serves as a center for finance and business all over the Southwest. Texas's many other cities include Austin, the capital.

Just north of Texas, the state of Oklahoma is also home to many cattle ranches and oil wells. Tulsa, Oklahoma, is sometimes called "the oil capital of the world." The state capital, Oklahoma City, attracted attention worldwide when its federal building was bombed in 1995.

Oklahoma has a special history. In the 1830's, the region was set aside by the U.S. government for Native Americans. Many tribes were forced to move to this "Indian Territory." There, the tribes set up their own forms of government. After the United States refused to accept the Indian area as a state, tribal leaders joined with white settlers to enter the Union. Today, over 60 tribes remain in the state.

Read the clues about Texas and Oklahoma.
Then complete the puzzle using the word list on the next page.

★ Across ★

2. The rank of Texas among the states in size and population
4. Plants where oil is processed; there are several in Houston
7. Name of the covered sports stadium in Houston
8. The nickname for Texas is the Lone _____ State.
9. Texas's biggest city
11. Valuable underground resource in both Texas and Oklahoma

1. Landform in most of Texas
2. Texas's first wildly successful oil well
3. Texas city; a financial center of the Southwest
5. Most common Texas crop
6. Area set up to receive Native Americans forced from the East—Indian _____
7. Capital of Texas
10. Oklahoma city; sometimes called "the oil capital of the world"

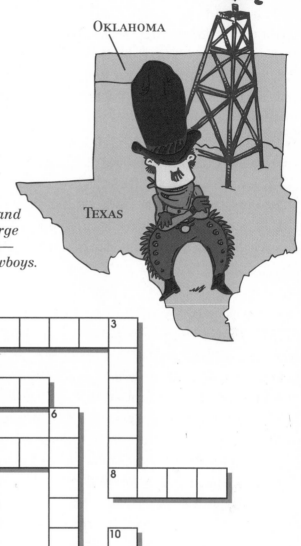

Many people in Texas and Oklahoma still wear large ten-gallon cowboy hats— even if they are not cowboys.

Word List

ASTRODOME	HOUSTON	REFINERIES	STAR
AUSTIN	OIL	SECOND	TERRITORY
COTTON	PLAINS	SPINDLETOP	TULSA
DALLAS			

North Dakota and South Dakota

Some of the greatest and saddest moments in Native American history took place in the land of the Dakota, also called the Sioux. In 1874, General George Custer discovered gold on Sioux land in the Black Hills (now South Dakota). The Sioux fought the army over that land and, at the Battle of the Little Bighorn, defeated Custer and his men. Later, however, the Sioux leader Crazy Horse was killed and the government took over the Black Hills.

Sioux and other tribes still live in the Dakotas. In 1973, a group called the American Indian Movement gained publicity for Native American rights when they took over the South Dakota Sioux village of Wounded Knee. It was at Wounded Knee that the U.S. Army killed a group of Sioux men, women, and children to end resistance in 1890.

The coming of the railroad and the Homestead Act, which offered free government land, brought settlers to Dakota Territory to farm. They found the vast Great Plains, varied only by oddly shaped, eroded hills called the Badlands in the west and the Black Hills in the southwest. Today, farming and ranching remain major ways of making a living. Wheat is the chief crop in North Dakota, as is corn in South Dakota. In North Dakota, the Garrison Dam on the Missouri River has opened many thousands of acres for farming.

Oil and minerals have also been found in both Dakotas, and gold is still being taken from the Black Hills. In fact, that is the location of the largest American gold mine, the Homestake Mine. Also in the Black Hills is Mount Rushmore, a mountain carved with huge stone portraits of George Washington, Thomas Jefferson, Theodore Roosevelt, and Abraham Lincoln.

Cities in the Dakotas are not large. The capitals of both states—Bismarck, North Dakota and Pierre, South Dakota—were once trading posts on the Missouri River.

Read the clues about North Dakota and South Dakota.
Then complete the puzzle using the word list on the next page.

★ Across ★

1. Precious metal found in the Black Hills by General Custer
4. The capitals of both North and South Dakota are on this river.
5. Name of the South Dakota hills where Mount Rushmore is located
6. Name of the large gold mine in South Dakota
7. Name of the mountain on which the faces of four presidents are carved
10. _____ Knee, a famous Sioux village

11. Initials of the Roosevelt whose face appears on Mount Rushmore
12. Main crop in North Dakota

★ *Down* ★

1. North Dakota dam on the Missouri that has allowed more farming
2. The act that provided free government land to farmers
3. The general who made a last stand at the Little Bighorn
5. Capital of North Dakota
8. Second word in the name of the Sioux leader represented in a mountain-sized statue being carved in South Dakota
9. Initials of the state for which Pierre is the capital

Sculptors have been carving a memorial to Crazy Horse on a mountain in the Black Hills since 1948. When finished, it will be the largest sculpture in the world.

Word List

BISMARCK	GARRISON	HORSE	TR
BLACK	GOLD	MISSOURI	WHEAT
CUSTER	HOMESTAKE	RUSHMORE	WOUNDED
	HOMESTEAD	SD	

Iowa, Kansas, and Nebraska

The states of Iowa, Kansas, and Nebraska are grouped along the Missouri River at the center of the United States. In fact, Kansas contains the center of the U.S.'s 48 adjoining states. These three states are mostly flat farm country. Iowa has the richest soil and wettest climate. Nebraska and Kansas include part of the Great Plains and are a little higher and drier with harsher winters. Big thunderstorms are a feature of the weather in all these states, sometimes accompanied by tornadoes.

Iowa, which is farther east, was settled earlier than the other two states and was admitted to the Union in 1846, with Des Moines as its capital. Homesteading and the expansion of the railroad brought settlers to Kansas and Nebraska. Congress decided to let the people of Kansas decide whether to enter the nation as a free or slave state. The settlers fought real battles over the issue, and the state gained the nickname, "Bleeding Kansas." At last, Kansas was admitted to the Union as a free state, with Topeka as its capital. Nebraska joined the United States after the Civil War. The nation's only unicameral (one-house) state legislature meets to make Nebraska's laws in its capital, Lincoln.

All three states are well-known for their agriculture. Iowa grows more corn and raises more hogs than any other state. It is also the place where rolled oats became the first quick breakfast cereal. The biggest cereal-making plant in the world today is in Cedar Rapids, Iowa. Kansas rivals North Dakota for the nation's largest total wheat harvest. Huge cattle ranches cover much of the land in Nebraska and Kansas.

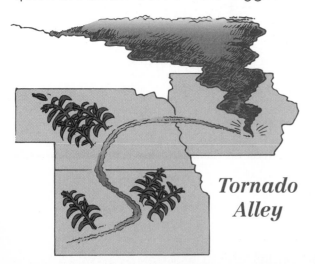

Tornado Alley

Life has been changing for families in farm states over the past few decades. Many Iowans, for example, now work at service jobs such as those in the insurance industry. Many people in Nebraska and Kansas work in manufacturing. In Wichita, Kansas's biggest city, for instance, workers put together more than half of the world's private airplanes.

Words about Iowa, Kansas, and Nebraska have been scrambled.
Rearrange the letters and write the correct word on each line.
Use the word list if you need help.

PEAKOT

_____

LACGUERRITU

_____

CENSNIARU

_____

THICAIW

_____

SELARPNAI

_____

SED NOMIES

_____

TAMARIGUUCFNN

_____

ERACLE

_____

ACRULINMEA

_____

THAEW

_____

SHEDMIONETAG

_____

NNOLCLI

_____

Word List

AGRICULTURE	DES MOINES	LINCOLN	UNICAMERAL
AIRPLANES	HOMESTEADING	MANUFACTURING	WHEAT
CEREAL	INSURANCE	TOPEKA	WICHITA

Minnesota, Wisconsin, and Michigan

Minnesota, Wisconsin, and Michigan are along the northern border of the United States, near the Great Lakes. The three states don't have many mountains, but all have some hills and plenty of streams and lakes. Minnesota claims more lakes than any other state—over 10,000!

Before the American Revolution, waterways served as highways to Native Americans, explorers, and fur traders in the Great Lakes region. Steamboats brought loads of immigrants, especially Scandinavians to Minnesota and Germans to Wisconsin. Today, the area's lakes and rivers are still major shipping routes.

Almost a hundred years ago, in Michigan, Henry Ford became the first American to make an affordable car using the assembly line. Soon Detroit became the car manufacturing capital of the world. So many people poured into the state to work in auto-related industries that the population of Michigan ballooned, and it is now about twice that of Minnesota or Wisconsin. Even smaller cities like Flint and Lansing, the capital, took part in car making. Although cars and trucks are still built in Michigan, many autoworkers have had to look for other jobs because of increasing foreign competition.

In Wisconsin, dairy farms are everywhere and cheese is an important product. So is beer, first made in this state from traditional German recipes. Milwaukee, Wisconsin's largest city, can ship its products on Lake Michigan. The capital, Madison, lies inland.

The Mississippi River begins in central Minnesota. The state's biggest cities—Minneapolis and St. Paul, the capital—lie across from each other on the river. These "Twin Cities" bustle with business and the arts, and they are home to more than a dozen colleges. The Mall of America in Bloomington also attracts many visitors.

These three states also have a wild side. They offer fishing, hunting, boating, and hiking. Isle Royale, Michigan's national park in Lake Superior, once had one of the world's largest herds of moose.

Use the word list to help you find the words about
Minnesota, Wisconsin, and Michigan that are hidden in the block below.
Some of the words are hidden backward or diagonally.

```
D F W Y D A I R Y F A R M S W Y
M I C H I G A N N O S I D A M P
A B T K V B C F E J S O U T I B
L A K E S Q F I I Z E N S A L L
L G L U C X T O E F M A O M W H
O L L A N S I N G P B N T H A I
F I S H I N G R E D L O P F U L
A P T R I S L E R O Y A L E K A
M R I L D K V O M D L N J V E T
E M O Z R J F Y A S I U X G E O
R H R O G L H E N T N E P C P S
I D T W I N C I T I E S A H X E
C K E C W G B A K U C R Q E S N
A W D X Q U V I H I M J V E D N
Z B W I S C O N S I N F R S C I
A N S E K A L T A E R G W E R M
```

Word List

ASSEMBLY LINE	FISHING	ISLE ROYALE	MICHIGAN
CAR	FORD	LAKES	MILWAUKEE
CHEESE	GERMAN	LANSING	MINNESOTA
DAIRY FARMS	GREAT LAKES	MADISON	TWIN CITIES
DETROIT	HIKING	MALL OF AMERICA	WISCONSIN

Illinois

Illinois is a busy state with farms, factories, and a successful transportation system. Illinois is the sixth most populous state.

Throughout Illinois's history, transportation routes have been the key to its success. The Mississippi River on the west and the Ohio River on the southeast border have allowed Illinois farmers and manufacturers to ship and sell goods from Canada to New Orleans and around the world. Even more valuable is the port of Chicago, one of the largest on the Great Lakes, with easy shipping routes eastward. The railroads gave Illinois a big economic boost as they brought grain and cattle from the West to Chicago for sale to eastern cities. Today, interstate truck routes and airplanes have joined the transportation web.

The city of Chicago, third largest in the nation after New York and Los Angeles, is a very exciting place. The first skyscraper was built there, and today, Chicago is home to the tallest building in the nation, the Sears Tower. Inside some of the skyscrapers, bankers are at work—this is the financial center of the Midwest. Once, poet Carl Sandburg called Chicago "hog butcher to the world." The slaughterhouses may have moved, but the Chicago Board of Trade remains the world's largest market for trading in grain and meat. O'Hare International Airport is among the busiest in the world. Culture in Chicago is lively, too. The city hums with jazz and the blues. The Art Institute of Chicago houses one of the finest art collections in the nation. And the Chicago Bulls basketball team is one of the nation's most popular.

There is a quieter side of Illinois south of Chicago. Most of the flat, fertile plains are farmland. Springfield, the state capital, sits in the middle of the state. There, you can visit memorials to Abraham Lincoln, perhaps the state's most famous citizen. To the south are hilly areas with woods and lakes.

Chicago is called the Windy City for a good reason!

Words about Illinois have been scrambled.
Rearrange the letters and write the correct word on each line.
Use the word list if you need help.

SPERASCKYR

_____

DARRLOAIS

_____

ZAJZ

_____

SPOTRAINTOTNAR

_____

IRDSNEGPFIL

_____

OHO RIERV

_____

SLUBL

_____

COLINNL

_____

FLARDAMN

_____

COGHACI

_____

RSEAS REWTO

_____

INARG

_____

Word List

BULLS	**GRAIN**	**OHIO RIVER**	**SKYSCRAPER**
CHICAGO	**JAZZ**	**RAILROADS**	**SPRINGFIELD**
FARMLAND	**LINCOLN**	**SEARS TOWER**	**TRANSPORTATION**

Indiana and Ohio

Soon after the Revolutionary War, Americans began to move across the Appalachian Mountains to the Ohio River valley and the land between it and the Great Lakes. This piece of land was soon made into states according to the Northwest Ordinance. This law, passed by Congress, allowed new states to enter the Union as equals of the original states if they met certain conditions. In 1803, Ohio was the first state created under these rules; land just to the west of Ohio became the state of Indiana.

Ohio grew in population more quickly than Indiana, and today, Ohio is full of cities both large and small. The largest cities in these two states were founded near water transportation. Cleveland became an industrial giant at the northern border of Ohio on Lake Erie, and Cincinnati grew as a major shipping point for goods on the Ohio River to the south. In Indiana, the city of Gary on Lake Michigan was closely linked with Chicago's trade.

Most land in Ohio and Indiana was scraped flat by glaciers thousands of years ago and is good for farming. In the east and south of Ohio, the Appalachian Plateau rises as a hilly region with steep ravines. Much of this land is covered with forests, and coal and oil are found there. Hills continue along the Ohio River at the southern borders of Ohio and Indiana. Huge salt deposits lie near Lake Erie, and beautiful limestone is quarried in Indiana. Service industries and manufacturing, such as steelmaking, are very important to both Indiana and Ohio.

Indianapolis, the capital and largest city of Indiana, is famous for its Indianapolis 500 auto race. Ohio State University, located in Columbus—the capital and largest city in Ohio—draws students and football fans to its large campus. The city of Cleveland, Ohio, has built a new theater district to draw visitors downtown.

Use the word list to help you find the words about Indiana
and Ohio that are hidden in the block below.
Some of the words are hidden backward or diagonally.

```
F B M D N A L E V E L C A B O A
C A L R T P C O L U M B U S U G
I S I L O P A N A I D N I T O N
N E F S R A T Z O A T H O V Q I
C N A F D L K R W S T R S I S R
I A R O I A K M F U A I E T R U
N G M L N C O I L C Z T S E M T
N I I T A H H C E R E E O I E C
A H N O N I I I K P R I D R T A
T C G Y C A O H I O R I V E R F
I I I A E N S W F J O O N E I U
A M W M R G T X U V N T N K C N
Y E D E X Y A B T O R O C A N A
L K T R J X T I N C U Z O L P M
V A Q L I M E S T O N E A G O S
W L A I N D U S T R I A L D M C
```

Word List

APPALACHIAN	COLUMBUS	INDUSTRIAL	ORDINANCE
AUTO RACE	FARMING	LAKE ERIE	OHIO RIVER
CINCINNATI	FORESTS	LAKE MICHIGAN	OHIO STATE
CLEVELAND	GARY	LIMESTONE	OIL
COAL	INDIANAPOLIS	MANUFACTURING	WATER

Pennsylvania

The English Quaker William Penn founded the colony of Pennsylvania, which means "Penn's Woods." He invited people from many parts of Europe to come and farm peacefully together, and he tried to treat the Native Americans fairly. Today, Pennsylvania is the nation's fifth largest state in population. Even though the state has so many people, plenty of countryside remains for hiking, skiing, and hunting in state parks and reserves. In the middle of Pennsylvania, the small city of Harrisburg serves as the state's capital.

The state includes a flat coastal plains area, a higher lowland called the Piedmont, and then the Appalachian Mountains, also called the Alleghenies in this state. On the western side of the state, the Appalachian Plateau, a hilly region, descends to the Great Lakes area and across the border with Ohio. The richest land is in the southeast, "Pennsylvania Dutch" country. The Dutch are really "Deutsch," or Germans, whose ancestors responded to advertisements made in Europe by Penn. Pennsylvania is a leader in dairy products, chickens, eggs, apples, mushrooms—and Christmas trees!

The state has two major cities, Philadelphia in the east and Pittsburgh in the west. Philadelphia, the largest, was actually planned by William Penn. It is still a port and a commercial center, as he meant it to be, but now it is one of the world's great cities. Many of the nation's largest corporations have headquarters in the city. Some of the great events in U.S. history took place here, including the writing of the Declaration of Independence and the Constitution. Today, you can visit the sites of these events and others within Independence National Historic Park.

Pittsburgh grew up where the Allegheny and Monongahela Rivers meet to form the Ohio River. The city sits atop underground coalfields that, along with iron ore, built the city as a steelmaker. Today, some steel is still made in the area, but the city's economy is now based on services, technology, and education (colleges and universities).

Read the clues about Pennsylvania.
Then complete the puzzle using the word list on the next page.

★ Across ★

2. Pennsylvania's largest city
5. Name of the national historic park where you can see famous Philadelphia buildings
8. The founder of Pennsylvania was one.
9. Pittsburgh grew up as a maker of this.
10. Pennsylvania's chief western city

11. Term for milk and milk products; Pennsylvania produces a lot

★ Down ★

1. River that joins the Monongahela to form the Ohio River
3. Capital of Pennsylvania
4. *Pennsylvania* means "Penn's ____."
6. The "Pennsylvania Dutch" are really of this ethnic background.
7. Founder of the colony of Pennsylvania

Important Historic Sites in Philadelphia

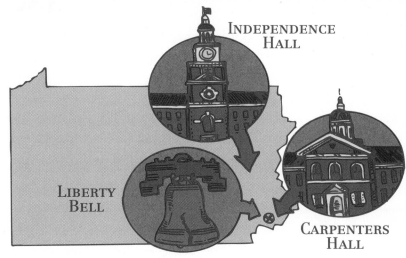

INDEPENDENCE HALL

LIBERTY BELL

CARPENTERS HALL

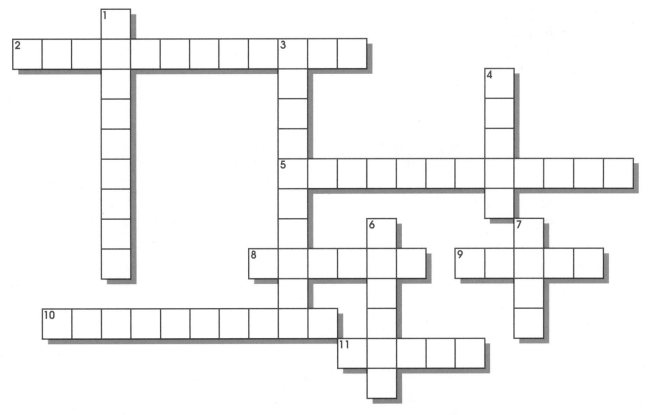

Word List

ALLEGHENY	HARRISBURG	PHILADELPHIA	STEEL
DAIRY	INDEPENDENCE	PITTSBURGH	WOODS
GERMAN	PENN	QUAKER	

Delaware and New Jersey

"What did Dela ware?" asks the old song. "She wore a New Jersey." In fact, these neighboring states have a lot in common. They share Delaware Bay and part of the Delaware River, which form the boundary between them. Both are old industrial states, with chemicals as a top product. Yet both states now depend less on industry, and more of the population is moving to suburban areas and to jobs in services. Both states have plenty of people—New Jersey is the most densely populated of all the states.

Delaware is the smallest of all the states except for Rhode Island. In 1787, Delaware was the first to ratify the U.S. Constitution, and so became the first state, with Dover as its capital. Much of southern Delaware remains quiet farm country, where chickens are the main product. Rehoboth, a town on the Atlantic, is a good place to enjoy the waves. Northern Delaware is much busier. Wilmington, at the mouth of the Delaware River, is the state's chief city. State laws give tax advantages to corporations, so many have located their headquarters there. DuPont has headed the list of chemical companies in Delaware for a very long time. Today, it is Delaware's largest employer.

Major Water Routes

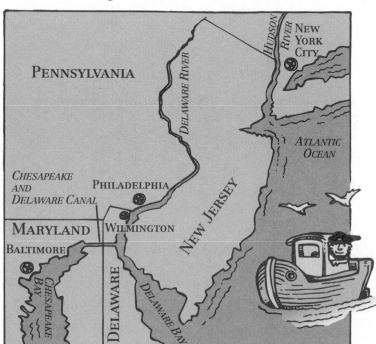

New Jersey lies between the giant cities of Philadelphia and New York, and much of its industry grew along that line. Trenton, the capital, sits midway along this line on the Delaware River. New Jersey farms supply many of the needs of the people of New York City and of the nation. Most farmland is in the southern part of the state. Atlantic City, on the coast, has become famous for casino gambling. Hills and mountains in New Jersey's northwest section offer good places to ski and hike.

Use the word list to help you find the words about
Delaware and New Jersey that are hidden in the block below.
Some of the words are hidden backward or diagonally.

```
A Z W I L M I N G T O N L S P D
T C O N S T I T U T I O N E L Z
L S W Q B M E L L R U Y P R D X
A Y E S R E J W E N G T E V E L
N D P V N F B V T A J V C I L A
T E F N Z I S N T B I K H C A I
I L H U M R O I D R X R I E W R
C A X C O P U G E U C H C S A T
C W N G U Q F R C B Y O K E R S
I A O D N M A A S U F R E E E U
T R U E T W E E X S M B N J B D
Y E K F A R M S I K S T S P A N
B I H L I D P K C L O B C R Y I
H U E T N J S W L N G R E V O D
I D C I S A D I J L K O Z Q D T
O A V L W C H E M I C A L S A I
```

Word List

ATLANTIC CITY	DELAWARE BAY	HIKE	SERVICES
CHEMICALS	DELAWARE RIVER	HILLS	SKI
CHICKENS	DOVER	INDUSTRIAL	SUBURBAN
CONSTITUTION	DUPONT	MOUNTAINS	TRENTON
DELAWARE	FARMS	NEW JERSEY	WILMINGTON

New York

They call it the Big Apple. It's New York City, the biggest city in the United States and the cornerstone of a big, busy state. After the Revolutionary War, New York City served as the first capital of the new nation. The large harbor at New York City invited trade from the beginning, and it became even more important after the Erie Canal was opened in the 1820's. The canal ran eastward from Buffalo on the shore of Lake Erie to Albany, the state capital, located on the Hudson River. The canal, then the railroad, and then trucks took increasing loads of goods from the middle of the country via Great Lakes ports to New York City. There, goods were bought, sold, and shipped all over the country and the world. A chain of industrial cities grew up along this water and railroad route, including Buffalo, Rochester, Syracuse, Utica, and others.

Today, although heavy industries like steel have closed many of their plants, New York remains a leading state in manufacturing, wholesale trade, communication, and finance. Some leading products are books and magazines—New York is the nation's chief publishing city. Another leading industry is clothing. And at the Stock Exchange on Wall Street in New York City, you can see every kind of American business being traded, and feel the pulse of the American economy as a whole.

Tourism is also a big business in New York. People come to the Big Apple for theater, famous art museums, music, shopping, and fun. They also come to see historical sites such as the Statue of Liberty in New York Harbor and Ellis Island, where many immigrants first arrived in the United States. The state of New York also includes farmland and beautiful natural spots away from the cities. There are several thousand lakes in New York, including Lake Ontario, which is one of the largest.

Read the clues about New York.
Then complete the puzzle using the word list on the next page.

★ Across ★

1. From the beginning, this haven for ships helped New York City trade.
3. Product of heavy industry; made less than in the past in New York
6. One of New York's largest lakes, along with Lake Erie
7. Name of forested mountains in the northeastern part of New York
8. Type of exchange on Wall Street
10. Name of the canal between Buffalo and Albany
12. One of the major cities at the western end of the canal

★ Down ★

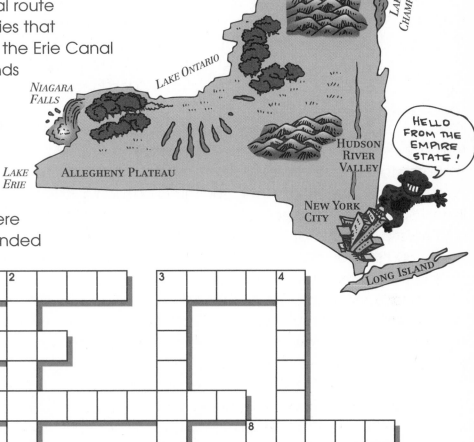

New York's Natural Attractions

2. Form of transportation built alongside the Erie Canal route
3. One of the industrial cities that developed because of the Erie Canal
4. The Statue of _____ stands in New York Harbor.
5. You read these; many are made in New York
7. Nickname for New York City—the Big _____
9. Capital of New York
11. Name of the island where many immigrants first landed

Word List

ADIRONDACKS	BOOKS	HARBOR	STEEL
ALBANY	BUFFALO	LIBERTY	STOCK
APPLE	ELLIS	ONTARIO	SYRACUSE
	ERIE	RAILROAD	

Connecticut and Rhode Island

Both Connecticut and Rhode Island have rich colonial histories. Connecticut's first constitution, the Fundamental Orders, set rules under which the colony governed itself. The orders served as one model for the U.S. Constitution. Rhode Island, the nation's smallest state, was founded by people seeking religious freedom from the Puritans in Massachusetts. Rhode Island became the first colony to formally declare independence from Britain.

Both states have prospered because of their Atlantic coastlines. Connecticut's long, sheltered coast along Long Island Sound afforded good harbors such as New London and Mystic, famous for shipbuilding and whaling in the early 1800's. Today, many commuters to New York live in southern Connecticut, in towns like Stamford.

Rhode Island's harbors are mostly in huge Narragansett Bay. Newport, on an island in the bay, has long been famous as a resort town and has boat races and music festivals. Today, you can visit Newport mansions where the rich vacationed beginning in the mid-1700's. The port city of Providence, on the mainland, is the state capital. Many people there work at making costume jewelry. Long ago, Samuel Slater built the nation's first fabric mill in Rhode Island, and soon all New England was humming with such mills. Today, though, most Rhode Islanders work in service jobs.

Industry remains important in Connecticut, which is a large producer of aircraft engines, submarines, and helicopters. The fertile Connecticut River valley cuts a farming belt north to south through the middle of the state. Hartford, the capital, sits on the river. The headquarters for many insurance firms are located there. Much of the rest of the state is hilly, especially in the northwest. That part of the Appalachian highlands is called the Berkshires, known as a good place to see autumn leaves.

Read the clues about Connecticut and Rhode Island.
Then complete the puzzle using the word list on the next page.

★ *Across* ★

2. Capital of Connecticut
3. Kind of jewelry made in Providence
6. Waterway off Connecticut's south shore—the Long Island _____
8. Connecticut's early constitution—the _____ Orders
11. Name of Rhode Island's very large bay

12. Connecticut leads in producing this kind of engine.

★ Down ★

1. Capital of Rhode Island
4. Fancy house; you can visit old ones in Newport
5. Mountains in Connecticut's northwest
6. Many people who live in this Connecticut town commute to New York for work.
7. Many large companies in this business are headquartered in Hartford.
9. Newport is located on one of these.
10. Last name of the man who built the first fabric mill in New England

Famous Universities in Connecticut and Rhode Island

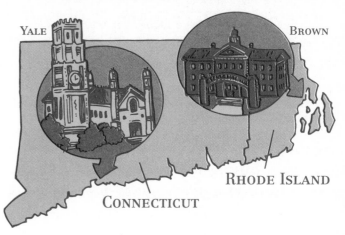

YALE   BROWN

RHODE ISLAND

CONNECTICUT

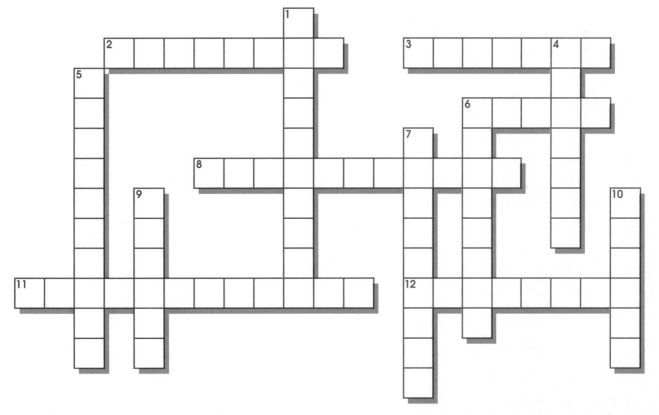

Word List

AIRCRAFT	**HARTFORD**	**MANSION**	**SLATER**
BERKSHIRES	**INSURANCE**	**NARRAGANSETT**	**SOUND**
COSTUME	**ISLAND**	**PROVIDENCE**	**STAMFORD**
FUNDAMENTAL			

Massachusetts

Massachusetts has a history full of firsts. It was the first of the colonies to enjoy democracy and town meetings, the first to sponsor public schools, the first to have a college and a library, and the first to act against the British in the Revolutionary War. Many reminders of the state's rich history are available to the public today, including Old Sturbridge Village, a re-creation of a typical New England town in the 1830s.

Massachusetts remains an important state despite its small size. Boston, the capital of Massachusetts, is an important city for the New England region and the rest of the nation. Massachusetts is home to many of the nation's finest colleges, including Harvard University—the first university to be founded in the United States. High-tech computer and electronics businesses have settled near such research institutions as the Massachusetts Institute of Technology (MIT).

The land in Massachusetts is low in the east and rises toward the west. From the southeast corner of the state, the sandy Cape Cod peninsula stretches out in a hook shape. South of it are the large islands of Martha's Vineyard and Nantucket. While the peninsula and islands were once home to fishing and whaling industries, today they are summer vacation spots. Provincetown, a town at the tip of the Cape, is known for its arts and theater.

The flat eastern part of the state is thickly populated, but the soil is sandy and rocky. It's no wonder many New Englanders turned to fishing or manufacturing instead of farming. Today, services and trade provide most jobs, though there is still some fishing—chiefly for cod and lobster. Farms tend to raise specialty crops, such as cranberries. The most fertile part of the state is the Connecticut River valley, which runs north to south. On the western side of the Connecticut River, the land rises to the rolling hills of the Berkshires.

Visitors can relive history at Plymoth Plantation, a re-creation of a 1627 Pilgrim village in Plymouth, Massachusetts.

Words about Massachusetts have been scrambled.
Rearrange the letters and write the correct word on each line.
Use the word list if you need help.

RAHRDAV

_____

HFGNISI

_____

PEAC DOC

_____

BKSHERIERS

_____

WORTNOVIPENC

_____

WONT NIEGMSET

_____

LUBCIP OLOSSCH

_____

BORETLS

_____

ATACINOV

_____

TUNCANTEK

_____

RBISCANERER

_____

STONOB

_____

Word List

BERKSHIRES	CRANBERRIES	LOBSTER	PUBLIC SCHOOLS
BOSTON	FISHING	NANTUCKET	TOWN MEETINGS
CAPE COD	HARVARD	PROVINCETOWN	VACATION

New Hampshire, Vermont, and Maine

New Hampshire, Vermont, and Maine make up the northeastern corner of the United States. They are all well known for their beautiful forests and mountains, and for their long, snowy winters attractive to skiers. Tourism is a major business in all three states. Though the states all have similar terrain, each has its own character.

New Hampshire was one of the original thirteen colonies. Its capital, Concord, is especially busy every four years because the state hosts the earliest presidential primary election in the nation. New Hampshire is also well known for its unusual tax laws—it has no state income tax or state sales tax. That is because most citizens of the state are conservative—they want to limit the powers of government.

Vermont was an area in dispute between New York and New Hampshire before Vermonters decided to form their own independent republic in 1777. Vermont helped fight the British in the American Revolution and afterward joined the Union as the fourteenth state. Vermont has no seacoast, though its largest city, Burlington, is on Lake Champlain. Montpelier, the capital, is in the center of the state. Vermont shares deposits of granite and marble with New Hampshire. Politically, however, the state is liberal—most Vermonters want government to help solve problems.

The area that is known as Maine once belonged to Massachusetts, but it became a state on its own in 1820. Lumber industries are the major source of income. Portland is the

largest city in Maine. In fact, most people live in the southwestern part of the state. L.L. Bean, the clothing and outdoor outfitter whose catalogs reach the whole country, is located in Freeport. North of the capital, Augusta, the population thins. Potato farms fill some northern counties. There are fewer fishermen along the coast than in the past, but the beauty of the area still draws many visitors.

Words about New Hampshire, Vermont, and Maine have been scrambled. Rearrange the letters and write the correct word on each line. Use the word list if you need help.

STERFOS

_____

TIOUMRS

_____

REBALLI

_____

CROONCD

_____

RISESK

_____

BLUPERIC

_____

RULMEB

_____

IMAPACHLN

_____

SMNOIUANT

_____

PEOERRTF

_____

TELNIECO

_____

TRAEING

_____

Word List

CHAMPLAIN	FORESTS	LIBERAL	REPUBLIC
CONCORD	FREEPORT	LUMBER	SKIERS
ELECTION	GRANITE	MOUNTAINS	TOURISM

Tennessee, Kentucky, and West Virginia

The Appalachian Mountains extend all the way from Maine to Georgia. They take up much of the land of Tennessee, Kentucky, and West Virginia. In fact, West Virginia is the most mountainous state east of the Rockies. You can enjoy the beauty of these mountains in Great Smoky Mountains National Park in Tennessee and North Carolina.

Settlement of these areas began when the earliest pioneers, including Daniel Boone, crossed the mountains from the East. Kentucky and Tennessee became states in the 1790's. West Virginia was then part of the state of Virginia. It did not become a state until the Civil War, when people in this region decided not to secede from, or leave, the Union with the rest of Virginia.

The beautiful Appalachians have yielded plentiful coal and wood products, but they are hard to farm, and miners in the mountains have faced bad conditions and long periods without work. Still, the mountain people have a proud cultural heritage including folk music, crafts, and stories.

Manufacturing has become the main source of income in all three states. Tourists also enjoy the mountains and come through historic towns like the capitals—Charleston, West Virginia; Frankfort, Kentucky; or Nashville, Tennessee. Some traditional ways of making a living are still thriving. In Kentucky, Thoroughbred horses are still raised and sold around the world from the Bluegrass region, and bourbon whiskey continues to be made. Tennessee has benefited from the dam and lake system created by the national Tennessee Valley Authority (TVA) to create inexpensive electricity, a project begun in the 1930's. Yet cotton still grows as it did a hundred years ago in eastern Tennessee. The first trade highways for these states were the Ohio and Mississippi Rivers, which continue to carry goods today.

**Read the clues about Tennessee, Kentucky, and West Virginia.
Then complete the puzzle using the word list on the next page.**

★ Across ★

1. Crop traditionally grown in eastern Tennessee

2. Kind of racehorse raised in Kentucky
4. First name of an early Kentucky pioneer
5. Nashville is called the capital of country _____.
6. Economic activity that brings most money to Kentucky, West Virginia, and Tennessee
9. Capital of Kentucky
10. The Great _____ Mountains National Park lies partly in Tennessee.

★ *Down* ★

1. Capital of West Virginia
2. Initials of the government system of dams and lakes along the Tennessee River
3. Kind of grass; name of Kentucky's horse country
7. West Virginia became a state after it refused to leave the _____ in the Civil War.
8. Mineral most mined in the Appalachian Mountains

The Appalachians, a popular area with tourists, are known for coal mining.

Nashville, Tennessee, is the capital of country music.

Word List

BLUEGRASS	COTTON	MANUFACTURING	THOROUGHBRED
CHARLESTON	DANIEL	MUSIC	TVA
COAL	FRANKFORT	SMOKY	UNION

Mississippi and Louisiana

Mississippi and Louisiana sit on either side of the Mississippi River as it flows to its end in the Gulf of Mexico. In these states, you can relive the history of the Deep South—and see how the South has changed. Mississippi's first very profitable crop was cotton, and cotton remains "king" of agriculture in the state today. That is because the state is perfectly suited to big cotton farms—the land is flat and fertile, the temperature warm all year, and rainfall plentiful. Today, however, most Mississippians work in services or manufacturing rather than agriculture. A small number of workers and machinery now do the farm work once done by slaves under the old plantation system. Near Natchez, you can see historic mansions built by plantation owners before the Civil War. And at Vicksburg, a port on the Mississippi, you can visit the site of the Civil War battle that marked a turning point in the war in favor of the Union.

Mississippi includes the forested Piney Woods region, where trees are cut down to make paper, turpentine, and other products. Along the Gulf Coast, shrimping and fishing boats are at work. The capital, Jackson, lies in the middle of the state and is the largest city.

Louisiana is famous throughout the world, mostly because of the colorful city of New Orleans. Louisiana's heritage is largely French—it was the cultural center of the Louisiana Purchase. The economic strength of the state was first based on its control of trade at the mouth of the Mississippi. River barges and oceangoing vessels still churn the river waters between Baton Rouge, the capital, and New Orleans. Trade continues to be the most important business in the state, followed closely by tourism. People flock to New Orleans to hear good jazz in the city where it was born, and to enjoy delicious foods—such as soup called gumbo—that combine French and American flavors. Many tourists also come to the city each year for Mardi Gras, New Orleans's biggest holiday, which is celebrated with parades and fun costumes.

Read the clues about Mississippi and Louisiana.
Then complete the puzzle using the word list on the next page.

★ Across ★

2. Slave labor was used to support this kind of large farm.
4. Second word in the name of New Orleans's famous holiday
6. Mississippi's top economic activity today, along with manufacturing

7. A forested area of Mississippi is called the _____ Woods region.
9. What parading people wear at Mardi Gras
10. French and American soup served in New Orleans
11. Near this city, you can see mansions from before the Civil War.
12. Body of water into which the Mississippi flows— _____ of Mexico

★ Down ★

1. Capital of Mississippi
3. A liquid product gained from Mississippi trees
5. Location of a major Civil War battle in Mississippi
6. Edible sea animal harvested from the Gulf of Mexico, along with fish
8. Nation that put its cultural stamp on New Orleans

Scenes from Mississippi and Louisiana

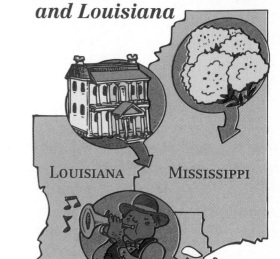

LOUISIANA   MISSISSIPPI

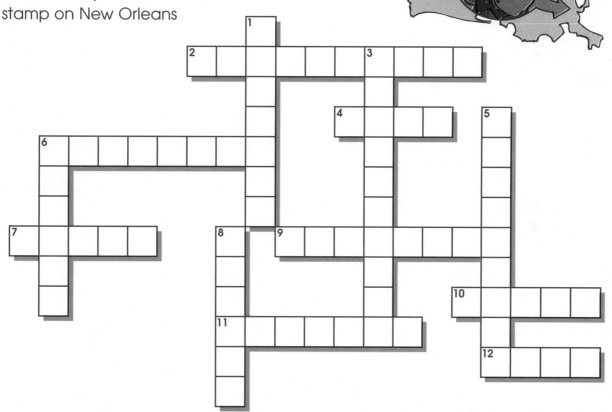

Word List

COSTUMES	GUMBO	PINEY	SHRIMP
FRANCE	JACKSON	PLANTATION	TURPENTINE
GRAS	NATCHEZ	SERVICES	VICKSBURG
GULF			

Missouri and Arkansas

Missouri and Arkansas lie along the western side of the Mississippi River and share a range of low mountains and hills, or highlands, called the Ozarks. South of the Ozarks in Arkansas are the Ouachita Mountains. They are full of water springs, including 47 hot ones at beautiful Hot Springs National Park.

These two states were part of the Louisiana Purchase, the huge piece of land sold to the United States by France in 1803. The city of St. Louis, Missouri, became a midwestern hub and a gateway for settlement of the West. At the far western edge of Missouri is Kansas City. This former cow town, now larger in population than St. Louis, still has a western look. Missouri's capital, small Jefferson City, lies in the center of the state.

Both states also have a foot in the southern region. During the Civil War, citizens from both states fought on both sides of the conflict, although Arkansas left the Union and Missouri did not. Much later, in the 1950's, Arkansas was in the spotlight during the struggle for civil rights. The United States Supreme Court ruled that public schools must accept students without regard to their race. In many places across the South, including Arkansas, black and white students had been attending separate schools. After the court ruling, several black students braved angry crowds to enroll at Central High School in Little Rock, the state capital, for the first time.

In the past, farming was the main way of life in both states. It remains a chief industry in Missouri, where nearly every crop grows. Manufacturing is now the most important industry in Arkansas. People there make a living processing food, making electrical appliances, and making paper—among other things. The Wal-Mart chain of stores got its start in the state. Today, however, Arkansas may be most famous as the birthplace of William (Bill) Clinton, a former governor who was elected president of the United States in 1992 and 1996.

Read the clues about Missouri and Arkansas.
Then complete the puzzle using the word list on the next page.

★ Across ★

2. Missouri's capital—_____ City
4. He was an Arkansas governor before he became a U.S. president.
7. Economic activity now more important than farming in Arkansas

10. First word in the name of Arkansas's capital
11. Arkansas has the only mine for these in the nation.

★ Down ★

1. Name of the Little Rock high school spotlighted in the Civil Rights era
3. Still a major economic activity in Missouri
5. Both Arkansas and Missouri were part of the _____ Purchase.
6. Mountains in southern Arkansas
8. Name of the monument arch in St. Louis
9. Popular dessert food introduced at the 1904 St. Louis World's Fair—_____ cream

The Gateway Arch in St. Louis, Missouri, reminds people of the city's history as a gateway for settlement of the West.

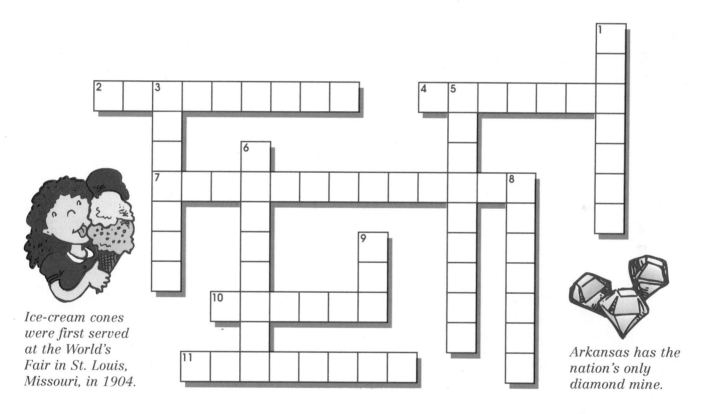

Ice-cream cones were first served at the World's Fair in St. Louis, Missouri, in 1904.

Arkansas has the nation's only diamond mine.

Word List

CENTRAL	FARMING	JEFFERSON	MANUFACTURING
CLINTON	GATEWAY	LITTLE	OUACHITA
DIAMONDS	ICE	LOUISIANA	

Alabama and Georgia

Alabama and Georgia are neighbors in the heart of the American South. Coastal plains cover the southern two-thirds of both states, although the land rises in a rolling area called the Piedmont. North of the Piedmont are hills and mountains that are part of the Appalachians. Settlers quickly found that the Piedmont and plains were prime cotton-growing lands. Georgia, one of the original thirteen colonies, developed an economy based on the plantation system and slave labor. This way of life extended to the area that became Alabama. Both states were part of the Confederacy during the Civil War. There have been many changes in both states since that time.

Boll weevils—insects that eat cotton crops—destroyed cotton harvests during the 1920's. Today, there is even a monument to the boll weevil in Alabama! Farmers tried other crops, such as peanuts, and some former farmland was returned to forest. Forest products such as paper and building lumber are important to both states today. Manufacturing and services now employ most people. Birmingham, Alabama, is a major iron and steel producer, partly because the coal, iron ore, and limestone needed to make steel are located in the surrounding area. Birmingham is now the largest city in the state.

In 1955, a bus boycott in Montgomery, Alabama's capital, touched off the Civil Rights movement. In time, that movement led to voting rights and to more opportunities in jobs and education for African Americans throughout the United States.

Martin Luther King, Jr., civil rights leader.

Atlanta, the capital of Georgia, has become the urban center of the southeastern part of the United States. Atlanta has always been important as a transportation hub and serves as the headquarters of Delta Air Lines. Today, almost half of all Georgians live within the greater metropolitan area of Atlanta.

Both Alabama and Georgia have areas of coast. Alabama's is on the Gulf of Mexico, where fishing boasts come in to Mobile Bay. Georgia's Atlantic coast attracts tourists, as does the wildlife refuge in the Okefenokee Swamp.

Words about Alabama and Georgia have been scrambled.
Rearrange the letters and write the correct word on each line.
Use the word list if you need help.

TALANTA

_____

SEFORT

_____

ELEST

_____

CASPAHALAPIN

_____

GONERTYMOM

_____

FILEDILW

_____

TAPNLOAINT

_____

AFEEDORNCCY

_____

GAMRIMINBH

_____

DOEMIPNT

_____

VICLI SHRIGT

_____

TOCNOT

_____

Word List

APPALACHIANS	CIVIL RIGHTS	FOREST	PLANTATION
ATLANTA	CONFEDERACY	MONTGOMERY	STEEL
BIRMINGHAM	COTTON	PIEDMONT	WILDLIFE

Florida

What is the most popular single-attraction tourist destination in the world? You can probably guess the answer—Disney World in Florida. Florida also has so many other attractions that it's no wonder tourism is the state's top moneymaker.

Mockingbird

27th state ★ Statehood: March 3, 1845

Orange Blossom

FL ★ The Sunshine State

Part of Florida's appeal is its climate and location. The state is a large peninsula that extends southward into the Atlantic Ocean. Attached to the peninsula is a northwestern panhandle of Gulf Coast land where Tallahassee, the state capital, lies. Because of its shape, Florida has an enormous continuous coastline that attracts people to its beaches and boat docks. Florida's climate is warm all year. In the far southern part of the state, including many small islands called the Florida Keys, the climate is tropical, which means it changes little with the seasons. Even in northern Florida, winter temperatures rarely fall below freezing. However, Florida is often in the path of hurricanes.

Florida caught the eye of Europeans in the early 1500's. Spain established the first permanent settlement in North America at St. Augustine, on the northeast coast. The Spanish first grew oranges in Florida; today, citrus fruits are the state's most valuable crop. Beginning in the 1800's, Florida became a destination for "snowbirds," people escaping from winter in the northeastern states. Others come to Florida to retire. Large communities of retired people have increased the population of cities like St. Petersburg. Florida has also become home to Hispanic people from south of the U.S. border, including many Cubans.

Visitors to Florida are likely to stop in the Orlando area, where there are many theme parks, including Universal Studios and Sea World. East of Orlando on the coast is the Kennedy Space Center at Cape Canaveral.

Read the clues about Florida.
Then complete the puzzle using the word list on the next page.

★ Across ★

1. Country that established the first permanent settlement in North America
5. Capital of Florida
7. Florida city where many theme parks are located
8. Name of islands below the southern tip of the Florida peninsula
9. People who winter in Florida's warm climate are given this nickname.
10. Severe kind of storm that sometimes blasts Florida
11. The northwestern Gulf Coast strip of Florida is shaped like a _____ handle.

★ Down ★

1. Universal _____ is a theme park in Florida.
2. Name of the "World" that is the world's top tourist destination; in Florida
3. Name of the Florida cape where spacecraft are launched into space
4. Florida city with many retired people: St. _____
6. Chief economic activity in Florida
9. Kind of land within Everglades National Park

At Everglades National Park, you can take an airboat through swampland to see pelicans, alligators, and other creatures.

Word List

CANAVERAL	ORLANDO	SNOWBIRDS	SWAMP
DISNEY	PAN	SPAIN	TALLAHASSEE
HURRICANE	PETERSBURG	STUDIOS	TOURISM
KEYS			

North Carolina and South Carolina

Statehood: November 21, 1789
12th state
Cardinal
Dogwood
NC ★ The Tar Heel State

Both the Carolinas have miles and miles of beaches. In both states, the wide coastal plain ends at the slightly higher, rolling red-clay country called the Piedmont. The Piedmont is divided from the plain along the "fall line," where early mill owners once set their waterwheels to take advantage of the descending streams. Many towns—such as both state capitals, Raleigh, North Carolina, and Columbia, South Carolina—grew up naturally along this fall line. West of the Piedmont lies the Appalachian mountain chain. North Carolina holds the chain's highest peaks, including the tallest, Mount Mitchell.

Statehood: May 23, 1788
8th state
Carolina Wren
Jessamine
SC ★ The Palmetto State

The Carolinas were among the thirteen original colonies. In fact, the first English settlement in the Americas was founded on Roanoke Island off North Carolina in 1585—although it mysteriously disappeared soon after. By the early 1800's, cotton and tobacco plantations supported by slaves had become a way of life. The first shots of the Civil War were fired at Fort Sumter, South Carolina, and after the war, a long period of poverty followed. In the years following the war, many textile mills employed people, as they do today, although low wages and competition from abroad have been problems.

North Carolina's Outer Banks

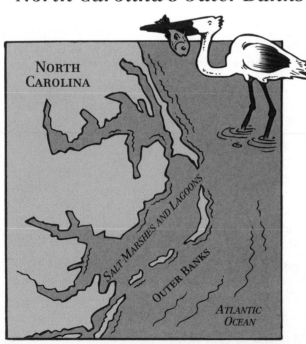

NORTH CAROLINA
SALT MARSHES AND LAGOONS
OUTER BANKS
ATLANTIC OCEAN

Today, most Carolina residents work in tourism and manufacturing. Tobacco is the biggest crop, and cigarette making is a large industry, especially around Raleigh in North Carolina. Since the 1970's, the population of each state has been growing, partly because of new electronics industries and university growth. In North Carolina, a "research triangle" has grown up around the University of North Carolina at Chapel Hill, Duke University, and North Carolina State. And visitors come to the Carolinas not only for the beaches but also to see historic sites such as the colonial era gardens and homes in Charleston, South Carolina.

Read the sentences about North Carolina and South Carolina.
Then complete the sentences by filling in each blank.
Use the word list if you need help.

★ The South Carolina city of _____ is famous for its colonial era gardens and houses.

★ The first mills along the fall line depended on _____ for power.

★ The University of North Carolina at Chapel Hill, Duke University, and North Carolina State form the North Carolina _____ triangle.

★ The islands off North Carolina are called the _____ Banks.

★ _____ is the major crop in both Carolinas.

★ The first shots of the Civil War were fired at Fort _____.

★ The _____ line lies between the coastal plain and the Piedmont.

★ Mount _____ is the tallest Appalachian mountain.

★ Salty _____ help separate the Outer Banks from the North Carolina mainland.

★ North Carolina was the site of the _____ English settlement in America.

Word List

Charleston	first	Outer	Tobacco
fall	marshes	research	water
	Mitchell	Sumter	

Virginia and Maryland

Virginia and Maryland have a geography similar to the rest of the states that line the Atlantic Ocean in the South. Flat coastal plains, sometimes called the tidewater region, give way to the slightly higher, rolling Piedmont. On the western edge of each state is part of the Appalachian range named the Blue Ridge. In Virginia, it is called the ridge and valley region. Maryland has a special physical feature, the Chesapeake Bay. The part of Maryland east of the bay is known as the Eastern Shore. Only the southeastern tip of Maryland extends out to the Atlantic, where Ocean City welcomes beachgoers. Between Virginia and Maryland flows the Potomac, on which Washington, D.C., is located. The national capital strongly affects both sides.

The capital of Maryland, Annapolis, is a small city on the western shore of the Chesapeake. Baltimore, to the north on the same side, is by far Maryland's biggest city. The area between Baltimore and Washington, D.C., is so urbanized that it is really one huge metropolitan area. In the past, Baltimore was host to heavy industries, but today, many people work for government agencies or in computer software or biotech industries.

Virginia is a much larger state, but it, too, is home to many government institutions and businesses that serve the national government. You can still visit many places to remember Virginia's rich history, such as Jamestown, site of the first lasting English colony, and colonial Williamsburg. The capital of the state, Richmond, was once the capital of the Confederacy. Civil War battlefields all over the state show how hard the war was fought there.

A good place to see natural Virginia is in Shenandoah National Park, where hardwood forests blanket the Blue Ridge. They turn lovely colors in the fall.

Fishermen work the waters of Chesapeake Bay, gathering crabs, clams, oysters, and many kinds of fish, but water pollution is endangering the catch.

Use the word list to help you find the words about Virginia
and Maryland that are hidden in the block below.
Some of the words are hidden backward or diagonally.

```
C P C H E S A P E A K E B A Y V
E T P W S K I J A M E S T O W N
A T C I P E F T A Z J U H G Y D
R N D F D T S O U T H C R D C B
J E N M E A Y M V I E U I E A A
Y M O P G N I A O T B P C O R T
G N T O D N S C O S H J H E E T
T R G T I A S I M X O C M K D L
I E N O R P B A L T I M O R E E
D V I M E O I O D A J X N B F F
E O H A U L O S P R G Q D P N I
W G S C L I T D N J M C U Q O E
A M A I B S E A T L A N T I C L
T T W W H R O C E A N C I T Y D
E U N B L D H A O D N A N E H S
R E A S T E R N S H O R E W C A
```

Word List

ANNAPOLIS	BLUE RIDGE	JAMESTOWN	SHENANDOAH
ATLANTIC	CHESAPEAKE BAY	OCEAN CITY	SOUTH
BALTIMORE	CONFEDERACY	PIEDMONT	TIDEWATER
BATTLEFIELDS	EASTERN SHORE	POTOMAC	WASHINGTON DC
BIOTECH	GOVERNMENT	RICHMOND	WILLIAMSBURG

Washington, District of Columbia

Washington, D.C., is the capital of the United States. The city of Washington is not a state. It is in a special district called the District of Columbia. This area of land, located between Virginia and Maryland on the bank of the Potomac River, is controlled by Congress. As the capital, Washington, D.C., is a symbol of unity for all the states. It is the center for the nation's government. Today, the District totals about sixty-eight square miles. The Washington metropolitan area is one of the largest urban areas in the nation; it includes suburbs in Virginia as well as those in Maryland extending up to Baltimore.

Washington, D.C., was planned by Congress to be the nation's capital, and Congress decided to name the city after the nation's first president. George Washington never lived there, but he appointed a French architect, Pierre L'Enfant, to design the city. In 1800, the government moved to Washington, and John Adams became the first president to live in the White House. The Capitol, intended to be the meeting place of Congress, was barely finished when the British burned it during the War of 1812. It was promptly rebuilt. Today, most Washingtonians make a living by working in government, providing services, or working in tourism. Young and old alike enjoy the Smithsonian Institution museums and other attractions located along the Mall. Visitors come to Washington all year, but a favorite time is in spring when the famous cherry trees, a gift from Japan, are in bloom around town.

Washington, D.C., was at first entirely controlled by Congress. Citizens now elect their own city council and mayor, but Congress still has the right to regulate the city and its spending. The people of Washington, D.C., elect a representative to Congress, but that person cannot vote on laws. Even though the city is so important to the nation, poverty and crime have been serious problems there.

Read the clues about Washington, D.C.
Then complete the puzzle using the word list on the next page.

★ Across ★

1. City where government is, such as Washington, D.C.
5. The Washington _____ is at the far end of the Mall from the Capitol.
6. People who burned the Capitol on the War of 1812
8. Name of the institution that has many museums in Washington, D.C.
9. Kind of pink blossoms famous in Washington, D.C.
10. Name of the river that borders Washington, D.C.
11. Washington, D.C.'s, only one has no vote in Congress.
12. Name of the grassy rectangle extending from the capitol

★ Down ★

2. Last name of the first president to live in the White House
3. Washington, D.C., is not in a state but in a _____.
4. Most people in Washington, D.C., work in services, tourism, or _____.
7. Group finally responsible for city government in Washington, D.C.
9. Building where Congress meets

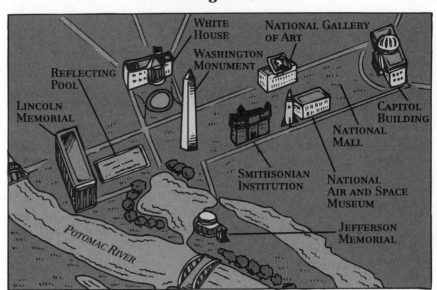

Washington, D.C.

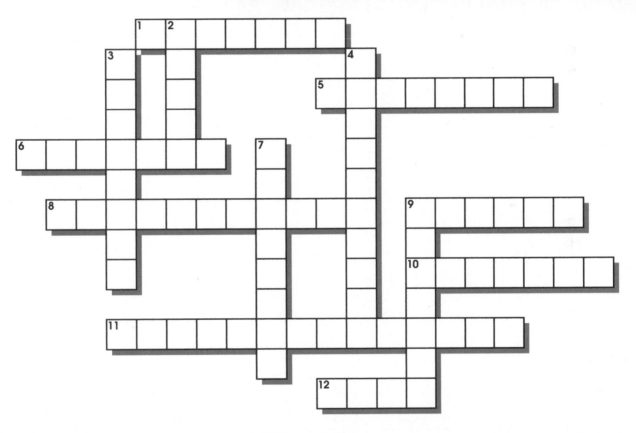

Word List

ADAMS	CHERRY	GOVERNMENT	POTOMAC
BRITISH	CONGRESS	MALL	REPRESENTATIVE
CAPITAL	DISTRICT	MONUMENT	SMITHSONIAN
CAPITOL			

U.S. States—Topics to Explore

You have read about only a small part of the unique history and geography that have shaped American's 50 states and Washington, D.C. Below, you will find a list of more topics related to the 50 states. Choose some topics from the list, or think of other subjects on your own, that you would like to learn more about. Use the following pages to take notes and create your own activities.

Other Topics About U.S. States:

- The Lincoln Memorial
- Yosemite National Park
- The Grand Canyon
- The Great Lakes
- The Appalachian Trail
- The Alaskan Pipeline
- The Sears Tower (Chicago)
- Ellis Island
- Colonial Williamsburg
- Ebbet's Field

Notes Page

Choose one of the topics from page 297, or think of a topic on your own, and write about what you know in the space below. Research your chosen topic further, using the library or the Internet to help you find information. Take lots of notes, as you will use these notes to create your own activity on the next page.

★ NOTES ★

Create Your Own Activity

Use this page to create your own activity based on the notes you took on the previous page. Share your activity with a friend.

Notes Page

Choose one of the topics from page 297, or think of a topic on your own, and write about what you know in the space below. Research your chosen topic further, using the library or the Internet to help you find information. Take lots of notes, as you will use these notes to create your own activity on the next page.

★ NOTES ★

_____

_____

_____

_____

_____

_____

_____

_____

_____

_____

_____

_____

_____

_____

_____

_____

_____

Create Your Own Activity

Use this page to create your own activity based on the notes you took on the previous page. Share your activity with a friend.

Notes Page

Choose one of the topics from page 297, or think of a topic on your own, and write about what you know in the space below. Research your chosen topic further, using the library or the Internet to help you find information. Take lots of notes, as you will use these notes to create your own activity on the next page.

★ NOTES ★

_____

_____

_____

_____

_____

_____

_____

_____

_____

_____

_____

_____

_____

_____

_____

_____

_____

_____

_____

Create Your Own Activity

Use this page to create your own activity based on the notes you took on the previous page. Share your activity with a friend.

State Flags

Do you know your state flags? Match each flag to its state.

a.

b.

c.

d.

e.

f.

g.

h.

i.

j.

_____ Louisiana

_____ Oklahoma

_____ New York

_____ Virginia

_____ Missouri

_____ North Carolina

_____ New Mexico

_____ Maine

_____ Minnesota

_____ New Hampshire

State Flags

Do you know your state flags? Match each flag to its state.

a.

b.

c.

d.

e.

f.

g.

h.

i.

j.

_____ Vermont

_____ Colorado

_____ Kentucky

_____ Wisconsin

_____ Mississippi

_____ West Virginia

_____ Utah

_____ Wyoming

_____ Iowa

_____ Idaho

State Flags

Do you know your state flags? Match each flag to its state.

a.

b.

c.

d.

e.

f.

g.

h.

i.

j.

_____ Michigan

_____ California

_____ Rhode Island

_____ Tennessee

_____ Washington

_____ Montana

_____ Arizona

_____ South Dakota

_____ Indiana

_____ Hawaii

State Flags

Do you know your state flags? Match each flag to its state.

a.

b.

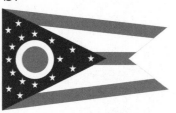

c.

d.

e.

f.

g.

h.

i.

j.

_____ Arkansas

_____ Florida

_____ Illinois

_____ Pennsylvania

_____ Ohio

_____ Nevada

_____ South Carolina

_____ Georgia

_____ North Dakota

_____ Kansas

State Flags

Do you know your state flags? Match each flag to its state.

a.

b.

c.

d.

e.

f.

g.

h.

i.

j.

_____ Connecticut

_____ Alaska

_____ Maryland

_____ Oregon

_____ New Jersey

_____ Alabama

_____ Massachusetts

_____ Delaware

_____ Nebraska

_____ Texas

Abbreviate the States

When you mail a letter or postcard to someone, the state in the address is always abbreviated using two capital letters. See how many postal abbreviations you know by filling in the correct abbreviation next to each state on pages 310 and 311.

_____ Alabama   _____ Delaware   _____ Indiana   _____ Maryland

_____ Alaska   _____ Florida   _____ Iowa   _____ Massachusetts

_____ Arizona   _____ Georgia   _____ Kansas   _____ Michigan

_____ Arkansas   _____ Hawaii   _____ Kentucky   _____ Minnesota

_____ California   _____ Idaho   _____ Louisiana   _____ Mississippi

_____ Colorado   _____ Illinois   _____ Maine   _____ Missouri

_____ Connecticut

John Q. Smith
123 Broad St.
Somewhere, OH 00000

USA 34

Jane Doe
123 Main Street
Anytown, OH 00000

Abbreviate the States

____ Montana ____ North Carolina ____ Rhode Island ____ Vermont

____ Nebraska ____ North Dakota ____ South Carolina ____ Virginia

____ Nevada ____ Ohio ____ South Dakota ____ Washington

____ New Hampshire ____ Oklahoma ____ Tennessee ____ West Virginia

____ New Jersey ____ Oregon ____ Texas ____ Wisconsin

____ New Mexico ____ Pennsylvania ____ Utah ____ Wyoming

____ New York

Dear Jane,

Jane Doe
123 Main Street
Anytown, OH 00000

USA
20

State Riddles

Read the riddles below about the U.S. states. You may know some of the answers right away—other riddles may be more difficult, so you will have to do some research. Then, solve each riddle by filling in the name of the state that is being described.

★ I am the biggest state. The highest peak in the U.S., Mt. McKinley, is located in me.

Which state am I?_____

★ I can "show" you a lot. Jefferson City is my capital. In the summer of 1993, much of

my land flooded. Which state am I?_____

★ Abraham Lincoln was born in me. A famous derby is held in me. The nation's gold

vault is in my Fort Knox. Which state am I?_____

★ La Salle claimed my area for France in 1682. The U.S. bought me from France in 1803.

I am the 18th state. Which state am I?_____

★ I am often called the Great Lakes State because I touch four of the five. My Battle

Creek is the largest producer of breakfast cereal. Which state am I?

_____

★ My Jamestown was the site of the first permanent English settlement in America.

Patrick Henry gave his famous speech in my Appomattox Court House. Which state

am I? _____

★ Montgomery is my capital. My state flower is the camellia. Which state am I?

_____

★ I contain the Grand Canyon. Phoenix is my capital. Without irrigation, half of me

would be desert. Which state am I?_____

★ I was the home of seven U.S. presidents. The Pro Football Hall of Fame is located in my

Canton. Which state am I?_____

State Riddles

Here are more riddles about the U.S. states. You may know some of the answers right away—other riddles may be more difficult, so you will have to do some research. Then, solve each riddle by filling in the name of the state that is being described.

★ I am big—220 times the size of Rhode Island! I have the most farms, farmland, cattle, horses, and sheep in the nation. Which state am I?_____

★ I am the "Land of Opportunity." Bill Clinton was born in me. Little Rock is my capital. Which state am I?_____

★ My people are "Hoosiers." I am the 19th state. The University of Notre Dame is located in me. Which state am I?_____

★ I got my name from the Indians. Bismarck is my capital. I am the Flickertail State. Which state am I?_____

★ I am the 50th state. My Pearl Harbor is very famous. Diamond Head is one of my most famous extinct volcanoes. Which state am I?

_____

★ I was the first state to secede from the Union. My Fort Sumter was the place where the Civil War began. I am the Palmetto State. Which state am I?

_____

★ I am the smallest state. Roger Williams founded me in 1636. I produce the most costume jewelry in the world. Which state am I?_____

★ I am the First State. I was named for Lord De La Warr. I was the first state to ratify the new constitution in 1787. Which state am I?_____

★ I am the Gopher State. My Mesabi Range contains much iron ore. St. Paul is my capital. Which state am I?_____

The National Anthem

"The Star-Spangled Banner" has been the National Anthem of the United States since 1931. Frances Scott Key wrote it long before that. During the War of 1812, when the British were bombarding Fort McHenry in Baltimore, Key wrote the words to rejoice that the "Stars and Stripes" (the U.S. flag) still flew over the fort.

The National Anthem consists of four verses. Most Americans are familiar with the first verse. See if you know it. Write the missing words in the verse below. You may use the word list if you need help.

Oh, say can you _____ by the

  dawn's early _____

What so _____ we hailed at the twilight's last _____?

Whose broad _____ and bright _____ thru' the perilous fight,

O'er the ramparts we _____ were so _____ streaming?

And the rockets' red _____, the bombs bursting in _____,

Gave _____ thru' the night that our _____ was still there.

Oh, say does that star-spangled _____ yet _____

O'er the land of the _____ and the home of the _____?

Word List

GLARE	BANNER	WATCHED	STARS
LIGHT	PROOF	SEE	PROUDLY
BRAVE	AIR	STRIPES	FLAG
GALLANTLY	WAVE	FREE	GLEAMING

U.S. Map

Here is a map of the United States. All of the state abbreviations have been filled in. Use the key on page 317 to color the map.

Color Key

Pacific States—green
Southwestern States—red
Midwest States—blue
Southern States—purple

Mountain States—brown
Atlantic States—yellow
New England States—orange

The Complete Book of

AMERICAN
Facts & Games

Grades 3-5

Answer Key

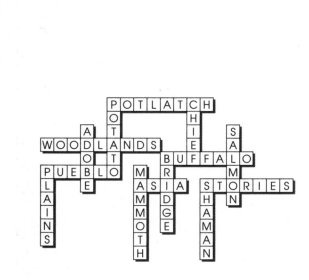

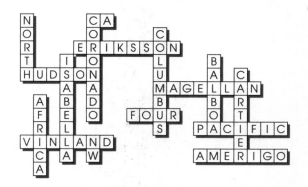

9

11

Word Search (13):

```
S H I P B U I L D I N G  G P Y M I
A L X D O C C A B O T O  L A U E
Q U A K E R F Q O H W L  T E D T
C Q E V L S P H G C M D  A N W O
P M F J E H L N D R P A  T R W N
H O Z R I S I R O U I N  O L M E
B L U U C M W J R H L M  R G E E
K A B J R B X I C G S D  N P T
H S V A K T T L C T R X  O G E I
T S F D B A E N S S I C  N P W N
U E T M N D Y V G N M O  S K E G
O Q S A Z J A M E S T O  W N N
M K J L I N B H V P L G  Y G Q F
Y F I M S E T T L E M E  N T S I
L H L Z S G N I D A R T  F E A I
P E N N S W O O D S R A  R I C E
```

13

Unscramble (15):

NHPSASI	NATSGUM
SPANISH	**MUSTANG**
TS UTENGUASI	IRLADOF
ST AUGUSTINE	**FLORIDA**
TSAAN EF	NADINI
SANTA FE	**INDIAN**
IRSPEIOD	ERPNIOE
PRESIDIO	**PIONEER**
LNRBLOEEI	SMINOIS
REBELLION	**MISSION**
THNTYICRAISI	RAFILOCIAN
CHRISTIANITY	**CALIFORNIA**

15

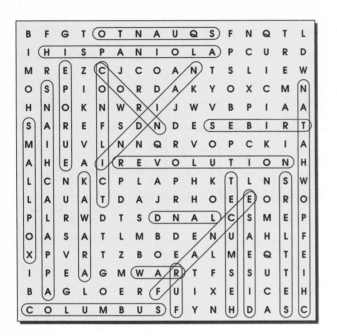

17

LERPEA	STIROTPA
REPEAL	**PATRIOTS**
SNICOLEO	NDANELG
COLONIES	**ENGLAND**
TXA	SROIET
TAX	**TORIES**
NTOBSO	BLIRTEY
BOSTON	**LIBERTY**
MULESA MADAS	SANDIIN
SAMUEL ADAMS	**INDIANS**
PMATS	MOGRNTEVEN
STAMP	**GOVERNMENT**

19

21

TSSATE	NOUSAILIA
STATES	**LOUISIANA**
SIVERAD	TANOTNALPI
ADVISER	**PLANTATION**
CEHTRIRCAUTE	LEMLIOTONC
ARCHITECTURE	**MONTICELLO**
INCRALTADOE	LIPTALICO
DECLARATION	**POLITICAL**
TUSETAT	PNDICEENNDEE
STATUTE	**INDEPENDENCE**
DIRTESPEN	AWREYL
PRESIDENT	**LAWYER**

23

25

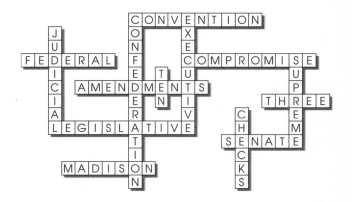

27

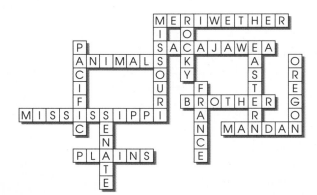

29

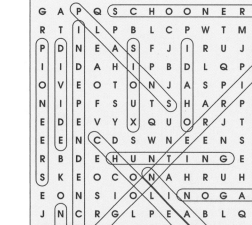

31

33

AAMLO	LETBAT
ALAMO	**BATTLE**
RENROIFT	LEMESTNTTE
FRONTIER	**SETTLEMENT**
PETINDNNEED	NUTISA
INDEPENDENT	**AUSTIN**
SHOUTON	TROKECCT
HOUSTON	**CROCKETT**
SLEGZONA	XCOMEI
GONZALES	**MEXICO**
LIGONEIR	MISONIS
RELIGION	**MISSION**

33

35

37

★ The cotton gin made growing cotton more ___**profitable**___.

★ Eli ___**Whitney**___ invented the cotton gin.

★ Nat ___**Turner**___ led a slave rebellion.

★ The ___**Underground**___ Railroad helped slaves escape.

★ Those who helped slaves escape on the Underground Railroad were known as ___**conductors**___.

★ One of every ___**four**___ families in the South owned slaves.

★ ___**Canada**___, a country north of the United States, was one of the areas to which some slaves escaped.

★ Plantation slaves worked in the fields, as craftsmen, or in the owner's ___**household**___.

★ Harriet ___**Tubman**___ is known as a famous African American conductor on the Underground Railroad.

★ Slave drivers were usually ___**slaves**___ themselves.

★ The ___**music**___ created by slaves became the basis of jazz and the blues.

37

39

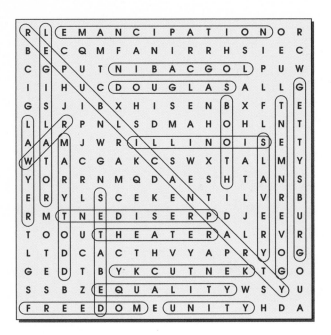

41

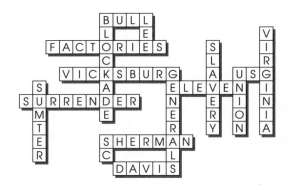

43

MARY		TBSED	
ARMY		**DEBTS**	
PROSREHRESCAP		PGRETSBAREGAC	
SHARECROPPERS		**CARPETBAGGERS**	
ERENDMEF		NMESTANDME	
FREEDMEN		**AMENDMENTS**	
DECREFNOYCA		REPOVYT	
CONFEDERACY		**POVERTY**	
THIGRS		NNIOU	
RIGHTS		**UNION**	
SREGNOSC		OSJHONN	
CONGRESS		**JOHNSON**	

45

TEOV		FGUSRAFE	
VOTE		**SUFFRAGE**	
VINCENTOON		THRIGS	
CONVENTION		**RIGHTS**	
TOMT		NITENETENH	
MOTT		**NINETEENTH**	
NSTONTA		YNOTAHN	
STANTON		**ANTHONY**	
DERMOFE		ECANES SLALF	
FREEDOM		**SENECA FALLS**	
UJRSNREOO		ITILNOOAB	
SOJOURNER		**ABOLITION**	

47

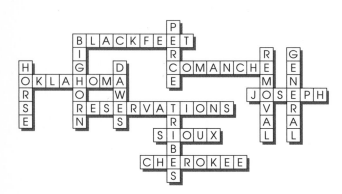

49

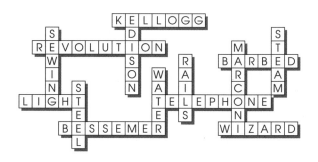

51

★ An uncontrolled rush of cattle is called a _____**stampede**_____.

★ Cattle thieves were called _____**rustlers**_____.

★ Cowboys used a well-trained _____**horse**_____ to help herd cows.

★ Cowboys threw a rope called a _____**lasso**_____ to catch cows.

★ Texas cowboys used a branding _____**iron**_____ to mark the cows to show ownership.

★ Cowboys wore leather leggings called _____**chaps**_____ to protect against brush.

★ A herd could travel about _____**fifteen**_____ miles in a day.

★ Community decisions made by cattle owners were called cow **custom**_____.

★ Cowboys raised _____**longhorn**_____ cattle in Texas.

★ Taking a herd to a distant location is known as a cattle **drive**_____.

53

55

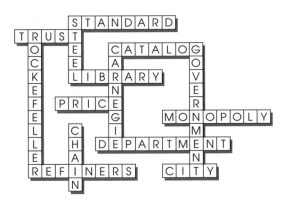

57

```
      S T A N D A R D
T R U S T E           C A T A L O G       O
O       E             A             V
C       E   L I B R A R Y           E
K       L             N             R
E     P R I C E       E   M O N O P O L Y
F         C           G           M
E         H A I N     I           E
L         A   D E P A R T M E N T N
L         N                       T
E R E F I N E R S     C I T Y
R         N
```

61

```
            I
J U V E N I L E           C
      H             C H I C A G O
    E N G L I S H   I
P   R               T     G A L L E R Y
L   I               I     A       U
A S E T T L E M E N T     R       L
Y R T     O X F O R D     B
G E R                     A
R A R                     G
O D       T               E
U I       O Y N B E E
N N       R
D G       E
```

59

★ **France** _____ gave the Statue of Liberty to the United States as a gift in 1886.

★ Chinese workers helped build the first **transcontinental** _____ railroad.

★ In sweatshops, hours were _____ **long** _____.

★ The _____ **Statue** _____ of Liberty stands in New York harbor.

★ Congress passed the first _____ **law** _____ to keep Chinese people out of the U.S. in 1882.

★ Someone who comes from another country to live permanently in a new country is called an _____ **immigrant** _____.

★ Most immigrants came from _____ **northwestern** _____ Europe before 1880.

★ A negative opinion of a group of people based on race is known as **prejudice** _____.

★ The quota system was designed to _____ **control** _____ all immigration.

★ Many Asian immigrants settled on the _____ **West** _____ Coast.

63

```
D P U R E F O O D A N D D R U G
F A I N A T I O N A L P A R K S
O S K H S R O U G H R I D E R S
R T G O V E R N O R E D Y B A F
E A J X T E D D Y B E A R U N H
S T H L T A Y L E F R N S D C J
T S A F E A O W E T E Q D E L I
S A R L D M I S E R E T U H E Z S
W R Y P E E T W H U R U K S N O L
R I O C R R E C V S V I E H A E M
I T M B A U G U H T C G T R U T F
T I C O U T O B M S B P E O Z N L
I N I H Q A T A P O P U L A R X T
N G Z H S N E W Y O R K C I T Y U
M S P A N I S H A M E R I C A N
```

77

SRUBBUS → **SUBURBS**	MESBLASY ELNI → **ASSEMBLY LINE**
TROYCAF → **FACTORY**	VROCENOY TELB → **CONVEYOR BELT**
MITE → **TIME**	SEENEINPXIV → **INEXPENSIVE**
KORREW → **WORKER**	STARP → **PARTS**
DOTHEM → **METHOD**	GAURNIFMUTCAN → **MANUFACTURING**
OMABILETOU → **AUTOMOBILE**	FENICTIFE → **EFFICIENT**

77

79

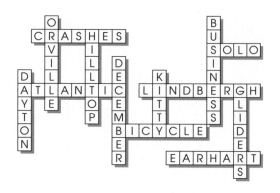

79

81

```
V W J T C U P S O L D I E R G M
A O L E N F O R K S E G D E R R
R M T L A L D I W L A P R C E L N
Q E P B T S T O I M H A L T
U N M G R S R E F O N O C M L I
L P C R I A E W A Y E V O R I P
N H L A T L O D N G W N F E G S
I I R B T I P L B N F F J S R T
R T B T N A L R I A W L M O A A
A A H T N A O S H O I U C T O B
W I L S O N A W C U C M X I N U
D N B E H C R W Y C U C M X I F
L L S J S E T H I T Z T D A O N
R G D M T S N X E C N A R F N I
O L E A G U E O F N A T I O N S
W F S B R M C R T B R C A B T K
```

81

83

GROMSNART → **ARMSTRONG**	DIGAFZETRL → **FITZGERALD**
SKIEPEASAES → **SPEAKEASIES**	OTHBIROPINI → **PROHIBITION**
WNE SRLONAE → **NEW ORLEANS**	PLARESFP → **FLAPPERS**
IMCSU → **MUSIC**	LANRUFE → **FUNERAL**
EDROCSR → **RECORDS**	WHATELY → **WEALTHY**
DORAI → **RADIO**	IEITRYELCCT → **ELECTRICITY**

83

Answer Key

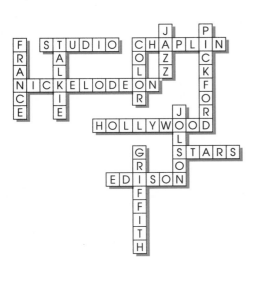

85

```
                  J        P
F   STUDIO    CHAPLIN
R   A         O        C
A   L    JAZZ O        K
N NICKELODEON L        F
C   K         O        O
E   I         R        R
    E    HOLLYWOOD      D
              J    O
              O  STARS
         GRIFFITH
         R    S
       EDISON
         F
         F
         I
         T
         H
```

87

```
WORK      T
R    SHARE HURSDAY
L    C     U
DEPRESSION R   O      S
O    O     S   C      T
R    M     D   T      O
L    O     A   O  WALL C
  MORGAN Y B  E  L  K
  MARGIN  HOOVER  L
       A
       N
```

89

★ Most migrants traveled _____**west**_____ after dust storms struck their farms.

★ A prolonged dry spell is called a _____**drought**_____.

★ A settler would dampen a _____**blanket**_____ to cover his windows during a dust storm.

★ The Soil _____**Conservation**_____ Service taught farmers to save soil.

★ The nickname given to migrants from Oklahoma was **Okies**.

★ The Grapes of Wrath was an important _____**book**_____ that helped show the plight of migrant workers.

★ Small farmers who got land from the government were known as **homesteaders**.

★ The famous photographer, Dorothea _____**Lange**_____ ,took pictures of migrant workers.

★ Dust storms destroyed this essential farm resource: **soil**.

★ The western plains states of Texas, Oklahoma, Colorado, New Mexico, and **Kansas** were nicknamed the Dust Bowl.

89

91

OSSUNIC **COUSINS**	ISANGVS **SAVINGS**
YETNORTA **ATTORNEY**	TOLRNCO **CONTROL**
REGVNROO **GOVERNOR**	RAFE **FEAR**
TREAG SIREONPEDS **GREAT DEPRESSION**	NEWMO **WOMEN**
LOPOI **POLIO**	NOTIRISEIM **MINORITIES**
WNE LEDA **NEW DEAL**	SPINKER **PERKINS**

91

93

BOLLAG	ANDORMNY
GLOBAL	**NORMANDY**
NAPJA	ENSWEHIREO
JAPAN	**EISENHOWER**
BECREEMD	GARYMNE
DECEMBER	**GERMANY**
REPLA RAHRBO	LISTOP
PEARL HARBOR	**PILOTS**
SMAPC	CMOATI
CAMPS	**ATOMIC**
TENSONCIMAOP	AISRHMHOI
COMPENSATION	**HIROSHIMA**

95

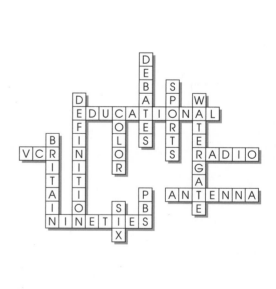

97

LODWR	ENWHORISEE
WORLD	**EISENHOWER**
TEOVIS	ETHER
SOVIET	**THREE**
ARKOE	NRIO
KOREA	**IRON**
LICRUHHLC	ERUNCLA
CHURCHILL	**NUCLEAR**
TIMCOUSMN	ONECYMO
COMMUNIST	**ECONOMY**
SPONAEW	LINERB
WEAPONS	**BERLIN**

99

101

SCROEV	DOCKSTOOW
COVERS	**WOODSTOCK**
NOTWOM	UTNYROC
MOTOWN	**COUNTRY**
MYRHTH	TOLSSENADEC
RHYTHM	**ADOLESCENTS**
RHISITB	LOPESG
BRITISH	**GOSPEL**
SUBLE	ORIDA
BLUES	**RADIO**
LIVES	EDREF
ELVIS	**FREED**

101

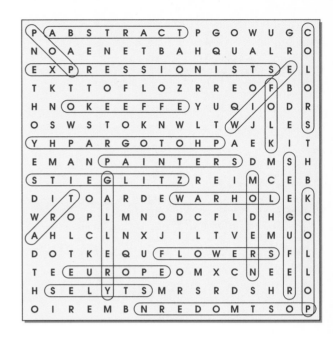

103

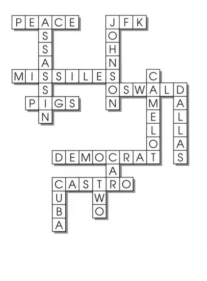

105

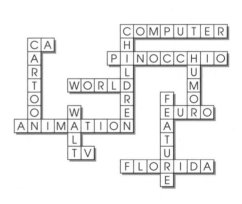

107

★ The temperature in Vietnam is usually __**hot**__.

★ President Johnson convinced __**Congress**__ to pass a war resolution.

★ Big protests followed the U.S. invasion of __**Cambodia**__, a neighbor of Vietnam.

★ Johnson said peaceful American ships were fired upon in the __**Tonkin**__ Gulf.

★ Vietnam is located in __**Asia**__.

★ Vietnam's large Communist ally is __**China**__.

★ Nixon coined the term __**Vietnamization**__ for replacing U.S. troops with Vietnamese ones.

★ Today, the exchange of goods, or __**trade**__, occurs between the U.S. and Vietnam.

★ Soldiers, as well as __**civilians**__, were sometimes dangerous in Vietnam.

★ __**South**__ Vietnam allied with the U.S. in the war.

109

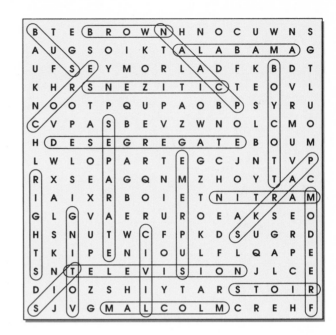

111

113

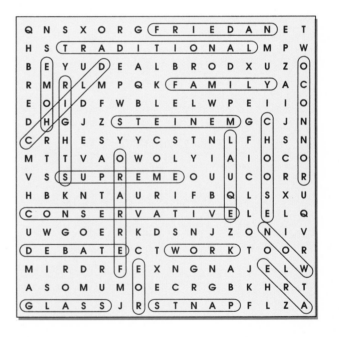

115

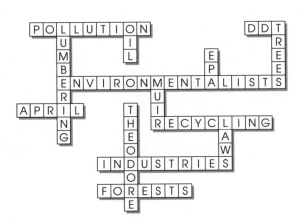

117

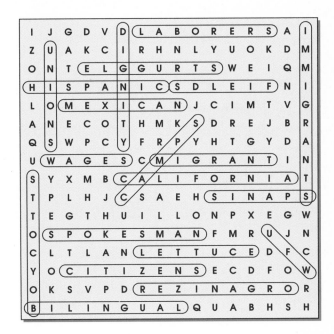

119

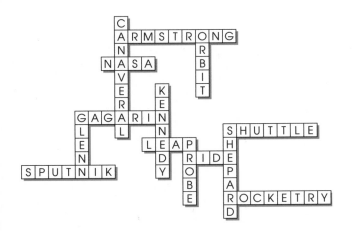

121

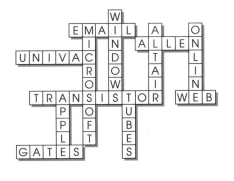

123

125

★ Bush helped form an ____**alliance**____ to fight the Persian Gulf War.

★ The hostage crisis of 1979 took place in ____**Iran**____.

★ Parts of ____**Yugoslavia**____ fell into ethnic conflict in the late century.

★ This former Yugoslav area, ____**Kosovo**____, is where the U.S. bombed attacking Serbs in 1999.

★ People kidnapped and kept for political reasons are called ____**hostages**____.

★ The U.S. went to war against Iraq in the ____**Persian**____ Gulf.

★ People who use terror to gain political ends are called ____**terrorists**____.

★ The initials of the international organization that fought and enforced the peace in the former Yugoslavia are ____**NATO**____.

★ Saddam Hussein said he had destroyed ____**arms**____, but the U.S. disagreed.

★ Iraq's invasion of ____**Kuwait**____ set off the Gulf War.

127

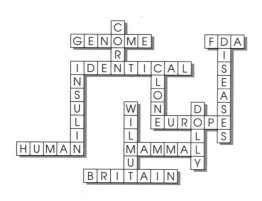

129

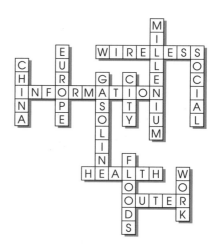

131

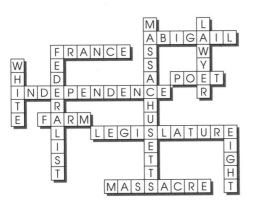

SABELNICEROT	OWNDCNUOT
CELEBRATIONS	**COUNTDOWN**
SEMTI QESRAU	GBU
TIMES SQUARE	**BUG**
TINFEOCT	MPOETSRCU
CONFETTI	**COMPUTERS**
SFKIRROEW	ANEPELPPI
FIREWORKS	**PINEAPPLE**
LOWDR	NEYDYS
WORLD	**SYDNEY**
FFLIEE ROWTE	SHEAMT
EIFFEL TOWER	**THAMES**

133

★ Washington fought for the British against the Indians and this country:

France _____.

★ Washington's home colony, or state, was _____ **Virginia** _____.

★ Washington was _____ **Chairman** _____ of the Constitutional Convention.

★ Alexander _____ **Hamilton** _____ served as Secretary of the Treasury under Washington.

★ The Whiskey Rebellion was a result of farmers refusing to pay a federal

tax _____.

★ Washington served as a _____ **general** _____ during the Revolutionary War.

★ Washington retired to his home, Mount _____ **Vernon** _____ after his presidency.

★ Washington worked to keep the nation _____ **neutral** _____ or free from alliances that might result in war.

★ Thomas Jefferson was Washington's Secretary of

State _____.

★ Washington married a young widow named _____ **Martha** _____

161

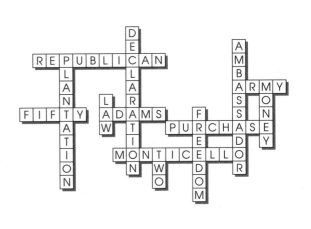

163   **165**

167

CERFAN	ULOVTRINEO
FRANCE	**REVOLUTION**
TRMINDATIINOSA	TGWSOHNIAN
ADMINISTRATION	**WASHINGTON**
SERGNOCS	MPTOOCA
CONGRESS	**POTOMAC**
ELODLY IMODNAS	RILDAFO
DOLLEY MADISON	**FLORIDA**
EROMNO RTCNEIDO	TOSUTIOCINNT
MONROE DOCTRINE	**CONSTITUTION**
NISAMOTSNIH	HITEW SHEOU
SMITHSONIAN	**WHITE HOUSE**

167

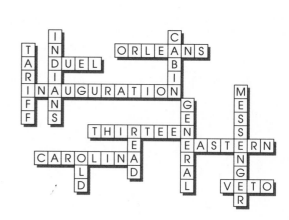

169

★ Van Buren was **Vice President** in Andrew Jackson's administration.

★ **Tippecanoe** was the site of the battle from which Harrison got his nickname.

★ Harrison was president for one **month** .

★ Van Buren spoke **Dutch** at home.

★ After his inauguration, Harrison admitted he was **ill** .

★ Tyler opposed the creation of a **national** bank.

★ The nation faced this economic problem while Van Buren was in office: **depression** .

★ Snappy sayings, or **slogans** , were an important part of Van Buren's campaign.

★ Van Buren lost for a second term because he could not improve the state of the **economy** .

★ **Tecumseh** was the Indian chief who was defeated by Harrison at Tippecanoe.

171

PISOMEMOCR	MICEOX
COMPROMISE	**MEXICO**
AANDCA	RANELEG
CANADA	**GENERAL**
ONINU	STAEMOCRD
UNION	**DEMOCRATS**
LVAEYSR	EREF
SLAVERY	**FREE**
SEWT	RAYLOT
WEST	**TAYLOR**
WIGSH	RIFONALCIA
WHIGS	**CALIFORNIA**

173

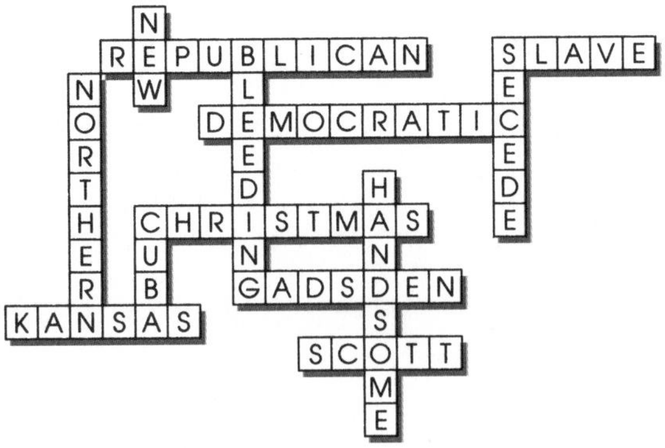
REPUBLICAN
SLAVE
NEW
NORTHER
DEMOCRATIC
SECEDE
BLEEDING
CHRISTMAS
CUB
HANDSOME
GADSDEN
KANSAS
SCOTT

175

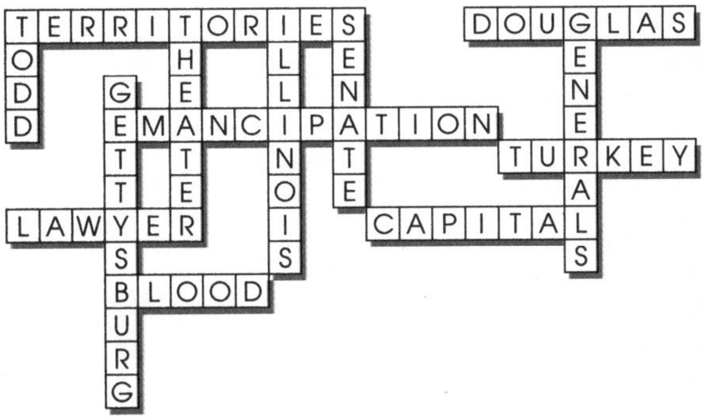
TERRITORIES
DOUGLAS
TODD
SENATE
ILLINOIS
GENERALS
EMANCIPATION
TURKEY
GETTYSBURG
LAWYER
CAPITAL
BLOOD

177

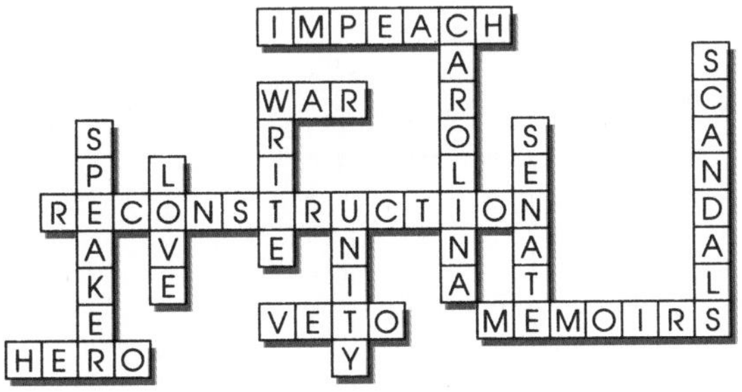
IMPEACH
CAROLINA
SCANDALS
WAR
WRITER
SPEAKER
LOVE
SENATE
RECONSTRUCTION
UNITY
VETO
MEMOIRS
HERO

179

- ★ The U.S. **postal** system was improved by Arthur.
- ★ Hayes was a **governor** in Ohio.
- ★ Garfield served seventeen years in **Congress** before he was elected president.
- ★ Garfield was fluent in **Spanish**.
- ★ Arthur improved this fighting force: the **Navy**.
- ★ Arthur helped reform **government** jobs.
- ★ Garfield was killed in the seventh **month** of his presidency.
- ★ **Electors** are the representatives who elect the president.
- ★ The civil **service** is the system of government jobs.
- ★ Arthur had eighty pairs of **pants**.

181

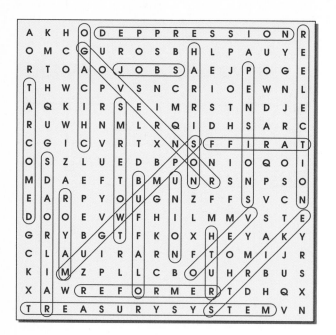

183

CRANHASTI
ANARCHIST

NOSERTA
SENATOR

VERSLI
SILVER

ROGERVON
GOVERNOR

FARIFT
TARIFF

SCTRANFEMUAUR
MANUFACTURERS

MAUG
GUAM

YREALW
LAWYER

BACU
CUBA

AIHAIW
HAWAII

CEMOONY
ECONOMY

CARBILUNEP
REPUBLICAN

185

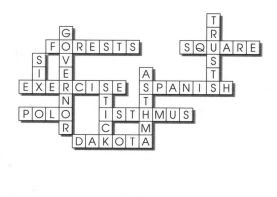

187

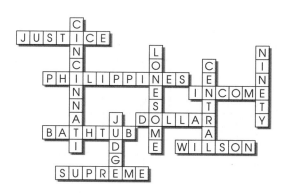

189

EAPEC
PEACE

AETRYT
TREATY

TINCREONP
PRINCETON

MRAGEN
GERMAN

REWOP
POWER

SNBKA
BANKS

SOREPOSRF
PROFESSOR

CISIDENOS
DECISIONS

SDIPTUES
DISPUTES

NOTREEUF
FOURTEEN

NETASE
SENATE

OKRSWRE
WORKERS

191

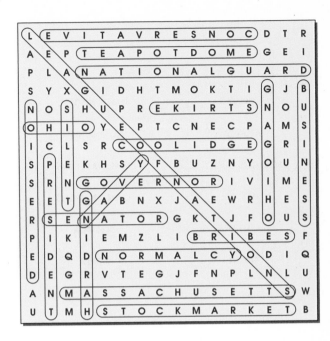

193

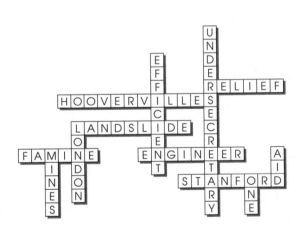

195

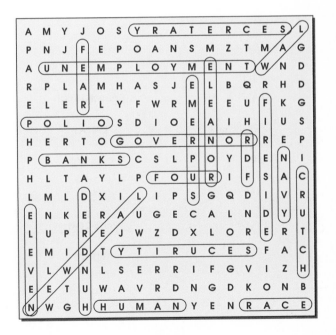

197

199

FILATIR	DNINEPEECNDE
AIRLIFT	**INDEPENDENCE**
MOICTA	MUSMCOMIN
ATOMIC	**COMMUNISM**
ICOSLA CUTRYESI	HLARAMSL APLN
SOCIAL SECURITY	**MARSHALL PLAN**
ETESMSKURE	TINDEU SITONNA
MUSKETEERS	**UNITED NATIONS**
MARHHOISI	TENASOR
HIROSHIMA	**SENATOR**
LIBNER	EKAOR
BERLIN	**KOREA**

201

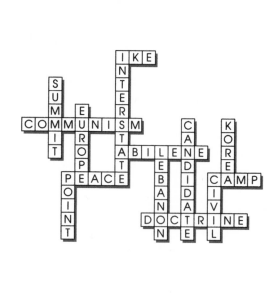

203

MASGCNRONSE	ITREGNSEEDOAG
CONGRESSMAN	**DESEGREGATION**
VRKHSCHEHU	SALADL
KHRUSHCHEV	**DALLAS**
THACSEMASTSUS	AMELTOC
MASSACHUSETTS	**CAMELOT**
DRAHRVA	LASWOD
HARVARD	**OSWALD**
YBA FO GPIS	CEPAE PORSC
BAY OF PIGS	**PEACE CORPS**
BESEATD	TILUPRZE
DEBATES	**PULITZER**

205

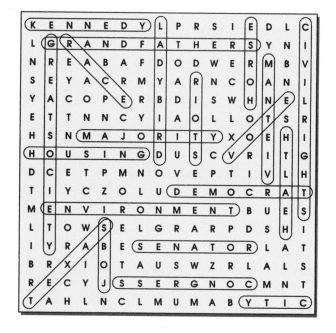

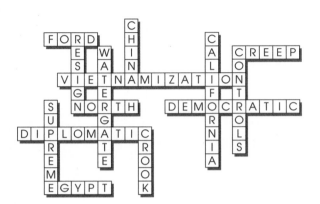

207

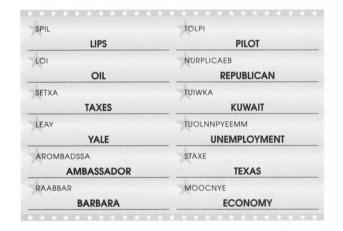

209

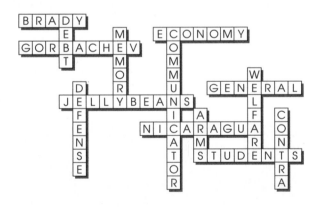

211

213

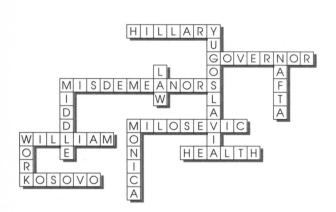

215

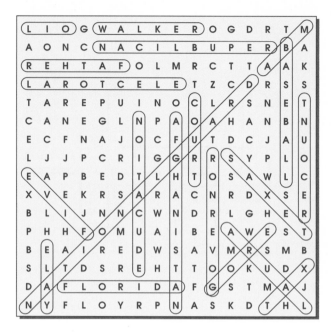

217

4	3	1	2
Zachary Taylor	Andrew Jackson	Thomas Jefferson	James Monroe

1	4	2	3
Theodore Roosevelt	Franklin D. Roosevelt	Woodrow Wilson	Herbert C. Hoover

2	1	4	3
Ulysses S. Grant	Abraham Lincoln	William McKinley	Grover Cleveland

227

3	2	1	4
Ronald Reagan	Richard Nixon	John F. Kennedy	William (Bill) Clinton

228

John Adams

James A. Garfield

William McKinley

William (Bill) Clinton

Herbert C. Hoover

James (Jimmy) E. Carter, Jr.

Martin Van Buren

Theodore Roosevelt

Name the presidents pictured above that match these statements. You may need to research some of the statements to write the name of the correct president.

★ We were born in Ohio. **James A. Garfield and William McKinley**

★ I served as governor of a state. **William (Bill) Clinton**

★ Our vice presidents became presidents after us. **John Adams, James A. Garfield, and William McKinley**

★ The three of us were in office on the first day of a new century. **John Adams, William McKinley, and William (Bill) Clinton**

★ I was born in the eighteenth century but died in the nineteenth. **John Adams**

★ I was born in the nineteenth century but died in the twentieth. **William McKinley**

★ We were both assassinated while in office. **William McKinley and James A. Garfield**

★ We both have the same first name. **William McKinley and William (Bill) Clinton**

229

Name the presidents pictured above that match these statements. You may need to research some of the statements to write the name of the correct president.

★ We were both born in New York. **Martin Van Buren and Theodore Roosevelt**

★ The two of us served as governors of states. **Jimmy Carter and Theodore Roosevelt**

★ We both served as vice president. **Martin Van Buren and Theodore Roosevelt**

★ The three of us were in office during times of economic trouble. **Martin Van Buren, Herbert C. Hoover, and Jimmy Carter**

★ The three of us served only one term each. **Martin Van Buren, Herbert C. Hoover, and Jimmy Carter**

★ We were both elected as Republicans. **Theodore Roosevelt and Herbert C. Hoover**

★ We were both elected as Democrats. **Martin Van Buren and Jimmy Carter**

230

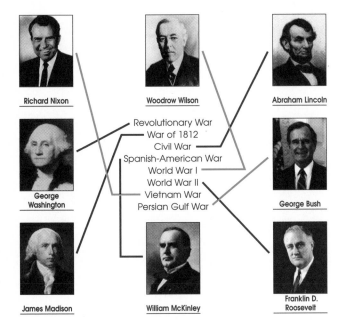

Richard Nixon
Woodrow Wilson
Abraham Lincoln
George Washington
James Madison
William McKinley
George Bush
Franklin D. Roosevelt

Revolutionary War
War of 1812
Civil War
Spanish-American War
World War I
World War II
Vietnam War
Persian Gulf War

231

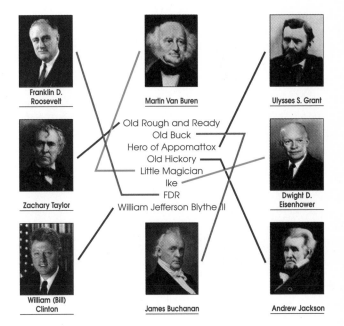

Franklin D. Roosevelt
Martin Van Buren
Ulysses S. Grant
Zachary Taylor
William (Bill) Clinton
James Buchanan
Andrew Jackson
Dwight D. Eisenhower

Old Rough and Ready
Old Buck
Hero of Appomattox
Old Hickory
Little Magician
Ike
FDR
William Jefferson Blythe III

232

Answer Key

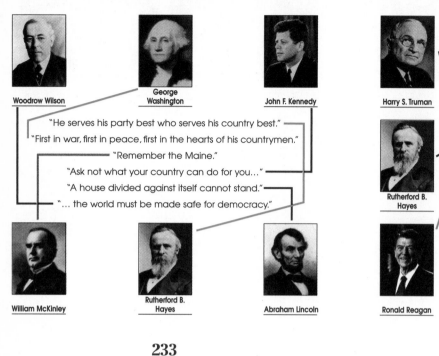

233

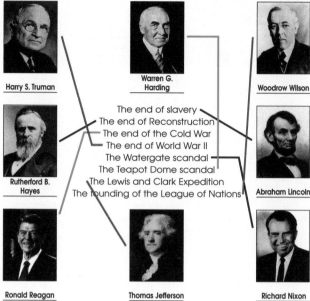

234

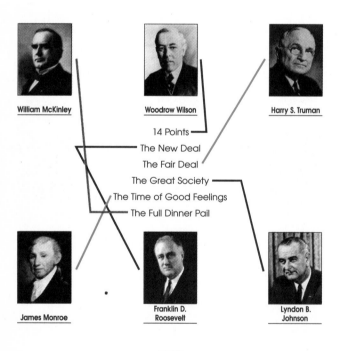

235

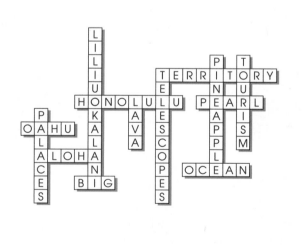

241

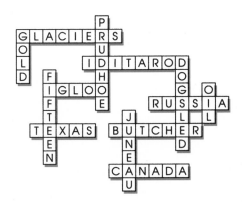

243

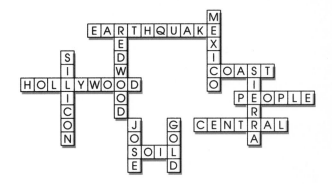

245

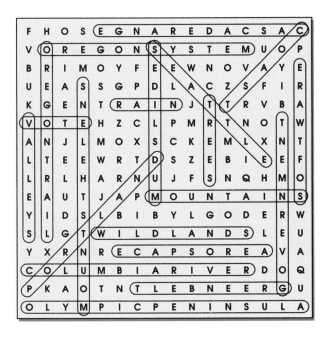

247

249

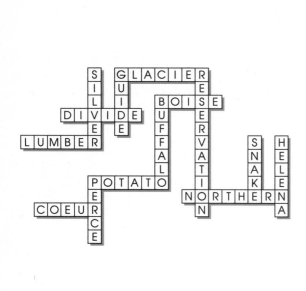

251

★ **Wind** _____ River is a large Native American reservation in central Wyoming.

★ Wyoming is home to _____ **Shoshone** _____ and Arapaho people.

★ Esther Hobart _____ **Morris** _____ sought equality for women in Wyoming Territory.

★ America's oldest national park, located in Wyoming, is
Yellowstone _____ .

★ The Colorado town of _____ **Aspen** _____ is famous as a ski resort.

★ The _____ **Anasazi** _____ were ancient Native American people who built cliff dwellings.

★ **Colorado** _____ has the highest average elevation in the United States.

★ Wyoming is known as the _____ **Equality** _____ State.

★ The U.S. _____ **Air** _____ Force has an academy in Colorado Springs.

★ Wyoming has fewer _____ **people** _____ than Colorado.

253

255

257

259

261

PEAKOT	TAMARIGUUCFNN
TOPEKA	**MANUFACTURING**
LACGUERRITU	ERACLE
AGRICULTURE	**CEREAL**
CENSNIARU	ACRULINMEA
INSURANCE	**UNICAMERAL**
THICAIW	THAEW
WICHITA	**WHEAT**
SELARPNAI	SHEDMIONETAG
AIRPLANES	**HOMESTEADING**
SED NOMIES	NNOLCLI
DES MOINES	**LINCOLN**

263

```
D F W Y D A I R Y F A R M S W Y
M I C H I G A N N O S I D A M P
A B T K V B C F E J S O U T I B
L A K E S Q F I I Z E N S A L L
L G L U C X T O E F M A O M W H
O L L A N S I N G P B N T H A I
F I S H I N G R E D L O P F U L
A P T R I S L E R O Y A L E K A
M R I L D K V O M D L N J V E T
E M O Z R J F Y A S I U X G E O
R H R O G L H E N T N E P C P S
I D T W I N C I T I E S A H X E
C K E C W G B A K U C R Q E S N
A W D X Q U V I H I M J V E D N
Z B W I S C O N S I N F R S C I
A N S E K A L T A E R G W E R M
```

265

SPERASCKYR	SLUBL
SKYSCRAPER	**BULLS**
DARRLOAIS	COLINNL
RAILROADS	**LINCOLN**
ZAJZ	FLARDAMN
JAZZ	**FARMLAND**
SPOTRAINTOTNAR	COGHACI
TRANSPORTATION	**CHICAGO**
IRDSNEGPFIL	RSEAS REWTO
SPRINGFIELD	**SEARS TOWER**
OHO RIERV	INARG
OHIO RIVER	**GRAIN**

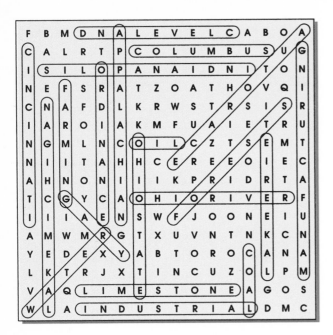

267

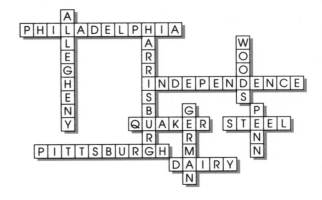

269

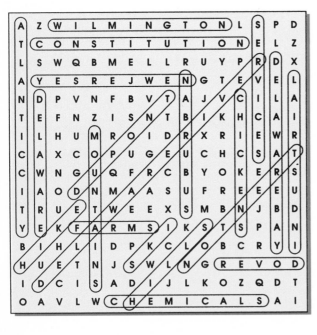

271

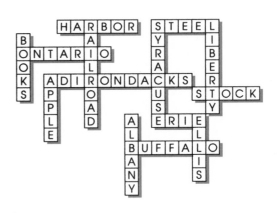

273

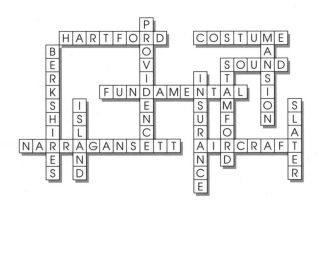

275

RAHRDAV	LUBCIP OLOSSCH
HARVARD	**PUBLIC SCHOOLS**
HFGNISI	BORETLS
FISHING	**LOBSTER**
PEAC DOC	ATACINOV
CAPE COD	**VACATION**
BKSHERIERS	TUNCANTEK
BERKSHIRES	**NANTUCKET**
WORTNOVIPENC	RBISCANERER
PROVINCETOWN	**CRANBERRIES**
WONT NIEGMSET	STONOB
TOWN MEETINGS	**BOSTON**

277

STERFOS	RULMEB
FORESTS	**LUMBER**
TIOUMRS	IMAPACHLN
TOURISM	**CHAMPLAIN**
REBALLI	SMNOIUANT
LIBERAL	**MOUNTAINS**
CROONCD	PEOERRTF
CONCORD	**FREEPORT**
RISESK	TELNIECO
SKIERS	**ELECTION**
BLUPERIC	TRAEING
REPUBLIC	**GRANITE**

279

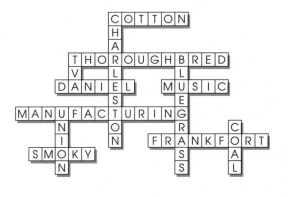

281

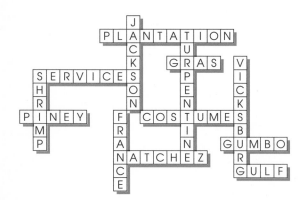

283

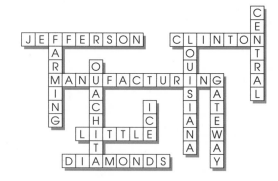

285

TALANTA	TAPNLOAINT
ATLANTA	**PLANTATION**
SEFORT	AFEEDORNCCY
FOREST	**CONFEDERACY**
ELEST	GAMRIMINBH
STEEL	**BIRMINGHAM**
CASPAHALAPIN	DOEMIPNT
APPALACHIANS	**PIEDMONT**
GONERTYMOM	VICLI SHRIGT
MONTGOMERY	**CIVIL RIGHTS**
FILEDILW	TOCNOT
WILDLIFE	**COTTON**

287

289

★ The South Carolina city of _____Charleston_____ is famous for its colonial era gardens and houses.

★ The first mills along the fall line depended on _____water_____ for power.

★ The University of North Carolina at Chapel Hill, Duke University, and North Carolina State form the North Carolina _____research_____ triangle.

★ The islands off North Carolina are called the _____Outer_____ Banks.

★ _____Tobacco_____ is the major crop in both Carolinas.

★ The first shots of the Civil War were fired at Fort _____Sumter_____.

★ The _____fall_____ line lies between the coastal plain and the Piedmont.

★ Mount _____Mitchell_____ is the tallest Appalachian mountain.

★ Salty _____marshes_____ help separate the Outer Banks from the North Carolina mainland.

★ North Carolina was the site of the _____first_____ English settlement in America.

291

293

```
  C P C H E S A P E A K E B A Y V
  E T P W S K I J A M E S T O W N
  A N C I P E F T A Z J U H G Y D
  R E D F D T S O U T H C R D C A
  J N M E A Y M V I E U I E A R B
  Y M O P G N I A O T B P C O E T
  G O T O D N S C O S H J H E E T
  T R T I A S I M X O C M K D L L
  I E O R P B A L T I M O R E I E
  D V M E O I O D A J X N B F F
  E O A U L O S P R G Q D P N I
  W G S C I T D N J M C U Q O E
  A M I B S E A T L A N T I C L
  T T W H R O C E A N C I T Y D
  E U N B L D H A O D N A N E H S
  R E A S T E R N S H O R E W C A
```

295

C A P I T A L
D   A   G
I   M   M O N U M E N T
S   B R I T I S H C   V
T   I   O   E
R   S M I T H S O N I A N C H E R R Y
I   C   G   N A
C   T   R   A P O T O M A C
T   R E P R E S E N T A T I V E
        S   S   I
            M A L L   O

305

a.
f.
__j__ Louisiana

__g__ Oklahoma

__d__ New York

b.
g.
__e__ Virginia

__h__ Missouri

c.
h.
__i__ North Carolina

__a__ New Mexico

d.
i.
__f__ Maine

__b__ Minnesota

e.
j.
__c__ New Hampshire

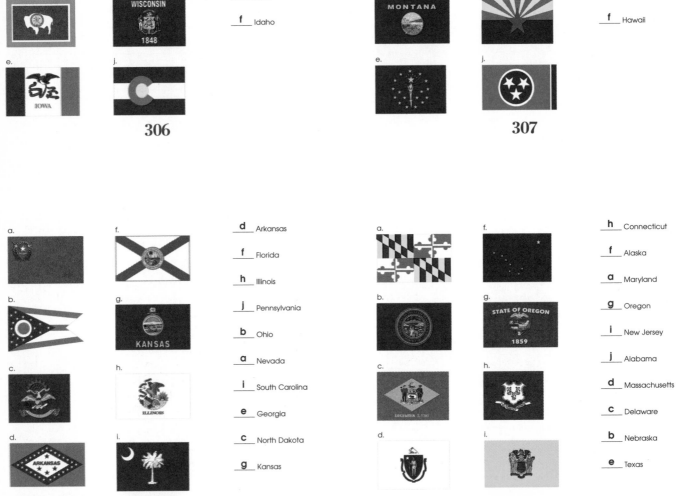

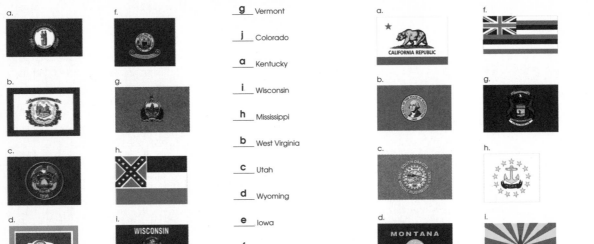

Page 306

a.
f.
b.
g.
c.
h.
d.
i. WISCONSIN 1848
e. IOWA
j.

g. Vermont
j. Colorado
a. Kentucky
i. Wisconsin
h. Mississippi
b. West Virginia
c. Utah
d. Wyoming
e. Iowa
f. Idaho

Page 307

a. CALIFORNIA REPUBLIC
f.
b.
g.
c.
h.
d. MONTANA
i.
e.
j.

g. Michigan
a. California
h. Rhode Island
j. Tennessee
b. Washington
d. Montana
i. Arizona
c. South Dakota
e. Indiana
f. Hawaii

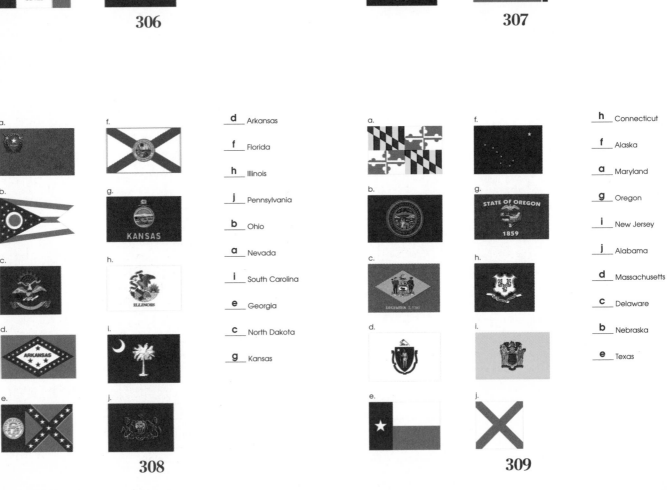

Page 308

a.
f.
b.
g. KANSAS
c.
h. ILLINOIS
d. ARKANSAS
i.
e.
j.

d. Arkansas
f. Florida
h. Illinois
j. Pennsylvania
b. Ohio
a. Nevada
i. South Carolina
e. Georgia
c. North Dakota
g. Kansas

Page 309

a.
f.
b.
g. STATE OF OREGON 1859
c. DECEMBER 7, 1787
h.
d.
i.
e.
j.

h. Connecticut
f. Alaska
a. Maryland
g. Oregon
i. New Jersey
j. Alabama
d. Massachusetts
c. Delaware
b. Nebraska
e. Texas

Answer Key

AL Alabama	**DE** Delaware	**IN** Indiana	**MD** Maryland
AK Alaska	**FL** Florida	**IA** Iowa	**MA** Massachusetts
AZ Arizona	**GA** Georgia	**KS** Kansas	**MI** Michigan
AR Arkansas	**HI** Hawaii	**KY** Kentucky	**MN** Minnesota
CA California	**ID** Idaho	**LA** Louisiana	**MS** Mississippi
CO Colorado	**IL** Illinois	**ME** Maine	**MO** Missouri
CT Connecticut			

MT Montana	**NC** North Carolina	**RI** Rhode Island	**VT** Vermont
NE Nebraska	**ND** North Dakota	**SC** South Carolina	**VA** Virginia
NV Nevada	**OH** Ohio	**SD** South Dakota	**WA** Washington
NH New Hampshire	**OK** Oklahoma	**TN** Tennessee	**WV** West Virginia
NJ New Jersey	**OR** Oregon	**TX** Texas	**WI** Wisconsin
NM New Mexico	**PA** Pennsylvania	**UT** Utah	**WY** Wyoming
NY New York			

310

311

312

I am the biggest state. The highest peak in the U.S., Mt. McKinley, is located in me.
Which state am I? **Alaska**

I can "show" you a lot. Jefferson City is my capital. In the summer of 1993, much of
my land flooded. Which state am I? **Missouri**

Abraham Lincoln was born in me. A famous derby is held in me. The nation's gold
vault is in my Fort Knox. Which state am I? **Kentucky**

La Salle claimed my area for France in 1682. The U.S. bought me from France in 1803.
I am the 18th state. Which state am I? **Louisiana**

I am often called the Great Lakes State because I touch four of the five. My Battle
Creek is the largest producer of breakfast cereal. Which state am I?
Michigan

My Jamestown was the site of the first permanent English settlement in America.
Patrick Henry gave his famous speech in my Appomattox Court House. Which state
am I? **Virginia**

Montgomery is my capital. My state flower is the camellia. Which state am I?
Alabama

I contain the Grand Canyon. Phoenix is my capital. Without irrigation, half of me
would be desert. Which state am I? **Arizona**

I was the home of seven U.S. presidents. The Pro Football Hall of Fame is located in my
Canton. Which state am I? **Ohio**

313

I am big - 220 times the size of Rhode Island! I have the most farms, farmland, cattle,
horses, and sheep in the nation. Which state am I? **Texas**

I am the "Land of Opportunity." Bill Clinton was born in me. Little Rock is my capital.
Which state am I? **Arkansas**

My people are "Hoosiers." I am the 19th state. The University of Notre Dame is
located in me. Which state am I? **Indiana**

I got my name from the Indians. Bismarck is my capital. I am the Flickertail State.
Which state am I? **North Dakota**

I am the 50th state. My Pearl Harbor is very famous. Diamond Head is one of my
most famous extinct volcanoes. Which state am I?
Hawaii

I was the first state to secede from the Union. My Fort Sumter was the place where
the Civil War began. I am the Palmetto State. Which state am I?
South Carolina

I am the smallest state. Roger Williams founded me in 1636. I produce the most
costume jewelry in the world. Which state am I? **Rhode Island**

I am the First State. I was named for Lord De La Warr. I was the first state to ratify the
new constitution in 1787. Which state am I? **Delaware**

I am the Gopher State. My Mesabi Range contains much iron ore. St. Paul is my
capital. Which state am I? **Minnesota**

Oh, say can you **see** by the

dawn's early **light**

What so **proudly** we hailed at the twilight's last **gleaming** ?

Whose broad **stripes** and bright **stars** thru' the perilous fight,

O'er the ramparts we **watched** were so **gallantly** streaming?

And the rockets' red **glare**, the bombs bursting in **air**,

Gave **proof** thru' the night that our **flag** was still there.

Oh, say does that star-spangled **banner** yet **wave**

O'er the land of the **free** and the home of the **brave** ?

315

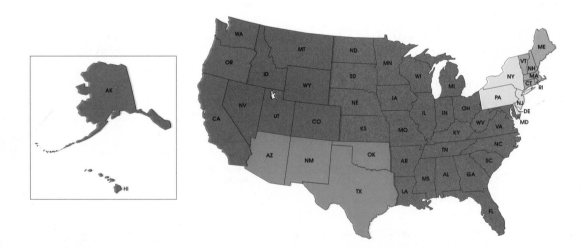

316-317